Criminals As Heroes

Criminals As Heroes: Structure, Power & Identity

Paul Kooistra

Bowling Green State University Popular Press
Bowling Green, Ohio 43403

Research for this book was made possible in part by funding from the Duke endowment.

Cover Design & Art by Greg Budgett and Gary Dumm

Contents

Preface   1

Chapter 1
  Introduction   7

Chapter 2
  Theories of the Heroic Criminal   15

Chapter 3
  Frank and Jesse James   43

Chapter 4
  Billy the Kid   74

Chapter 5
  Butch Cassidy   99

Chapter 6
  The Heroic Criminal of the 1930s   119

Chapter 7
  American Social Bandits:
  Identity, Power, and Structure   141

Chapter 8
  The Modern Heroic Criminal   160

Notes   181

Index   196

Preface

In 1974 I was an undergraduate sociology major trying to choose a suitable subject for my senior thesis. I happened upon a popular biography of Jesse James and was fascinated by what I read. In criminology classes I had been introduced to such concepts as "habitual offenders" and "mass murderers." These terms were used to describe particularly troublesome criminals. I also noticed that from time to time the media and politicians would invoke these same concepts as metaphors for evil. Yet here I was reading about a lawbreaker who certainly fit the definition of habitual offender and mass murderer, and he was being presented as a heroic figure. Why was this?

I was also struck by similarities that existed between the tales about Jesse James and the content of a popular movie, Butch Cassidy and the Sundance Kid, which had been released a few years earlier. I wondered how criminals like Jesse James and Butch Cassidy differed from other murderers and thieves so that at least for some people they were considered heroic. And I wondered how I could possibly explain this phenomenon of the heroic criminal as a senior thesis.

As it turned out, I decided this was much too complex an issue for me, a college senior. There did not seem to be a handy theoretical framework to use, and there seemed to be very little in terms of a body of research upon which to build. I was unable to imagine how even to begin a sociological analysis of outlaws. So I chose a much simpler empirical study about power tactic preference. By invoking the appropriate questions in a questionnaire and conjuring up the proper statistical tests, I was able to ensure a good grade with much less effort. The paradox of the criminal as hero was for a time put aside as a research question.

My interest in this issue was revived while I was in graduate school at the University of Virginia. I thought about doing a dissertation on this subject, but again I felt hesitation and a little embarrassment. This, after all, did not appear to be mainstream sociology. In fact, it did not appear to be "mainstream" anything—not history, not psychology, not anthropology. At best, it seemed an exotic branch of folklore. Not only did there appear to be little scholarly interest in legendary criminals; there also seemed to be little popular interest in outlaws like Jesse James.

1

But throughout the 1970s, outlaws increasingly became part of the content of popular culture. The rock group, the Eagles, released a concept album which chronicled the rise and fall of the Doolin-Dalton gang. Warren Zevon penned a ballad about Frank and Jesse James. And there were several other examples of rock groups using outlaws for metaphors describing their position in American culture either through original songs or by reviving old classics such as Woody Guthrie's "Pretty Boy Floyd." Several movies were released such as The Long riders and The Great Northfield Raid which revitalized the outlaw myth. It did seem that these lawbreakers, long after their careers had ended, still fascinated the American public. And my interest in this topic was again rekindled.

But still this was not a topic that one would be advised to choose to start a professional career in sociology. More than one scholar to whom I mentioned my interest in a sociology of outlaws looked at me a bit suspiciously. And my initial attempts to find any research on this issue of criminal-as-hero were not very successful. I found, for instance, one theorist who suggested that heroes became criminals because of their names! Jesse James was popular thanks to the magical properties of alliteration! Billy the Kid was blessed with a great nickname! Somehow, I suspected there must be more to it than this. And I thought that Oedipus complexes and physical attractiveness did not completely explain how particular lawbreakers became legendary figures.

A turning point came when I took a special topics course with University of Virginia anthropologist Chris Crocker. Here, for the first time, I became aware of Eric Hobsbawm's provocative study of "primitive rebels." Hobsbawm linked the emergence of "social bandits" like Jesse James to particular social conditions and used a comparative method to argue his case. I did not agree with everything Hobsbawm wrote, but I at least had discovered a theoretical framework from which to begin. And more important, I felt I could now mount a compelling argument that a sociological analysis of heroic criminals was a very worthwhile endeavor. Explaining the popularity of Jesse James and other American Robin Hoods became the basis of my dissertation.

And so began a long and difficult task. I spent hour after hour pouring over hundreds of old newspapers on microfilm, cordially obtained for me by the inter-library loan office at the University of Virginia library. (Later, librarians at Quinnipiac College, Yale University, University of Florida, and Furman University would spend hours tracking down and obtaining obscure sources for me.) Many times I wished I had chosen a simple empirical study. Often, I would be briefly tempted to change dissertation topics, but I found myself fascinated with what I was discovering about America's folk hero criminals. After five years of research and writing, a dissertation was completed.

I have read in numerous prefaces the acknowledgements an author makes to those who have helped him or her, but until I undertook this topic I never fully appreciated just how much intellectual debt any author has to others. I made ample use of the resources available to me at the University of Virginia. I would pose the paradox of the heroic criminal to anthropologists such as Roy Wagner, Victor Turner, Charles Purdue, and Mimi George; and they would provide invaluable insights. I would visit the history department, and historians such as David Shi and Dorothy Ross would sharpen my thinking and give me guidance. And of course the sociology department was an endless source of support. Graduate students such as John S. Mahoney, Amy Aldred, and Tom O'Leary were repeatedly subjected to rehearsals of what I was about to write, and patiently gave advice. Faculty members such as Frank Arnhoff, Jeanne Biggar, David Bromley, Ted Caplow, Randall Collins, Murray Milner, Steve Nock, Marshall Shumsky, and Joel Telles provided thoughtful suggestions. Later, comments from Jacqueline Whitmore at Santa Fe Community College (Gainesville, Fl), Joan Gordon at Quinnipiac College, Alan Hill at Delta College (Bay City, MI), and Dan Cover, Gene Johnson, Brian Siegel, and William Leverette, Jr. of Furman University were helpful.

Perhaps the greatest source of help was my dissertation committee at Virginia. Thomas Guterbock, Chris Crocker, Robert Bierstedt, and Gresham Sykes gave freely of their time and knowledge and deserve much credit for whatever merit this work may have. Only they know the almost miraculous transformation that occurred between the original version of this product and its final form. These scholars not only helped refine this work, but also my ability to think and write. Special thanks must go to Gresham Sykes for literally spending hours at a time answering my queries and providing impromptu seminars on sociological and criminological theory, and life in general. I learned far more sitting in his kitchen than I did in many of the courses I took in college or graduate school. I would like to also acknowledge John Schorr and Charles Vedder at Stetson University, and Richard Allinson.

Dissertations, unfortunately, are not the most readable form of prose. Several years were spent refining the work, adding detail in some areas and streamlining others. Special thanks must be given to John Crabtree at Furman University for providing critical support on a number of levels. Thanks also must be given to Steve Richardson, Amy Hunt, Elizabeth Kelly, and J. Glen Clayton of the Furman University library for help in acquiring obscure newspapers, books, and magazines. Cheryl Abernathy assisted in the assembling of the index. Pat Browne provided expert editorial assistance and helped me rewrite this work, translating it from "dissertationese" into a form of English that hopefully is more pleasing to read.

I also appreciate the efforts of Kay Zahrai of the Oklahoma Historical Society, Martha Minor from the Kenneth Spencer Research Library at the University of Kansas, Jean Hudon of the Texas History and Archives Department at the Dallas Public Library, John Lovett from the Western History Collections at the University of Oklahoma library, and Fae Sotham from the State Historical Society of Missouri. A portion of the preparation of the book was funded by the National Endowment of the Humanities, through a Furman University Faculty Development Grant.

Finally, I would like to thank my family for their support in helping me write this book. My wife Carol took time out from her studies as a medical student to help type early drafts of the manuscript, and her sharp comments helped me refine some of the less cogent portions of the work. Later, her emotional support helped me carry the book to its conclusion. I must also thank our son, Tristan, who has been the perfect baby and allowed his father to sneak off to the word processor from time to time. Without his cooperation, this work would still be in progress.

The *Daily Graphic* cover. From the collection of the Library of Congress. Reprinted with permission.

Chapter 1

Introduction

The public, as opinion polls show, has often considered crime to be one of the country's most serious social problems. Politicians have invoked the "crime problem" in every major political campaign of the past few decades. The media have shocked and terrified us repeatedly with sordid tales of criminal evil. Violent crime, especially murder and robbery, is considered the most heinous form of lawlessness (cf. Rossi, et. al., 1974). Murderers and thieves harm not just their immediate victims but also subvert the moral basis upon which society rests. They are spectres of evil that terrorize honest citizens, forcing people to live in fear behind locked doors, to spend large amounts of money to protect themselves, and even to abandon their homes and neighborhoods when the threat of crime seems too great. It is little wonder, as Edwin Schur (1969:9) points out, that we think that "crime is something done to society, criminals are the enemy of society, society is at war with crime."

Nonetheless, throughout history we find a handful of individuals who have robbed and killed in clear violation of law, but who were not considered wicked or depraved. Instead, these robbers and murderers were viewed as social heroes, and not just during their lifetime but for decades afterward. They have been popular media creatures whose criminal exploits have been celebrated in song, newspapers, books, plays, movies, and even television dramas. These are lawbreakers who have been transformed from ordinary criminals into legendary Robin Hood figures of epic proportions.

Outlaws such as Billy the Kid, Jesse James, and Butch Cassidy typify American criminals who have been cast as heroic figures. Billy the Kid, a convicted mass murderer, was described by the lawman who killed him as:

Bold, daring and reckless, he was open-minded, generous, frank and manly. He was a favorite with all classes and ages, especially was he loved and admired by the old and decrepit, and the young and helpless. To such he was a champion, a defender, a benefactor, a right arm. (Garrett, 1954:8).

Miguel Otero (1935:215), a former governor of New Mexico, also had met the young felon and spoke highly of him:

7

To be frank, I found myself liking the Kid....
He had his share of good qualities: he was pleasant to meet; he had the reputation of always being kind and considerate to the old, the young, and the poor; he was loyal to his friends and, above all, loved his mother devotedly.

Is there a mistake here? Are these men talking about a man who killed at least six people, including a sheriff he ambushed? It is hard to believe that a law officer and governor could have such respect and admiration for a man who seems to be a psychopathic killer.

Jesse James, who was responsible for numerous deaths and scores of bank and train robberies, has similarly been extolled. A leading spokesman for the Missouri Democrats, John Newman Edwards, wrote stirring editorials praising Jesse and his outlaw kin for over ten years. The death of this by-then fabled bandit, carried out by paid gunmen in the employ of the Missouri political establishment, provoked Edwards to write in the Sedalia Democrat (April 4, 1882):

Not one among all the hired cowards, hard on the hunt for blood money, dared face this wonderful outlaw, one against twenty, until he turned his back to his assassins, the first and only time in a career which has passed from the realms of an almost fabulous romance into that of history.

As a result of the adulations of men like Edwards, Jesse James was a national celebrity even before his death. His murder was greeted by headlines usually reserved for officials of the state. The New York Daily Graphic (April 11, 1882) far removed from the brigand's homeland, parodied the public reaction to the outlaw's death with a cartoon featuring the bandit's tombstone, upon which was enscribed:

The most renowned murderer and robber of his age. He quickly rose to eminence in his gallant and dangerous profession and his exploits were the wonder and admiration and excited the emulation of the small boy of the period. He was cut off in the prime of his strength and beauty...by the shot of a base assassin of whom the Governor of the State of Missouri was an accomplice.

Jesse James earned the wonder and admiration of more than small boys, however, and almost one hundred years after his demise, new ballads were still being penned which praised and glorified him (Zevon, 1973; Kennerly, 1980). It is likely that Jesse James will continue riding across literary landscapes for at least another hundred years.

Butch Cassidy and his band of associates, known as the "Wild Bunch" or "Hole-in-the-Wall Gang," have also been glorified for almost a century. Virtually all forms of media have celebrated the exploits of this assemblage of criminals. Of Butch Cassidy, Horan and Sann (1954:204) write: "of all the outlaws of the West, probably Robert LeRoy Parker, known to frontier history as Butch Cassidy, is the most likeable." Another writer claims that "among cowboys and cattlemen of the old frontier, (Cassidy's) name stood for daring, resourcefulness, and a certain chivalry" (Kelly, 1938:4). And according to Lula Parker Betenson (1975:xi, xiii), Butch Cassidy was blessed with a charismatic personality. "His friendly singular charm and his interest in people—the struggling people—won him their protection from the law.... I can honestly say that I have not found one person who knew him personally who will say a bad thing about him." Certainly Cassidy has many friends in the movie industry because the 1969 film, Butch Cassidy and the Sundance Kid, grossed over 75 million dollars on its way to becoming the most popular Western ever made.

Jesse James, Billy the Kid, and Butch Cassidy are the most popular American Robin Hoods, but there are others—Sam Bass, the Daltons, Bill Doolin, John Wesley Hardin, Bonnie and Clyde, John Dillinger, and "Pretty Boy" Floyd, for instance—who have also been portrayed as heroic criminals. (cf. Adams, 1954, 1979; Nash, 1975).[1] Although these criminals lived in different times and places, a set of legends that has surrounded them is basically the same: they are driven to a life of crime either as a victim of injustice or for commiting an act which the state, but not the community, considers as criminal; they are considered by large portions of the public as moral and honorable men; these brigands are men who violate the law but who represent a "higher" justice; they rob from the corrupt rich and give to the deserving poor; others are harmed only when "justice" requires it or in self-defense; The legitimacy of the state is not challenged, only the corrupt practices of the oppressors of the people. Regardless of how many men they murdered or robberies they committed for personal gain, these are attributes imputed to the heroic criminal.

This book is an examination of several of America's most noted Robin Hood figures. Its purpose is to explain why the anomaly of the heroic criminal exists and to examine how such creatures come into being. This endeavor begins by looking at previous efforts to explain why we make heroes out of criminals. The heroic criminal is a phenomenon that has captured the interest of scholars from a wide range of intellectual disciplines. Historians, folklorists, psychologists, literary critics, anthropologists, criminologists, and sociologists have explored this subject. Not surprisingly, a variety of explanations have been given which may be grouped into three categories: psychological, cultural, and sociological. Each of these perspectives offers important insights concerning the criminal as hero. Chapter two examines these explanations in detail, but it may be useful to discuss briefly the three perspectives here.

Psychological explanations account for the existence of heroic criminals by claiming that narratives about these figures serve a critical psychological function for those who read or write such tales. The most persuasive of these theories is one which proposes that through such stories we may vicariously release rebellious feelings generated by the restrictions imposed by authority, either in the form of parents or of agents of the state. The eventual demise of these rebels, often violent in nature, reminds us that in the long run, crime "does not pay." This kind of explanation is illuminating but incomplete. Only certain criminals are elevated to heroic status. This perspective cannot account for why particular kinds of criminals become heroes, while most others do not.

Cultural explanations posit that the American Robin Hood reflects the values of a group of people, and his conflicts in some way represent the important struggles of his time. The heroic criminal is a cultural product to be explained by the values he symbolizes. His courage, loyalty, cleverness, and success account for his heroic status. Cultural explanations, in fact, tell us *how* we make heroes out of criminals— by linking them with cherished ideals in much the same way modern advertising campaigns connect products to popular images. But this type of explanation does not tell us why we make heroes out of criminals unless we assume that they truly epitomized the values they are held to represent. It is a tremendous leap of faith to assume that legends are accurate accounts of the deeds and character of criminals who have been fashioned into heroes.

Sociological explanations suggest that the heroic criminal is a product of particular structural conditions. Robin Hood criminals appear when large numbers of people become disenchanted with the quality of justice represented by law and politics. This popular unrest does not occur randomly but is the consequence of specific social conditions such as famines, rapid social change, blatant and excessive political corruption, economic depressions, or other strains that disrupt the day-to-day existence of many people who are not used to worrying about basic needs. Under these conditions numerous heroic criminals may appear.

Although this type of explanation does not tell us why a particular criminal is selected from the heap of common thieves and murderers and fashioned into a heroic figure, it provides a good starting point for such an inquiry. To understand why criminals are cast as heroes, one must go beyond the already constructed legends of fabled brigands to an examination of the actual behavior of the men chosen for the Robin Hood role and of the particular social context in which they acted out their criminality. Of prime importance are the social interpretations of their lawlessness. Who were their supporters and who were their opponents. How did people perceive the victims of these criminals? What was the social background of these heroic criminals? What was the political nature of those who became American Robin Hoods? These are questions which are essential to address to understand why and how criminals become heroes.

To answer these questions, I begin by examining the general social conditions under which American Robin Hoods emerged. I argue that this anomaly, the heroic criminal, is a cultural product that is called into existence by certain structural conditions. At times when large numbers of people have had their sense of order and security disrupted, particularly by economic upheavals such as depressions, then a legitimation crisis occurs. Widespread portions of the public feel "outside the law" because the law is no longer seen as an instrument of justice but as a tool of oppression wielded by favored interests. Social justice and state law are in antithesis, and people turn to symbolic representations of justice outside the law such as the Robin Hood criminal. These social bandits recall a sense of justice based upon kinship and community rather than one based upon impersonal bureaucratic procedures established by the state. During such times, a national "market" for such symbolic representations of justice exists.

I then offer an explanation of why and how certain lawbreakers become fashioned into heroes to meet this "demand." I begin with an examination of the particular social setting in which the heroic criminal emerges and suggest how these conditions, his social identity, the identity of his victims, and the nature of his criminal acts, helped shape social definitions of his criminality. Finally, I look at the powerful figures whose careers are entwined with the careers of these criminals and describe how entrepreneurs skilfully market these lawbreakers to a receptive public.

It should be noted that unraveling the "true" story of the heroic criminal is *not* my concern. This work is not intended to be a collection of "revisionist" biographies about Western figures. It adds very little to what is known about the life of these criminals. I have not uncovered previously unknown letters or manuscripts penned by these outlaws, or interviewed their relatives in hopes of uncovering some previously untold tale. I have found no old photographs showing the James gang playing softball on the fields of Minnesota shortly before the Northfield raid! Instead, I have relied heavily upon previously penned biographies of these criminals. Particularly important in this regard were accounts of these brigands which were written, read, and acknowledged as "true" accounts—biographies and newspaper stories written at the time these outlaws were plying their trade. My concern is not so much with what the criminal actually did but with what people believed about him and how they asserted those beliefs to others. What acts was he credited with performing, what motives were imputed to him, and what qualities he was presumed to have? An important part of this work is delineating the differing versions of reality that emerged about such criminals and suggesting why people came to embrace a particular version as being "true." I see the heroic criminal as a byproduct of group conflict and propose that varying interpretations of his criminality reflect this conflict. The Robin Hood criminal is, in a way, a political criminal.

The major portion of this treatise consists of case studies on the life and times of Jesse James, Billy the Kid, and Butch Cassidy. These lawbreakers were chosen on the premise that they are the most famous of the American Robin Hoods. It is assumed that factors responsible for the development of a heroic criminal will be most clearly evident in these cases.

Also examined are a number of 20th century criminals to see how they compare to the romanticized frontier bandits. Among these are a number of criminals—John Dillinger, "Pretty Boy" Floyd, and Al Capone—who emerged as heroic figures during the depression years of the 1930s. Finally, I study more recent lawbreakers such as Patty Hearst and Gene Hart, Bruce Griffith, and Bernhard Goetz—some well-known and others not—to see in what ways, if any, that these criminals typify the contemporary American Robin Hood.

This approach to understanding the heroic criminal is not without drawbacks. Three problems immediately come to mind. First, it is not always easy to determine where historical fact yields to fanciful legend. One may easily confuse the legendary hero with the real criminal. I hope this is a minor problem because my concern is not so much with what the outlaw actually was like or with what he really did; I am more interested in what people believed about him. It is not my intention to participate in the glorification of lawlessness or the futhering of myth. My inclination is to believe that in actuality there was little that is heroic about men who essentially killed and robbed with impunity. However, many people did find something noble in the nature of these murderers and thieves, and I consider it worthwhile to find out why.

Second, it is sometimes difficult to determine the extent of popular support given to these criminals. We have yet to find, for instance, a public opinion poll measuring the popularity of Jesse James. However, by uncovering the social backgrounds of those making public declarations in the media about the outlaw, we may infer generally what groups sympathized with and glorified the outlaw. And occasionally, the media accounts of the lawbreaker provide us with information about the dimensions of his popularity.

Finally, there is a sampling problem to confront. Through the use of the case study method, I am looking at a small number of criminals and searching for common elements and patterns shared by each that might account for selection as an American Robin Hood. They represent perhaps extreme cases rather than the "typical" romanticized criminal, and criminals are certainly glorified in ways other than turning them into Robin Hoods (which I will touch upon in the concluding chapter). Furthermore, there is no systematic way of determining why these particular criminals were chosen over other lawless men of their time for the part of a cultural hero. But where possible, I have noted criminals who shared many characteristics in common with the American Robin Hoods and have described the features these criminals lacked which may have prevented them from gaining entry into the realm of American Folklore.

Despite such problems, this approach seems more promising than cultural or psychological explanations of why we make heroes out of criminals because it places the lawbreaker in the social context from which his criminality initially derived its meaning. If one wishes to understand why and how people fashion heroes out of criminals, one should go beyond already constructed legends and examine the actual behavior of the outlaw, the identity and activities of those who helped turn the criminal into a public figure, and the audience that initially found something heroic about his lawlessness.

One last matter to consider here is the reason for examining heroic criminals. What may we possibly learn from such an endeavor? First, we may better understand how social conditions affect public perceptions of criminality by noting the times and places in which such heroic criminals emerge and become popular. We may observe how cultural products like the Robin Hood criminal are linked to particular structural conditions, and we may gain insight into the types of structural conditions that lead to the condoning, rather than the condemning, of extra-legal attempts to define and enforce social justice.

Second we may see how crime definitions are socially constructed. We may examine the common characteristics and motives assigned to these criminals and compare these with what historical evidence would suggest be more plausible motives and attributes. The themes surrounding the Robin Hood criminal may be viewed as socially constructed rationalizations that enable the public to justify the lawlessness of these lawbreakers as well as their glorification.

Third, an analysis of the origins of legends surrounding the Robin Hood criminals will demonstrate both the problematic nature of the meaning of crime and the political nature of attempts to define criminality. Upon examining the early tales of the Robin Hood criminals, we find disagreement over what label to apply to these men—immoral demon or saintly hero. Just as today where one man's "freedom fighter" is another's "terrorist," so too are the parameters of group conflict evident in the differing interpretations of the nature of these notorious criminals from our past. Of particular importance here is the role played by "moral entrepreneurs" who assert to the public a view of social reality concerning the nature, cause, and significance of the heroic criminal (Becker, 1963).

Fourth, we may observe the important role played by the media in shaping public perceptions of crime and the criminal. Much of this public understanding is shaped by the media rather than through direct personal experience. Numerous studies have shown how the media, in particular the press, distort the incidence and prevalence of crime, sensationalizing violence and oversimplifying crime issues (Cf. Cavender 1981; Fishman, 1978; Garofalo, 1981; Graber, 1980; Winick, 1978). At least part of the public concern about crime and many of the crude stereotypes of criminals that exist may be attributed to the mass media. The Robin Hood criminals provide a clear illustration of how the media may systematically distort crime for political or economic reasons.

Finally, we may note the interconnections between media portrayals of crime, public perceptions of criminality, and the political use of lawlessness as a social issue. Each of these elements is linked together in a circular fashion, each looking to the others in order to understand the meaning of criminality. Consequently, our understanding of crime may become hindered by collective fantasies fashioned by media exploitation and political propaganda. By recognizing how our knowledge of crime may sometimes be distorted, we should be better prepared to uncover scientific truths concerning illegal behavior.

Chapter 2

Theories of the Heroic Criminal

Heroes satisfy a basic human need. Throughout history and in all societies, we find evidence of hero worship. In antiquity, the hero was a god in a man's body whose performances were all the more remarkable because they were accomplished within the confines of human frailty. Figures such as Roland and Beowulf represented Man at his best; they were individuals struggling not only with external forces but also with their own human weaknesses (cf. Campbell, 1968; Leeming, 1981). In more modern societies such as the United States, heroes have been identified as paragons of success, group loyalty, and individualism (Klapp, 1962). Our heroes have also been endowed with god-like qualities and have been hailed as representatives of moral virtue and extraordinary strength, courage, and insight. Historical figures such as George Washington, Thomas Jefferson, Abraham Lincoln, Robert E. Lee and Nathan Hale have been canonized and might be considered the secular saints of a civil religion (cf Bellah, 1970). Others such as Daniel Boone, Thomas Edison, Clara Barton, and Charles Lindbergh are American heroes who have typified abstract American values. Heroes express the kinds of things of which a culture approves. They are human expressions of idealized social values.

It is perplexing, however, that among our cultural heroes we find a number of notorious criminals, men who, had they appeared in our midst today, would have been reviled as mass murderers and habitual offenders. Normally murderers and thieves are viewed as immoral creatures with little redeeming value. Yet outlaws like Jesse James, Billy the Kid, Butch Cassidy; gangsters such as Al Capone; and bank robbers such as John Dillinger have been fashioned into cultural heroes. Why do we make heroes out of such men? A number of scholars from a variety of disciplines have pondered this question and have offered an assortment of explanations. Their answers may be grouped into three basic categories: (1) psychological explanations; (2) cultural explanations; and (3) sociological explanations. In this chapter, I will examine and evaluate these accounts, determining what contributions each makes to solving the puzzle of how and why we make heroes out of criminals. Then I will develop a theoretical framework from which to analyze the shaping of heroic criminals.

Left to right: Bill Powers, Bob Dalton, Grat Dalton, and Dick Broadwell, 4 of 5 men who attempted to rob two banks at Coffeyville, Kansas on Oct. 5, 1892. Emmett Dalton, who was with them survived 21 bullet wounds, served time, pardoned. Western History Collections, University of Oklahoma Library. Reprinted with permission.

Jesse James in 1875. Western History
Collections, University of Oklahoma Library.
Reprinted with permission.

Frank James. State Historical Society of
Missouri. Reprinted with permission.

Frank James, (seated), Jesse James, (front right), Fletcher Taylor. State
Historical Society of Missouri. Reprinted with permission.

Psychological Explanations

A number of thinkers have used a psychoanalytic perspective to explain why people fashion heroes out of criminals. This orientation stresses the functions that such figures serve for both the audience reading or hearing about the criminal and for the narrators who construct and relate such stories. The psychoanalytic perspective posits that the heroic criminal is a response to fundamental problems facing the human species. Although such explanations do not deny the subtle shadings of culture on a social product such as the heroic criminal, there is an inclination to turn inward, searching and probing the human psyche to discover the etiology of such an anomaly as the heroic criminal.

One interesting psychoanalytic explanation of the heroic criminal focuses upon the sexual implications of the lawbreaker, with a particular interest in the libidinal implications of the outlaw's gun. As in the case of many other narratives, tales of the Robin Hood criminal are suspected of being tied to the Oedipus complex and function as a "safety valve" that releases the tensions entangled in this sexual conflict. The refusal of the heroic criminal to abide by the rules of the state is, from this perspective, symbolic of the son's rejection and denial of his father. Kenneth Munden (1958:128), who has written the most developed psychoanalytic interpretation of the cowboy myth, proposes that the "hero represents the son who is challenged by the father and the siblings, who are defeated and killed." Bankers are cast as thinly disguised father figures, and detectives represent the jealous siblings also vying for the attention of the mother. The fact that so few women are found in Westerns is explained, according to Munden, as an indication of incestuous wishes toward the mother that are denied and repressed.

The sexual nature of the gun also figures prominently in this type of interpretation of the outlaw. Henry Schein (1975:330) points out: "Bad men draw it too often but too slowly. Like Casanova, they shoot in all directions without finding their mark. The hero...shoots seldom, but never misses. As a protector of the community, he cannot afford to be promiscuous." The outlaw hero, like an austere Puritan, only uses his gun when absolutely necessary and morally proper.

The sexual undertones of legends concerning the heroic criminal have convinced a number of scholars that the virile masculinity such lawbreakers represent accounts for their popularity in our culture. John Cawelti (1975:58) has argued that "the tendency to admire gunfighter heroes and the actual social incidence of violence with guns are both symptoms of a more complex cultural force: the sense of decaying masculine potency which has long afflicted American culture." Robert Hine (1973:281) similarly has proposed that "as the role of women broadened in the 20th century, both men and women looked with nostalgia to an unquestioningly male-dominated society" typified by the Western gunfighter.

Undoubtedly the underlying sexuality of the heroic criminal and his gun excites and fascinates many readers of such tales, and perhaps accounts in part for the interest such figures seem to have for young adolescent males. However, this kind of explanation may be criticized on a number of grounds.

First, there is the tendency to select elements from narratives that support this type of argument and to ignore aspects of these tales which seemingly contradict it. Through this selection process, it becomes quite easy to construct a case, often glibly referred to as "the myth," which fits the theory quite well. Consider, for example, claims about the paucity of females in "the cowboy myth," as Munden (1958) puts it, and how this is taken as evidence of denial and repression of the "mother figure." How, then, do we explain the fact that a number of women—Belle Starr, Annie Oakley, and "Calamity Jane" for example—have played a prominent role in Western legends? How do such figures relate to our sense of "decaying masculine potency." How do we account for the fact that the James boys' one-armed mother is a significant feature in their legends, or that both of these virile outlaws married "for love" during their outlaw careers, "captured at the altar" as one newspaper put it (St. Louis Dispatch, June 9, 1874). In the 1930s, Bonnie Parker and "Ma" Barker emerged as noted gunslingers on the wrong side of the law. Certainly the "masculinity" such women exhibited was not the basis for turning them into minor cultural heroes! Furthermore, female outlaws who have been fashioned into heroes have been found in other cultures in enough numbers, says Eric Hobsbawm (1981:136), "to make us suspect that they are at least in certain parts of the world a recognized phenomenon." Explanations for the existence of heroic criminals that stress their sexual implications, especially those that invoke the Oedipus complex, fail to account for the existence of women who break the law and are fashioned into heroes.

A second problem with this type of explanation is its method of "proof by analogy." Put simply, elements in a narrative are seen as symbolic representations of objects that they closely resemble. Thus guns are phallic symbols because they have a long thin shaft, "ejaculate" bullets, "erupt" when stimulated by hand, and so on. Many of these parallels are brilliantly constructed and very persuasive; however, they may also become contrived and overstated. Munden (1958:135), for example, claims that notching the gun, as an indication of a kill also has sexual meaning: "Symbolically, it can only mean one thing: an incision on the phallus, an act of mutilation." He further contends that this symbolic act of "self-castration" results from "the arousal of guilt feelings for the death of the father" symbolized by murder. And of course there is still the issue of latent homosexuality to consider since the gunman typically points his phallic symbol at other men!

The problem here is that just because objects share similarities in form or function, they are not necessarily linked together symbolically. Outlaws in Westerns may be wearing masks, for instance, in order to fend off traildust and not because they are struggling to deny oral fixations. Horses and automobiles may be used because of their capacity to transport outlaws quickly from the scene of the crime and not because they hold any deep sexual meaning. Stories portraying outlaws riding with their legs wrapped around horseflesh, brandishing their pistols, covering their mouths with cloth, and murdering detectives and bankers may be simply reflecting what outlaws were doing at the time and not redressing any deep-seated psychological problem of the author or reader.

Another troublesome feature of some psychoanalytic interpretations of the heroic criminal is their "catch 22" methodology resulting from judicious use of the concept of repression. If evidence supporting an explanation is lacking, its absence may be explained by claiming repression. Thus, because so few women are found in Westerns, this is considered proof of intense childhood desires for the mother and the fear and shame that accompanies this. But if we find women in Westerns, this may also prove that conflicts surrounding the Oedipus complex are present. This kind of logical chicanery promotes the belief that it is the data, and not the theory, that are being tested and reformulated.

A somewhat different psychoanalytic explanation of the heroic criminal holds that he is a product of wish-fulfillment. The figure of the Dashing Outlaw for instance is seen as someone "in whose person all might find recklessly displayed their own hidden defiances, their private longings to be something both worse and better than they had it in them to be." (Jackson, 1955:xx). In a similar vein, William Settle (1966:2-3) writes:

> How did these cold-eyed bandits who gunned down unarmed men and terrorized the countryside become the stuff of legend? The answers may lie in the motives and attitudes of Americans who, according to one theory, find Jesse James fascinating because, through reliving his exploits, they release vicariously something of their own rebellion against the restrictions of modern society.

It is because the criminal is a lawbreaker that we make a hero out of him. He is a man who refuses to bow down to the tyranny of authority, and that is why we glorify him. And the inevitable triumph of law over the criminal—who almost always suffers a violent and lonely death— is a reminder that desires to rebel, when translated into action, are neither tolerated nor advised. Tales of the heroic criminal, in a sense, serve as "safety valves" where aggressive impulses are channeled and cleansed.

This argument is persuasive, but is incomplete. While we undoubtedly find psychological release by vicariously experiencing the rebellious deeds of the lawbreaker, we choose to undergo this experience with a very limited number of criminals. We do not imagine ourselves dining with Albert Fish on the bodies of children he molested and then cooked; nor do we admire the handiwork of Edward Gein, who fashioned lampshades from the skin and soupbowls from the skulls of the women he killed. And we certainly do not view ourselves prancing in the moonlight, our underpants filled with vaginas from deceased women (Nash, 1975:116-21; 124-128; Levin and Fox, 1985)! Certainly these criminals are fascinating, but we do not make heroes of them. Only a handful of criminals who committed particular types of crimes against certain victims are fashioned into heroes. To understand why we glorify a criminal, we need to examine the social context in which he played out his life. We need to consider the cultural background from which interpretations of the criminal derived their meaning.

Cultural Explanations

A broader perspective of the heroic criminal is taken by cultural explanations of this phenomenon. Rather than emphasizing the appeal the lawbreaker is presumed to have to the individual, cultural accounts suggest that the popularity of criminals results from the fact that they are symbolic expressions of cherished cultural values. The hero is a concrete example of how social ideals of a rather abstract nature might be manifested in a more concrete, but still pure and noble form. Criminals who are fashioned into heroes, then, are promoted for such a role because they embody traits that have wide social appeal.

Henry Nash Smith (1950:111) in his excellent analysis of the symbolic and mythical qualities of the American West, posits that the fictional outlaw Deadwood Dick became enormously popular partly because he embodied the "popular ideal of the self-made man." Criminologist Richard Quinney (1970:263) proposes that the heroic criminal exists because he reflects certain values such as "aggressiveness, cleverness, and the ability to 'outdo' others in some way." Historian Richard White (1981:406) suggests that outlaws like Jesse James became cultural heroes because of the manliness they exhibited:

The portrait of the outlaw as a strong man righting his own wrongs and taking his own revenge had a deep appeal to a society concerned with the place of masculinity and masculine virtues in a newly industrialized and seemingly effete order.

And as George Orwell (1969:52) points out, those criminals who were highly successful at their chosen lawless profession were accorded the same honor as the Robber Barons who were seen plundering citizenry with the blessings of the law. Biographies about criminals like the James boys are similar in style and tone to biographies written about the Rockefeller family; and organizational geniuses like Henry Ford are described in ways not unlike organized crime figures such as Al Capone. Perhaps crime, as Daniel Bell (1962:128) put it, is mirror casting a contorted image, "caricaturing the morals and manners of society." Criminals who capture the ideal American virtues of individuality, success, cleverness, or courage may become American heroes regardless of the content of their actions.

Certainly the legends of heroic criminals are filled with flattering portrayals of these brigands. Although these men robbed and killed, we are told over and over that they did it with style. Moreover, these fabled outlaws are endowed with an assortment of endearing qualities—loyalty to friends, compassion for the downtrodden, courage in the face of danger, honesty (most of the time), and cleverness in abundance. Men of such character, naturally, would be logical candidates for the role of cultural hero. The analysis of narratives about heroic criminals provides the basis for cultural explanations of why heroes become criminals. It is assumed that tales about such lawless figures are popular because they contain themes that appeal to the interests or reflect the values of a large and diverse audience. Discovering these themes embedded in the text is the key to explaining why we make heroes out of criminals.

This approach poses a number of problems, however. A major problem is the failure to account for why we need to have criminals serve as models of cherished social values. Courage, cleverness, success, loyalty, individuality, innovativeness, and masculinity can be found in generous amounts among lawful citizens who are not robbing and killing. Why do we need to make heroes out of lawbreakers who allegedly have such traits? Certainly the belief that these criminals possessed such traits makes them more appealing, but are these qualities the basis for their heroic stature?

It is doubtful. Consider, for instance, the idea that these criminals became heroes because they were successful at their vocation. Undoubtedly, if these fabled brigands were not somewhat successful, they would never have achieved heroic status. Had they died in their first robbery, for example, no one would have ever taken note of them. But were they really models of success? Billy the Kid was killed at the age of 21. Jesse James was shot in the back by a trusted companion. Butch Cassidy allegedly was gunned down in a small South American village. Virtually every American Robin Hood has suffered a violent and premature death. Certainly this is a far cry from Henry Ford or Andrew Carnegie. And even among thieves, the successes of these outlaws pale before the triumphs of some of their now-forgotten criminal contemporaries. Charles Silberman (1978:27) points out: "In terms of the scale of their operation and the amount of money taken, the big city professional thieves make folk bandits such as Jesse James look like adolescent street muggers." In sixteen years of robbing banks and trains, the James gang earned about $250,000. During these same years, on at least four occasions professional safecrackers managed to steal several times that amount in a single robbery of an Eastern bank. These criminals might have made far better models of success than a bandit like Jesse James, but they are all but forgotten.

There are many criminals who seemingly exemplify idealized cultural values, but they are not heroes. A highly successful corporate offender, a clever rapist, or an innovative child molester does not gain our admiration. The prolific serial killer achieves notoriety, but he does not earn our adoration. We are very selective about the criminals we choose to accept as heroes. Only certain lawbreakers who do specific things to particular types of victims are glorified. Clearly this suggests that the basis for considering criminals as heroes has something to do with their criminality and not simply with their imputed character. Cultural explanations fail to recognize this because they emphasize only selective aspects of the tales of fabled brigands. This often results in a lack of perspective since elements are taken out of the context from which they derive their meaning.

Another shortcoming of cultural explanations is that they fail to question the relationship between legend and reality. Instead, they assume that the tales of these criminals are reasonably accurate accounts of their character and actions. These lawbreakers became heroes, in short, because they were heroic. While the actual content of their actions was illegal, their manner of conduct was inspirational. Their calmness in the face of danger, their courage and determination, and their fierce loyalty to friends and principle were things at which to marvel.

Undoubtedly the presentation of outlaws as admirable men was important in gaining for them widespread admiration. Through the performance of spectacular feats, outlaws did become media sensations. The Santa Fe New Mexican (May 4, 1881) described a daring jail escape made by Billy the Kid as "as bold a deed as those versed in the annals of crime can recall. It surpasses anything of which the Kid has been guilty so far that his offenses lose much heinousness in comparison with it, and it effectively settles the question of whether the Kid is a cowardly cut-throat or a thoroughly reckless and fearless man." A similar amount of hyperbole was given to the activities of the James gang by the St. Paul Pioneer Press (Sept. 20, 1876), in describing the bandits' success at eluding the pursuit of hundreds of men following the Northfield robbery:

Truth is stranger than fiction, and no novel writer would dare invent such situations for his characters as these six men have passed through. The feats of Turpin, Shepherd, and the more recent Joaquin, and even the bloodcurdling and enormous achievement of the dime novels pale before the accomplishments of these desperate outlaws.. . .

Such determination, daring and perseverence was worthy of a better cause, and cannot but evoke admiration even of those who must desire their extermination. Probably no men were ever more desperately set upon, nor more intrepid daring ever displayed by mortal.

Similar declarations of amazement and praise may be found concerning such lawbreakers as Butch Cassidy, John Dillinger, "Pretty Boy" Floyd, and any other American lawbreaker who has been cast as hero. But as Michael Schudson (1978:5) astutely noted about the press in late 19th century America, "there was as much emphasis in leading newspapers on telling a good story as on getting the facts. Sensationalism in its various forms was the chief development in newspaper content. Reporters sought as often to write 'literature' as to gather news." The press in the past (and certainly in the present) has often treated crime as entertaining drama, often misrepresenting such tales as informative news. From newspaper accounts such as these, the fashioning of heroic criminals began.

Sensationalist accounts have a tendency to play fast and loose with the facts. For instance, Orrin Klapp (1962:50) suggests that Billy the Kid did not make a good villain because he was "blonde, blue-eyed, well-built, and rather handsome; women fell for him." Dixon Wecter (1941:350-1), however, points out that an authenticated picture of the young desperado "dissipates the legend that he was a dapper man of steel. He there appears as an adenoidal farm-boy with a rifle." Another historian has described the Kid as a "buck-toothed moron" (Horan, 1976:15). Legends have a tendency to give "face-lifts" to the characters that star in their dramas.

And historical evidence suggests that the "face-lifts" went beyond reconstructing physical appearances. Little proof exists of charitable acts performed by these figures; but there is an abundance of evidence concerning uncharitable deeds. Jesse James, the archetypical American Robin Hood, provides a good example. During the course of his criminal career, some sixteen people were killed. The first documented murder, committed in an 1869 bank robbery at Gallatin, was done probably for no other reason than to frame a former comrade-in-arms for the robbery (Settle, 1966:38-40, 55). A Clay County neighbor was slain simply because he was suspected of aiding detectives in their hunt for the outlaw. Yet glorifications of Jesse James overlooked or rationalized these acts, and the victims were depersonalized. It is as if banks and trains were killed rather than human beings with wives and children.

Our admiration for these figures should also be tempered by the fact, moreover, that for every laudatory description of them one may also find accounts that revile these very same lawbreakers. According to one biographer, Jesse James spent his childhood "burying small animals alive" (Buel, 1893:110). Another chronicler of Jesse James began his biography by rhetorically asking:

What language can furnish the vocabulary which contains enough lurid words, wild synonyms, ensanguinary adjectives, and murderous verbs to do justice to this horrible monster; this insatiable vampire who has drank enough blood to print, in red, an entire edition of this narrative (Gordon, 1891:9).

Clearly not everyone viewed Jesse James as a symbolic representation of cherished social values.

Billy the Kid also had his share of detractors. The Las Vegas Daily Optic (May 4, 1881) wrote of the young outlaw:

His name has long been the synonym of all that is malignant and cruel.... With a heart untroubled to pity by misfortune, and with a character possessing the attributes of the damned, he has reveled in brutal murder and glorified in shame.

The paper further described the outlaw as a "young demon" to whom "the drooping forms of widows and the tear-stained eyes of orphans" meant nothing. The death of Billy the Kid was almost universally hailed by the New Mexico press as a milestone in the civilization of the territory. The New Southwest (July 23, 1881) for instance, observed that "the vulgar murderer and desperado known as Billy the Kid has met his just desserts at last" and ended its eulogy by saying "the fact is he is a low-down vulgar cut-throat, with probably not one redeeming quality."

Indeed, virtually every criminal who has been labeled a hero has also been cast in the role of a villain. Among the diverse tales of notorious criminals, two diametrically opposing legends may be sorted out—one praising him as a saint and the other condemning him as a demon (cf Steckmesser, 1965). Which of these versions captures the real outlaw? Probably neither. As Orrin Klapp (1962:13) points out, the construction of reputations of notorious criminals is usually based upon conventional tales, themes and anecdotes: "So it often results that there is something very similar about...outlaws like Billy the Kid, Jesse James, Pancho Villa, John Dillinger, or Al Capone." These celebrated criminals are actors in archetypical story forms. They are more closely akin to literary symbols than to real men. They are cultural products, and their actual behavior, motives, and attributes may be quite different from those imputed to them by entrepreneurs constructing the legend. For example, the noted California bandit, Joaquin Murieta, described by one writer as "California's most enduring myth," may never have existed (Jackson,

1955:xi). Murieta may have been the product of one writer's imagination and the blending together of newspaper accounts concerning several Mexican bandits who were terrorizing the California gold fields. His "biography" was first published in 1854. Other publications catering to mass audiences borrowed freely from this fiction and quickly turned Murieta into a national figure who has even been accorded space in several California state histories. The fact that a criminal who may never even have existed was fashioned into an American Robin Hood suggests that the actual deeds and characteristics of heroic criminals played only a minor part at best in elevating them to such lofty status. A good public relations man and a receptive audience may be far more important.

Still another problem afflicting cultural explanations of the heroic criminal is their tendency to select out aspects of a narrative which are then identified as the major "theme" which accounts for the popularity of a figure or of a particular story form. One difficulty with this method is that it takes elements of a story out of their context. Furthermore, as John Cawelti (1975:5) points out, the concept of theme "fails to provide us with any way of determining which themes are more important than others or even how one theme is related to another.... This becomes particularly problematic when we encounter themes which seem to contradict each other in the same work." By focusing upon thematic messages in tales of heroic criminals, it becomes possible for one author (Fishwick, 1969:96) to see a gunman like Billy the Kid as a symbol of the pastoral epoch "doomed by the railroad, the tractor, and the homesteader. He went down grimly with both guns roaring defiance and death;" while another author (Mottram, 1976) sees the gunman as an example of modernizing America because he relies upon technology to survive. Or as another example, we find Martin Nussbaum (1960:26) describing the western hero such as the outlaw as a "vanishing symbol of individualism in an age of togetherness and conformity;" while Robert Warshow (1975:338-50) describes the outlaw as "the last gentleman," bound by the code of honor and the "pressure of obligation."

We should not be surprised at the varying and even contradictory themes that are offered as explanations for the popularity of the heroic criminal. Tales of notorious criminals will hold different meanings for different audiences. It is essential to realize, as Will Wright (1975:185) has pointed out, that the heroic outlaw is a basic American myth and not simply a real person. And myths, as the eminent French anthropologist Claude Levi-Strauss (1966:38-9) observes, are by their very nature ambiguous and open-ended:

> The diversity of sequences and themes is a fundamental attribute of mythic thought....
> Unconcerned with neat beginnings and clear goals, mythic thought does not effect complete
> courses; it always has something more to achieve.

It is this open-ended quality that enables the tales of heroic criminals to have continued relevance in changing social climates and for diverse audiences. Through the process of what Robert Escarpit (1968:424) has termed "creative treason," new versions of outlaw tales are constructed with embellishments attractive to modern audiences. Legends of outlaws such as Jesse James will mean different things to different readers depending upon the tales consulted, the values of the reader, and the social context in which the tales are read. As Anthropologist Victor Turner (1977:128-9) has noted, myths have a "multi-vocal character, having many meanings, and each is capable of moving people at many psycho-biological levels simultaneously." It is the great broadness and rich depth of meaning that give legends of the heroic criminal their popularity and the Robin Hood criminal his symbolic power.

Finally, one last limitation of cultural explanations for the heroic criminal is that the approach encourages parochialism. By turning one's attention to a search for themes embedded in a narrative, one overlooks the fact that the Robin Hood criminal is found world-wide. He has been encountered in Australia (O'Malley, 1979), in Viet Nam (McLane, 1971), and throughout Europe and Asia (Hobsbawm, 1969). Given that the Robin Hood criminal is what Eric Hobsbawm (1959:5) has rightfully called "a universal and virtually unchanging phenomenon," it seems unlikely that the basis for this heroic criminal has anything to do with peculiarly American social values, attitudes, or experiences. This universality suggests that the heroic criminal touches a nerve rooted in human experience and is something that originates from a source that transcends any particular culture.

So we cannot assume that stories about heroic criminals accurately reflect a behavioral reality. Cultural explanations of the heroic criminal cannot tell us why we make heroes out of criminals. This kind of explanation does explain *how* criminals are fashioned into heroes, however. By drawing upon standard stories that comprise the Robin Hood motif, a series of rationalizations which excuse the lawlessness are presented. He is "driven" to a life of crime. He only robs the corrupt rich and gives to the deserving poor. He only harms others in self-defense or when social justice requires it. And at the same time, the criminal-to-become-hero is adorned with an assortment of cherished social qualities, virtues which make him more appealing and permit us to forget that this individual is a murderer and thief. Finally, his biography and the biography of his victims are constructed in such a way that their social roles are reversed; he is seen as a man with whom we may easily identify. And his victims are seen as enemies of social justice. Thus he becomes transformed into a figure through whom people may vicariously rebel. As the context in which his lawlessness unfolded loses its relevancy, new twists are added to the outlaw and his actions which permit him to maintain his heroic status. Thus, the legend is created and perpetuated.

To understand why we make heroes out of criminals, we need to take a more holistic view than that offered by psychological and cultural explanations of this phenomenon. Probing into the depths of the reader's mind, unraveling the motives of authors, or searching the pages of a literary product is not enough. We need to turn our attention to the social conditions in which the outlaw played out his life, to the interpretations and opinions of the lawbreaker held by his contemporaries, to the nature of support and opposition given to the criminal, and where possible, to the actual behavior of the outlaw. In particular, we need to uncover commonalities in the structural conditions under which such criminals appear and from which the criminality of such figures derives its meaning. The heroic criminal is best seen as a cultural product that thrives under certain structural conditions, social circumstances that transcend a particular society and may be found at various times and in various places throughout the world. To explain why we make heroes out of criminals we must look at why and how certain criminals became legendary figures.

Sociological Explanations

Sociological explanations for why a criminal becomes a heroic figure examine the social setting in which his actions took place and consider how social conditions influence the interpretations of the lawbreaker's character and deeds. A number of scholars have been sensitive to the role social structure plays in the formation of heroic criminals. Perhaps the most brilliant analysis of the heroic criminal has been done by Eric Hobsbawm (1959, 1969). In an early work, Hobsbawm described this type of criminal as a "social bandit" who robbed from the rich as a form of "pre-political" social protest. An analysis of the appearance of such bandits in Europe and Asia led Hobsbawm to conclude that these lawbreakers were the product of certain social conditions. The social bandit was a symbol of justice who emerged "when a peasant society which knows no better means of self-defense is in a condition of abnormal tension and disruption" (Hobsbawm, 1959:5). These conditions were identified as famines, wars, or periods of modernization that threatened to destroy or transform a rural society based on traditional authority. For Hobsbawm, the Robin Hood criminal is a rural creature, found in peasant societies, and above all the product of particular social conditions.

These brigands are also judged to be relics of the past, for Hobsbawm feels that the structural conditions that gave life to them no longer exist in the modern world. Modernization, with its improved police methods, efficient communication systems, and rapid transportation deprives would-be Robin Hoods of the conditions needed for success (Hobsbawm, 1969:5). Furthermore, modernization is accompanied by the politicization of the peasant. Armed with a political consciousness and equipped with organizations to articulate his discontent, the rural farmer no longer needs the symbolic and ineffective form of political protest represented by social banditry. According to Hobsbawm (1959:23), the heroic criminal "appears only before the poor have reached political consciousness or acquired more effective methods of social agitation." The days of the Robin Hood criminal are over, says Hobsbawm, for today's world no longer contains the social conditions necessary to give life to social banditry. Modernization in the form of Marxism or unionism have spread virtually to all corners of the world.

Hobsbawm's work on social banditry is a brilliant attempt to link a cultural product—the heroic criminal—to particular structural conditions. However, it seems that social bandits have continued to emerge in modern industrialized societies populated by politically aware "peasants" with well organized rural-based political machines. Historian Richard White (1981) has argued that outlaws such as Jesse James, the Daltons, and John Wesley Hardin represent American social bandits at a time when there was nothing resembling a peasantry in this country. Pat O'Malley's (1979, 1981) analysis of Australian bushrangers such as Ned Kelly has come to much the same conclusion. Even Hobsbawm (1981:150-2) has subsequently modified his position to allow that social bandits may have existed in the United States as late as the 1930s because such figures were part of American popular culture, although he argued that they now are "extinct, for all practical purposes."

There is, however, no reason to believe that American Robin Hoods cannot exist and even thrive in modern societies. More elaborate criminal justice systems may have no effect on the absence or presence of social bandity. Indeed, in some ways certain aspects of modernity, particularly the growth of the "culture industry" and mass media, have greatly expanded the possibility for the existence of criminal celebrities. (These are themes that I will develop further in the last chapter.)

Nor is there any reason to believe that the development of more effective forms of political protest among agrarian poor would eliminate the appearance of the social bandit. There is no cause to assume that political protest is a zero-sum phenomenon; if organized expressions of popular dissent exist, informal and less articular modes such as social banditry will not necessarily be silenced. Social bandits such as Jesse James and Billy the Kid in the 1870s, the Daltons and Butch Cassidy in the 1890s, and "Pretty Boy" Floyd and John Dillinger in the 1930s emerged concurrently with agrarian political organizations that proved quite effective. In the 1890s, the Populist party was powerful enough to elect six governors, control the legislatures of eight states, and bring to office some 50 Congressmen. In 1896 the Populist cause was represented by William Jennings Bryan, arguably one of America's most skilled orators, who was influential enough to be nominated for the Presidency by the Democratic party. While Populists never succeeded in placing a candidate in the White House or controlling Congress, it would be an error to consider them as an ineffective political force at the time when American Robin Hoods emerged in this country.

It seems, then, that social bandits are quite capable of appearing in advanced societies and existing concurrently with more organized and efficient forms of agrarian political protest. There are some problems with Hobsbawm's analysis in regard to the political nature of social banditry and also the effect of modernity on this phenomenon. Yet it may be that the general structural pre-conditions he outlines as necessary for the emergence of the heroic criminal—particularly severe economic strains—still hold. What then is the political nature of the Robin Hood criminal? Upon examination, it seems that social banditry has a very indirect and somewhat confusing relationship to agrarian politics. In this next section I will examine the relationship between American social banditry and Populist protest, and also consider the structural conditions under which American Robin Hoods have emerged.

The Political Nature of the American Robin Hoods

To begin with, it is interesting to observe that the heroic criminal makes his appearance in agricultural regions of the country. Studies have found this type of criminal throughout the world but almost exclusively in rural settings (Hobsbawm, 1959; McLane, 1971; O'Malley, 1979, 1981; White, 1981). In the United States, the Robin Hood criminal has almost always emerged in the Midwest and the West, the domain of the farmer. Even the big-time bank robbers of the 1930s like Dillinger and Floyd, although they practiced their trades in both rural and urban settings, were from the Midwest and from rural origins. Not only are such figures existing concurrently with agrarian political protest, but they are appearing in the region from which this protest eminates.

There seems to be good reason for the appearance of American Robin Hoods in this region, once considered the backbone of the country and domain of Jefferson's heroic American. The farmer saw his status tumble as the businessman and financier rose in status. Accompanying this shift in status was a shift in power. Legislative acts such as the Coinage Act of 1873 were condemned by agrarian segments of the population as laws which favored the monied interests of Wall Street and stood contrary to the interests of the farmer. W.H. Harvey's popular tract, *Coin's Financial School*, described the coinage act as the "crime of 1873." Some twenty years later, William Jennings Bryan gave voice to the disenchantment of the displaced farmer in his famous "Cross of Gold" speech. Considering that agrarian groups perceived laws as little more than crimes and invoked religious metaphors such as crucifixions as ways of expressing the impact such statutes had on them, it is not difficult to understand how certain criminals could become transfigured into heroic figures symbolic of justice for portions of the agrarian population.

The transformation of "badman" into a good and a noble man was greatly facilitated by the fact that the victims of the outlaw were identical to the alleged oppressors of the farmer. During the 19th century, the banks, monopolies of various sorts, and the railroads were identified as those "social cormorants" that were "farming the farmers" (Fine, 1929:59). These institutions became widely recognized metaphors for corruption and social evil—symbols of organized injustice. Banks charged murderous interest rates to the impoverished farmer, and then bankers gathered like buzzards around the settler's property (so it was believed) to seize it when payment could not be made. Similar horror stories emerged about the railroads. Some railroads drained the public treasury of a community and then declared insolvency while a handful of speculators escaped with the money; or, even worse, caused some towns to wither away because the railroad chose not to build in that direction. Even some municipalities that were favored by the railroad found its presence to be a mixed blessing; the tracks became tentacles that wrapped around the economic life of a settlement and made demands, such as tariffs, or threatened embargoes that could not be ignored. Land monopolies demonstrated how monied interests could attain vast tracts of land without the customary expenditure of hard work and with little fear of failure, surely a hateful sight to those who journeyed West and risked their fortunes and their lives to develop a parcel of land. The land corporations were most despicable when they used their power to drive squatters away from their family homes and killed those who dared to resist (cf. Fulton, 1974; Glasscock, 1929; Hollon, 1974; Mercer, 1954 repr.; O'Connor, 1973). During these years the famous outlaws of the West preyed upon banks, railroads, and corrupt monopolies that exploited the "common man."

During the 1930s, when a new wave of American Robin Hoods emerged, the list of social institutions that corrupted the law and victimized the farmer had dwindled to one: the banks (cf. Chandler, 1970; Cooper, 1934; Shover, 1965). Correspondingly, the criminals of the period who rose to heroic stature were almost exclusively bank robbers.

The heroic criminal and organized agrarian political movements, such as the Populist movement in the United States, seem to find their genesis in the same cause: agrarian discontent with existing political and economic practices. The American Robin Hood emerged in the same regions of the country as organized agrarian political protest groups, and the victims of the outlaw were commonly identified by such political groups as the institutions that were corrupting the law and causing the unfortunate plight of the farmer.

To see the heroic criminal as some bizarre appendage of formal agrarian political organizations would be misleading, however. In fact, the heroic criminal is paradoxically both *more* and *less* than a political figure symbolizing agrarian discontent.

At least in the United States, populist leaders generally denounced outlaws and felt that the glorification of criminals was undesirable (cf. Settle, 1966:66-7; White, 1981:396). Robbing banks and trains was not viewed as a particularly effective form of political protest, and the politicization of bandits such as Jesse James was seen as something that diffused action by converting it into a form of vicarious rebellion. Furthermore, by entangling populist protest with criminality, it made the moral claims of agrarian dissenters appear less legitimate and more questionable. Thus, a number of writers have considered the heroic criminal as a symbolic figure who tends to obstruct rather than to promote organized social and political protest (Blok, 1972: 496; Hobsbawm, 1969:24-9; Oberschall, 1973:202). Therefore, the Robin Hood criminal is somewhat less than a political figure capable of mobilizing agrarian political discontent.

On the other hand, if the Robin Hood criminal is to be fashioned into a national cultural hero, he must appeal to more than an aggregate of embittered farmers. Anton Blok (1972:500), in fact, argues that it is the urban middle class rather than the hapless peasantry that idolizes the Robin Hood criminal. However, the small town merchant and the urban laborer, and others must also be able to find some meaning in the actions and identity of the criminal in order for him to become a national figure. And it is because he is *more* than a political figure expressing agrarian discontent that such a criminal becomes fashioned into a Robin Hood figure. He expresses the discontent of a wide spectrum of people. Of course, he appeals to many people for reasons that have nothing to do with politics, but the political nature of the Robin Hood criminal is the *fundamental* reason why a criminal becomes fashioned into a social hero. Seeing the Robin Hood criminal as a political figure helps us understand *why heroic criminals appear at certain times* and provides us with insight into why the *form* and *content* of the legends about Robin Hood criminals take the shape they do. Furthermore, we can understand *why particular criminals are chosen* to play the role of a Robin Hood criminal.

The Structural Context

One of the most striking facts about the American Robin Hoods is that they do not emerge randomly. As we have already noted, they appeared, like their counterparts throughout the world, in a rural agrarian setting. In the United States, these outlaws roamed the Midwest and West. But they also appear in clusters at particular times. During the 1870s, Clay Allison, Sam Bass, "Black Bart" Bolton, King Fisher, John Wesley Hardin, Billy (the Kid) Bonney, "Wild Bill" Hickock, Frank and Jesse James, Belle Starr, Ben Thompson, and the Younger brothers emerged and became public figures within the space of a few years. An epidemic of heroic criminals did not break out again until the 1890s when the Daltons, Bill Doolin, Tom Horn, Butch Cassidy, and the Wild Bunch appeared and thrilled the nation with their exploits. Finally, another wave of popular lawbreakers arrived in the 1930s when John Dillinger, "Pretty Boy" Floyd, Al Capone, Bonnie and Clyde Barrow, Ma Barker, and "Machine Gun" Kelly became prominent figures. Outside of these periods, hardly any heroic criminals appear (See Table 1).

These three periods have something in common: an economic depression that was widespread throughout the country. Indeed, the Robin Hood criminal has been observed emerging during economic depressions in Europe and parts of Asia (Hobsbawm, 1959, 1969), Australia (O'Malley, 1979) and in Viet Nam (McLane, 1971). It is easy to see how a depression would produce social definitions of certain laws and particular political practices as unjust. Undoubtedly there is always a portion of the population who feels that the law is unjust, and some degree of corruption, like the poor, is with us always. But during a depression or some other form of societal strain where the daily lives and routines of large numbers of people are disrupted, suddenly corruption and political insensitivity become more visible and odious to the general public. The middle-class merchant or more affluent farmer, for example, may suddenly find his modest economic holdings swallowed up by taxes or interest rates he can no longer afford to pay. Suddenly national politics and legal declarations that were never a matter of concern become unpleasantly relevant. Political malfeasance is no longer apathetically accepted but is passionately condemned. In such times, moreover, a large and relatively influential group exists which adds its voice to those who are customarily dissatisfied with political and economic arrangements.

In such times the perception of the law and political office as tools in the hands of interest groups becomes widespread. And as historian Kent L. Steckmesser (1966:348) suggests, the law becomes seen as "the tool of a gang, or it comes to represent a social system in which injustice is the rule." Under these conditions, figures of justice may be fashioned who are outside the law, and these heroic criminals may appeal to large numbers of people, not just the unhappy farmer. Depressions which occur concurrently with or shortly follow periods of political corruption create a market where there is a large demand for symbolic champions of justice outside the law, and this is why heroic criminals appear in

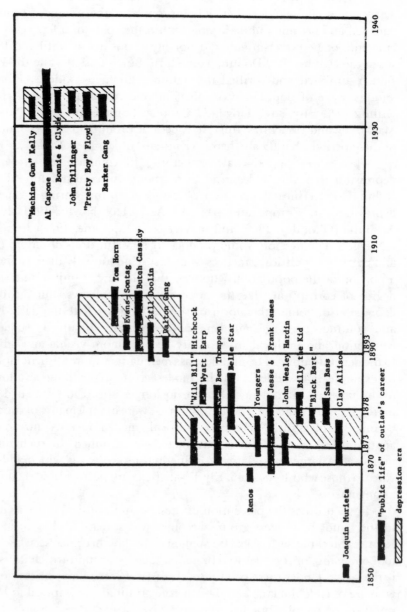

TABLE I. Robin Hoods in American History

John Newman Edwards. State Historical Society of Missouri.
Reprinted with permission.

Bob Ford. From: H.H. Crittenden, compiler, *The
Crittenden Memoirs* (New York: G.P. Putnam's
Sons, 1936). Reprinted with permission.

clusters during particular periods of time, to satisfy the popular demand. The American Robin Hood is a cultural product—a political symbol— who emerges under particular structural conditions.

Symbolic Politics and the form of Legend

Seeing the Robin Hood criminal as a political figure also enables us to understand why legends of the heroic criminal take the *form* they do. The outlaw of legend and literature is a "social product" constructed by the media and the popular imagination. Tales about such a criminal, as we suggested earlier, tell us what people want to believe about him and not necessarily what he did and why. These legends might be seen as *socially constructed* rationalizations for glorifying criminals which are quite similar to the neutralization techniques that Gresham Sykes and David Matza (1957:664-70) suggest make it possible for individuals to justify illegal acts. Outlaws are "driven to a life of crime" (denial of responsibility). They never harm the common folk, and, in a sense, don't really steal because these Robin Hoods are only taking property from the corrupt and redistributing it to the poor to whom it rightfully belongs (denial of injury). Furthermore, as Hobsbawm (1969:35) observes, in legend these outlaws only kill "in self-defense or in just revenge." Those who lost life or property to the outlaw only received what they were due in much the same way a convicted criminal receives punishment from the court. Such a convict is not considered a "victim" of the court, and Robin Hood criminals are the personification of an effective court in which justice is swiftly administered (denial of the victim). In fact, it is the political system and its representatives that are evil and corrupt and not the heroic criminals (condemnation of the condemners). Finally, while Robin Hood criminals disobey the law, they are faithful to higher moral duties. They act not just in the interest of friends and family but are the defenders of a whole class of people, the oppressed (appeal to higher loyalties). Legends of such outlaws take great pains to show that although they break the law, when all aspects of their criminality are considered, they are really paragons of virtue. These legends then, are not historically accurate accounts of an outlaw but might better be seen as originating from propaganda designed to convince the public that the outlaw and what he stands for are morally good.

Not all the legendary accounts of the Robin Hood outlaws portray these men as admirable figures, however. For every tale that shows such men to be saints, a tale can be found which describes these men as beastly savages with no redeeming qualities (cf. Steckmesser, 1965). This also can be understood by recognizing the political nature of such tales. As scholars of communications ranging from orally transmitted myths to mass media have noted, through complicated processes of selective exposure, selective perception, and selective retention, an audience tends to accumulate messages that will strengthen and reinforce its particular constructions of social reality and ignore or reject anomalies that threaten the way it makes sense of the world.[1] Thus, as Inciardi, et. al (1977:55-6) observe about outlaw tales:

(V)ariations in folklore accounts between groups and across areas and time, provide information to elaborate on the social dimensions underlying definitions of crime. The comparison of folklore versions and official interpretations of bandits offers a clue to determining the outlines of group conflict and consensus and their impact on definitions.

The variation in tales concerning outlaws originates from groups with conflicting social values and political interests, and this leads them to disagree about the moral and political implications of the legendary outlaw.

It should be understood, however, that not all outlaw tales are full of political messages or are designed to convey moral truths. Over time, the outlaw of legend becomes a literary figure with a life of its own. Writers may utilize such figures for no other purpose than to make money. Audiences turn to outlaw tales for entertainment alone. Legends are fractured in many directions for different audiences and for different reasons, some not even remotely political. Nonetheless, at their origins, the legends of heroic criminals are political. In order to understand the phenomenon of the heroic criminal we need to begin not with legends, but with the men and social groups behind the legends. By this I mean the outlaw about whom such tales were constructed, the men who were responsible for initiating these legends, and the audience that found meaning in the criminality of the outlaw.

Symbolic Politics and the Content of Legend

By seeing the Robin Hood criminal as a political figure, one is also able to explain the *content* of legends concerning the heroic criminal. He does not just go around robbing and killing everyone. His victims are only those individuals or institutions that are widely recognized at the time as corrupters of the law and oppressors of the common folk. The villains in this moral tale are easily recognized because they are the same villains that people read about in their newspapers and hear being denounced by political groups of the time. These victims are widely recognized metaphors for institutional evil.

One can also understand how certain individuals are selected from the great mass of robbers and murderers and fashioned into Robin Hood figures. Their social identity is such that they can be easily fitted into the role. This may be in part because of certain personal characteristics that they possess, but of much greater importance is the fact that their identity can be infused with political meaning. They can be portrayed as a common man who was victimized by injustices perpetuated by those who were corrupting the law. They can be fashioned into a symbol of social and political discontent, and this is what separates them from common robbers and murderers.

Thus, as anthropologist Claude Levi-Strauss (1963:268) suggests, legends such as those of the heroic criminal are perpetuated in two ways. Traditional figures may be revived and new versions of their life may be told; or old tales may be given new life by inserting contemporary figures in them. There exists an "organic contiguity apparent among mythology, legendary tradition, and what we must call politics." The Robin Hood criminal and his victims are simply the latest actors participating in an ancient morality play that is concerned with the relationship between law, justice, and the individual. Their political and social qualities have earned them their roles and have provided the context in which the tale unfolds. The tale itself is a political fable, and the forms taken by it are shaped by and directed toward social groups in conflict over the meanings of crime and justice. Finally, the popularity of the outlaw legends are determined to a great extent by the social and political situations in which they emerge. When large numbers of people feel that the law and political office are tools in the hands of special interest groups, and these tools are seen as being wielded against the interests of "the people," then there exists an ideal market for symbols of justice outside the law: Robin Hood criminals. Under such conditions, legends are created and flourish.

A Theoretical Framework: Structure, Identity, and Power

A structural explanation for the emergence of heroic criminals provides a good starting point, but by itself it is incomplete. It accounts for why there may be a demand for extra-legal symbols of justice, but cannot explain how certain lawbreakers were chosen to meet that demand. In the chapters to follow, I will examine several American Robin Hoods to determine what things they have in common which might account for their emergence as heroic criminals. In particular I will look for attributes which made each of these men suitable for the role of an American Robin Hood. To do this, I will use a theoretical framework borrowed from the sociology of literature. As Robert Escarpit (1972:1-2) notes, to maintain a sociological perspective when analyzing literary products one must recognize that "each and every literary fact presupposes a writer, a book, and a reader; or in more general terms, an author, a product, and a public." The relationships between these are complex, but it is necessary to consider each to gain a full understanding of the social significance of works of literature. The Robin Hood criminal, while not simply a literary product, might be considered a cultural product that is quite similar. To fully understand how and why certain criminals become heroes, it is useful to examine (1) the Robin Hood criminal as product—who he was, what he did, and to whom he did it—; (2) to look at the author(s) of this product—who was marketing this figure to the public—; and (3) to describe the public that found social significance in the identity and actions of the Robin Hood criminal.

In considering the Robin Hood criminal as a cultural product, three important factors deserve consideration. The first of these is the social identity of the criminal. A social identity is a socially constructed definition of who a person is. It is comprised of the statuses he holds and the way he performs in those statuses. A social identity has dynamic qualities and is always being shaped and altered. More importantly, it lends itself to variations in interpretation. Through selective exposure, perception, retention, and differences in weighting which elements are most critical in determining who a person is, people will arrive at differing interpretations of a person's social identity.

To be fashioned into a Robin Hood figure, a criminal must possess characteristics that can be drawn upon to present him as a member of a group that suffered injustices at the hands of the state. Furthermore, he must be cast as a "common folk" and not as a member of a deviant subculture; he is someone with whom large numbers of people can identify. Finally, he must appear to be acting in the interests of others and not just for personal gain. The social identity of a lawbreaker may be partly determined by what he says, but what he does and the statuses he holds play a more significant part in determining whether he is perceived as a Robin Hood.[2]

A second factor is the social identity of the victims of the criminal. These are individuals or institutions that can easily be portrayed as "enemies" of the people. These are the forces in society that are held responsible for the corruption of the state, adulterers who have led to the divorce between law and justice.

Third, the nature of the criminal acts must also be considered as a factor in shaping the way lawless behavior is perceived. Factors such as the intensity and extent of suffering a criminal act causes, how much personal benefit the criminal gains from his lawlessness, and how the behavior relates to the moral standards of the community will determine how the behavior is judged.[3] If the Robin Hood criminal is to be a figure of justice outside the law, then his crimes are, in a sense, really seen as punishments meted out to deserving victims. But if his actions are too violent and exceed fairness, his behavior will be difficult to rationalize and justify. A criminal who robs the corrupt rich may become a Robin Hood figure. A criminal who kills their children and rapes their wives will not.

Another important dimension of the Robin Hood criminal is the resources of power and influence available to support him and assert his heroic nature to others. As William Goode (1978:252) points out, "the relative resources of individuals or groups in prestige processes may have considerable effect on who gets how much praise or dispraise.... The greater the resource in money, prestige, or political influence, the more people can sway officials, reporters, and others to turn their attention away from the deviation, or persuade to treat it as a minor offense, calling for only a small loss in esteem." Goode has in mind the favored treatment that upper-class juvenile offenders or corporate criminals receive from the legal system in comparison to less advantaged social groups, but the same principle holds true for heroic criminals. As Blok (1972:498) observes in his analysis of social bandits in Sicily:

> Protection of Bandits may range from a close though narrow circle of kinsmen and affiliated friends to powerful politicians, including those holding formal office as well as grassroots politicians. Protection thus involves a power domain. Of all the categories the peasants are the weakest.... It may hence be argued that unless bandits find political protection, their reign will be short.

Here Blok is talking about resources which provide forms of protection such as hiding the outlaw from authorities, tipping him as to the actions of law enforcement officials, and providing legal defense or political immunity. These might be thought of as defensive measures to protect the Robin Hood criminal.

But the criminal who becomes a Robin Hood figure also benefits from a different use of power and influence whereby he is promoted rather than protected and where his outlaw "reign" is not only lengthened but the boundaries of his fame are extended. As Marshall Fishwick (1954:228) notes, "behind every hero is a group of skillful and faithful manipulators." The Robin Hood criminal is the beneficiary of shapers of public opinion in the form of newspaper editors, authors, or celebrities who turn the criminal into a cause. In recent years we have seen the trials and tribulations of criminals such as Joan Little, Rubin "Hurricane" Carter, and Jack Abbott presented to the public by luminaries such as James Reston, Bob Dylan, and Norman Mailer. The criminal who becomes a cultural hero has more than the support of the poor and oppressed. His career is entangled with powerful and influential people. Often such entanglements in and of themselves and serve to increase the notoriety of the criminal.

The Robin Hood criminal, however noble his character might be, needs these "moral entrepreneurs," as Howard S. Becker (1963) terms them, to become a cultural hero. He cannot mount soapboxes and inform people why he became a criminal and what motivates his actions. He needs others to "market" him to the public and to articulate his character and motivations. The modesty of heroic criminals can be preserved when others, particularly prestigious or skilled communicators, can extoll his virtues.

But the heroic criminal may also be marketed by powerful enemies who use him or his crimes as symbols of evil or corruption. The stature of the criminal may be raised by the attention given to him by his detractors. His worth may be determined by the quality of his foes. When the outlaw is challenged only by local law enforcement officials, his fame will be minimal. When he becomes the topic of condemnation by state or national political figures, by national organizations that wage war on crime, or by powerful institutions, the outlaw may become a hero of epic proportions.

Finally, it is important to consider the audience that finds meaning in the social and political issues embodied in the criminality of the Robin Hood outlaw. There are numerous lawbreakers who have been considered as heroes by some social group or community (Abrahams, 1970:61-85; Dance, 1978:224-46; Levine, 1977:407-20; Miller, 1958). The ghetto pimp may be a hero to the local teenage crowd. Charles Manson was certainly a heroic figure to his Family of drifters and outcasts (Bugliosi, 1974)! But in order to emerge from obscurity and become a national hero, the criminal must appeal to large numbers of people. Even powerful promoters will fail to create a heroic criminal if the public is not receptive. To understand how and why criminals become heroes, one must consider the types of social conditions that create a market for such figures and determine who considers the lawbreaker as a hero.

Conclusion

To summarize, what I am arguing is that in order to understand why and how certain criminals are transformed into cultural heroes, a broader perspective is needed than that provided by psychological or cultural explanations. Psychological explanations provide some insight into why tales of these figures are popular, but they do not adequately explain why certain types of criminals are chosen as Robin Hoods. The powerful symbolism contained in outlaw narratives undoubtedly attracts and stimulates the audience, and explains in part *how* certain criminals may be transformed into heroes; however, psychological explanations are too simple.

A similar problem arises with cultural explanations of heroic criminals. This perspective illuminates *how* certain criminals are fashioned into heroes: by constructing legends about them which serve as both socially constructed rationalizations legitimizing their lawlessness and as embellishments adorning the character of these criminals with cherished social values so as to make them socially attractive. But cultural explanations do not explain why certain types of criminals become heroes unless we believe that their actual behavior was justified and their actual character was a true reflection of cultural ideals. These beliefs, as I have noted, are not reasonable.

A sociological perspective provides the broader view needed to account for the Robin Hood criminal, and it is the framework I will use to examine the heroic criminal. I begin my analysis with an examination of the social conditions in which certain lawbreakers are chosen as heroic figures and with a consideration of those factors instrumental in their selection for such a role. These factors include (1) the social identity of the outlaws and their victims, the nature of their lawlessness, (2) the promoters and opponents of the outlaws, (3) and the audience that supported and identified with their lawlessness. Such an examination will reveal that the heroic criminal is less than a paragon of prized virtues and more than a vehicle for the vicarious expression of rebellion. He is a symbol of justice outside the prevailing legal definitions of morality. The heroic criminal eventually takes on other meanings and is enjoyed for other reasons, but the political nature of such a criminal is the fundamental reason for his existence. The political character of the Robin Hood criminal explains why he appears at certain times and why legends about him take the form they do. Furthermore, we can understand content of these legends, including why a particular criminal becomes a Robin Hood figure, by recognizing the political basis of the heroic criminal.

Chapter 3

Frank and Jesse James

No other outlaw figures in this country have captured the public's imagination as Frank and Jesse James have. In his annotated bibliography on Western outlaws, Ramon Adams (1969) cites over 300 books and pamphlets about the Jesse James alone, far more than have been listed for any other outlaw. Jesse James has become the standard to which other American criminals—like Butch Cassidy, John Dillinger, and even Al Capone—are compared. A century after Frank and Jesse James robbed their last bank, ballads, movies, and books still glorify the desperate deeds of these bandits. Jesse James may rightfully be considered *the* American Robin Hood.

Why did Frank and Jesse James become the stuff of legend? Undoubtedly, the fact that they were successful at their vocation had something to do with their notoriety. For over 16 years they went uncaptured while robbing dozens of banks and trains. The particular series of events which marked their public careers in crime also deserve consideration: the destruction of their family home and harm to innocent family members at the hands of railroad detectives, Jesse James's controversial assassination engineered by the Missouri political establishment, and the outlaws' shrewd attempts to foster a Robin Hood image by the style of their robberies and the content of their literary efforts published in Missouri newspapers.

Of greater significance, however, is the broader social and political context in which their actions took place. The James boys, like several famous outlaws of the time—the Youngers and John Wesley Hardin to name a few—were easily portrayed as Southerners living under the rule of foreign despots, Radical Republicans, during the Reconstruction period. To a larger number of Missourians, the actions of these outlaws had political meaning. These criminals were true rebels continuing the struggle against the despised Yankees who controlled Southern political and legal systems. These bandits were good men who were driven to outlawry because of injustice; they were persecuted because of their identity as Confederate guerillas, falsely accused and denied fair protection of the law. As a result, they became symbols of the proud and recalcitrant South. The fact that they claimed as their victims the banks and railroads, which were cast as social villains oppressing the poor, only added to

43

these outlaws' heroic nature. And the fact that these social institutions employed Pinkerton detectives, an organization that served the North during the Civil War as spies, broadened and intermingled the symbolic and political aspects of the James gang. To some these outlaws were evil figures, mass murderers and thieves who violated the law with impunity; but to many others, they were noble figures representing a just cause.

The South has been characterized following the Civil War as a region where political corruption was widespread and social order was precariously maintained. As a popular history textbook notes: "With the collapse of the Confederacy, civil administration all but disappeared throughout the South.... There were few courts, judges, sheriffs, or police officers with any authority, and vandalism went unrestrained except by public opinion or lynch law" (Morison, et. al., 1977:321). It was a time of vigilantism and mob rule. The Republican rule of the South during Reconstruction lacked legitimacy and constitutional authority. Former Confederates were excluded from the political process, making easy comparison with the plight of the colonies at the onset of the American Revolution. Violence was epidemic; the threat of violence almost routine (Cf. Andrews, 1971; Rable, 1984; Trelease, 1971).

While conditions throughout the South were similar, social bandits did not appear everywhere. Their emergence was confined to the borders of the Confederacy: Missouri, Kansas, Oklahoma Territory, Arkansas, and Texas. Perhaps the nature of the war and differences in the composition of the population in these border states account for this fact. These areas differed from most of the South in that pockets of pro-Union supporters could be found living in close proximity to supporters of the Confederacy. In these regions the war literally was one of neighbor against neighbor. Acts of brutality and destruction exceeded in intensity that witnessed in other parts of the South. Scalping and decapitation were practiced to promote terror. Animosity was not directed toward generals acting with at least some semblance of legitimacy; it was focused upon local citizens who had formed what amounted to terrorist bands and operated with blatant disregard for the customary rules of warfare. The hatred that developed for the leaders and members of these terrorist bands was probably as great as that felt for more distant and abstract figures who served as symbols of evil for the two sides, particularly Abraham Lincoln and Jefferson Davis.

Furthermore, these depredations were carried out by people who lived in close proximity to their victims both during and *after* the war. Their very presence thus served as a constant reminder of the brutalities of the conflict and facilitated post-war reprisals. Feud violence such as the legendary Hatfield-McCoy struggles in West Virginia and Kentucky, resulted from wartime grievances (Brown, 1969:48-50)

These conditions played a critical part in the development of Frank and Jesse James as legendary heroes. The nature of the civil war in the Missouri region, the fact that these outlaws could be cast as righteous avengers under the infamous Confederate guerilla chieftain Quantrill, and political events which transpired after the war contributed immensely to their popularity. Several other criminals of this region, coming from similar backgrounds, also achieved a popular following, although never quite to the extent of the James boys. The fact that these robbers preyed on banks and trains, two vilified institutions during the depression years of the 1870s, also helped build public sympathy and contributed to their Robin Hood image. The notoriety and acclaim given to Frank and Jesse James, both during their lifetimes and after, resulted from a number of factors, not the least of which was their amazing success at their profession. While other robbers may have carried off more loot, no one has even come close plying their trade for the 16 years that Frank and Jesse James did. Most significant, however, were the peculiar events which took place in the lives of these criminals, events so bizarre that they were truly stranger than fiction. These events held political meaning for large numbers of people, including powerful politicians, media spokesmen, and the outlaws themselves.

To understand fully the political significance of Frank and Jesse James, one must begin with an examination of the political and social conditions that existed in the Missouri region prior to the Civil War. In 1854 Congress had opened the Kansas and Nebraska territories to settlement and left the issue of whether slavery would be permitted to the territories' residents. A New England Emigrant Aid Company was formed to send anti-slavery immigrants to the region and swing the balance of power on the slavery issue in favor of the abolitionist North. This did not sit well with settlers who had moved to Kansas from slave states such as Missouri or who lived on the Missouri-Kansas border. The Missouri press and politicians like David Atchinson called for Southern men to occupy Kansas and assure its status as a slave state by voting in Kansas elections and by intimidating anti-slavery forces. The marshaling points for proslavery factions were Clay, Jackson, Bates and Vernon counties in Missouri, counties which were also to be the home turf of the James gang.

The presence of two competing economic and ideological factions fighting for domination of a small geographical area yielded predictable results. About the same time that South Carolinian Preston Brooks was beating Senator Charles Sumner of Massachusetts senseless on the Senate floor, John Brown was busy massacring five proslavery men and boys in Kansas, and proslavery men were pillaging the town of Lawrence, Kansas—a settlement of the New England Emigrant Aid Company.

Violent conflicts in the region broke out sporadically right up to the Civil War.

The Civil War only served to increase and intensify conflict in the border states, and from 1861-1865 Missouri was under martial law. Two governments existed; a Confederate government in exile and a pro-union government that lacked legitimacy and was ineffective in tempering the excesses of the military rule. In September of 1861, pro-union forces under the leadership of Kansan James Lane virtually destroyed the Missouri town of Osceola by looting everything that could be carried away and torching everything that remained behind. Lane's brigade essentially was a terrorist gang, and its conduct, as union general H.W. Halleck observed, "has done more for the enemy in this state than could have been accomplished by twenty thousand of his own army. I receive almost daily complaints of outrages committed by these men in the name of the United States and the evidence is so conclusive as to leave no doubt of their correctness" (cited in Wilson, 1975:85-6). Southern guerillas intensified their activities and atrocities committed by one side were quickly matched by violence performed by the other.

To combat the growing problem of guerilla warfare, Halleck took a number of steps. First, he decreed that anyone caught in acts of sabotage would be summarily executed, and anyone accused of such acts would be given a military trial with death the sentence for the guilty. Then, in mid-June of 1862, Southern sympathizers became subjected to a system of fines to pay for deaths and damages inflicted by Confederate guerillas. For every Union soldier or citizen killed, a fine of $5000 would be levied; woundings would range from $1000-$5000. The cost of property destroyed would also be tallied and charged to local Southern supporters (Parrish, 1973: 52). In July a decree was passed forcing all males ages 18-45 to enlist in the state militia. Those who refused were listed as disloyal. Thus it became virtually impossible for anyone to remain neutral. Property was sometimes seized because of personal vendettas unrelated to political leanings. Criticism of military policy was grounds for arrest. Under these unfortunate policies, bonds and taxes imposed against alleged southern sympathizers probably exceed two million dollars in under six months (Parrish, 1973:67).

In the summer of 1863 matters intensified. Brigadier General Ewing, given the task of solving the guerilla problem in Missouri, decided to arrest and jail families of Confederate "bushwackers" and their supporters. On August 14 a three story building that was serving as a jail collapsed, killing several women and injuring many others. Rumors quickly spread that the structure had been deliberately weakened; the women were, in effect, murdered. And so one week later, 450 guerillas under the leadership of William Clarke Quantrill rode into Lawrence, Kansas, pillaged the town, and murdered over 150 citizens.

The Union reaction to this act of vengeance was severe. On August 25, General Order No. 11 was issued. All persons living in Jackson, Cass, Bates, and Vernon counties, who lived beyond one mile of a town, were given 15 days to evacuate their homes. What remained was either carried off or put to torch by Jennison's Kansas. Homes, barns, and fields were burned to the ground. The area, later the home ground of the James gang, became known thereafter as the "burnt district." The events of August would be remembered by both sides for a long long time.

Both Frank and Jesse James, along with several of their future criminal associates, served in Quantrill's guerilla band during these turbulent years. In 1865, with the surrender of the Confederacy, what was to be done with guerillas was uncertain. In Missouri they were promised amnesty under military law, but there were no such assurances under civilian law. In some communities, notices were posted advising known guerillas to look elsewhere for residency. Some were indicted by highly partisan grand juries for wartime crimes, and others were accused of postwar crimes and lynched (Cf. Parrish, 1973:139). Many former Confederate guerillas, including Frank James, avoided this persecution by moving from their home state after the war.

What happened to Jesse James immediately following the war is uncertain. Unsubstantiated but widely accepted is the story that Jesse was shot and left for dead as he surrendered to Federal troops, thus giving rise to the belief that he turned to outlawry because he was not given amnesty after the war. However, many Confederate guerrillas, even better known at the time than Jesse James, did make the transition to law-abiding citizen after the war, which makes this tale seem to be more of a convenient fiction than historical fact.

Four quiet years passed. The handful of bank robberies that occurred in Missouri after the war were sometimes attributed to former Confederate guerrillas, but never to Frank and Jesse James. Then in December of 1869 the bank at Gallatin, Missouri was robbed and the cashier was gunned down in cold blood. Cashier John Sheets fought for the Union during the war and was involved in a gunfight that claimed the life of noted guerrilla "Bloody" Bill Anderson, under whom the James boys had fought. According to eyewitnesses, the bandits had cursed Sheets, blamed him for the death of a brother, and executed him. Jim Anderson, brother of "Bloody" Bill and a noted guerrilla in his own right, was the logical suspect. However, evidence in the form of a fine horse left by one of the robbers pointed to Jesse James as the man responsible for the robbery. A party was dispatched to arrest Frank and Jesse James at their Clay country home, but after some spirited gunplay and fine horsemanship, the brothers eluded their pursuers.

Popular feeling ran strongly against the James brothers in the Gallatin region after the robbery. The Liberty Tribune (December 17, 1869) reported that "should the miscreants be overtaken it is not probable that a jury will be required to try them. They will be shot down in their tracks, so great is the excitement among citizens...." In part this reaction resulted from Gallatin's Union leanings during the war and Sheets's popularity among its citizenry. Also relevant was the fact that banks of the time did not insure their depositors against loss. Thus, when a bank was robbed, the savings of the local citizenry were removed along with the bank's assets. People had an understandable tendency toward extreme displays of displeasure when confronted with the fact that their life savings had just left town on the back of some stranger's horse! Several ex-guerrillas accused of bank robbery had already been shot down by irate citizens or taken from jail cells and lynched by people who had traveled long distances to hasten the course of "justice." And so when the Gallatin Missourian (December 16, 1869) commented that the murderers were two brothers by the name of James who were bragging that they "had killed the sheriff and defied everybody," it seemed that these outlaws were going to be permanently retired even before their careers got started.

Unlike other border bandits, however, Jesse possessed a keen appreciation of the power of public opinion and an intuitive sense of how it might be shaped. Like a consummate politician, he took up the pen to deflect public ill will away from himself and his brother. An open letter was directed to the governor which proclaimed innocence and implied political persecution. He and his brother were being set up by men with political revenge in mind, men who were waving a "bloody shirt" at them because of war-related grievances. The Liberty Tribune (June 24, 1870) made Jesse's letter available to its readers:

Governor McClurg

Dear Sir: I and my brother Frank are charged with the crime of killing the cashier and robbing the bank at Gallatin, Mo., Dec. 7, 1869. I can prove by some of the best men in Missouri, where I was the day of the robbery and the day previous to it, but I well know if I want to submit to an arrest I would be mobbed and hanged without trial. The past is sufficient to show that bushwackers have been arrested in Missouri since the war, charged with bank robbery, and they most all have been mobbed without trials....

Governor, when I can get a fair trial, I will surrender myself to the civil authorities of Missouri. But I will never surrender to be mobbed by a set of bloodthirsty poltroons....

Within a month, the Liberty Tribune (July 22, 1870) published a list of alibis furnished by Jesse James and commented that "those who have read Jesse James' defense generally believe him innocent." This may have been more likely wishful thinking or partisanship on the part of the pro Democratic ex-Confederate factions controlling the paper.

However, very little effort was made to capture the James brothers. Although they did not completely shed the outlaw label, they did disappear from public view for almost a year.

Then on June 3, 1871 several men robbed the bank at Corydon, Iowa while most of the town were attending a fiery political oration on the evils of Black Republicanism. On the way out of town, one of the bandits was kind enough to interrupt the speaker to announce the bank had been robbed. This was viewed as a hoax, and several minutes passed before the message was confirmed. The posse which formed was able to get close enough to the bandits to exchange shots, and physical descriptions of the robbers, as well as the direction in which they fled, led to widespread opinion that Frank and Jesse James were among the guilty (Richmond Conservator, June 17, 1871).

Once again Jesse James took to the pen to defend himself. A letter was sent to the Kansas City Times offering a set of alibis. Jesse also spelled out the political nature of the charges being leveled at him. He refused to surrender because the "degraded" Radical Republicans were sure to lynch him. It was James' contention that he was a political criminal, a man branded an outlaw because of his wartime service to the Confederacy (Richmond Conservator, July 8, 1871).

Another quiet year passed. Then on September 26, 1872 the James gang was credited with a crime which played a major role in propelling them to legendary status: the robbery of the Kansas City Fair. The loot totalled less than $1000, and a young girl wounded by a stray bullet was the only casualty. There seemed to be nothing inherently heroic about this crime. But it did attract the attention of a Missouri newspaper editor named John Newman Edwards, a Confederate war hero and a prominent figure in the Missouri Democratic party. The day following the robbery, Edwards wrote of it in the Kansas City Times (Sept. 27, 1872) as a "deed so high-handed, so diabolically daring and so utterly in contempt of fear that we are bound to admire it and revere its perpetrators." Such a crime was, according to Edwards, "chivalric; poetic; superb" and surpassing any exploit in our criminal history.

Not content with this ebulliative tribute, Edwards two days later published an editorial entitled "The Chivalry of Crime" in the Kansas City Times (Sept. 29, 1872):

There are men in Jackson, Cass, and Clay—a few there are left—who learned to dare when there was not such word as quarter in the dictionary of the Border. Men who have carried their lives in their hands so long that they do not know how to commit them over into keeping of the laws and regulations that exist now, and these men sometimes rob. But it is always in the glare of the day and in the teeth of the multitude. With them booty is but the second thought; the wild drama of the adventure first. These men never go upon the highway in lonesome places to plunder the pilgrim. That they leave to the ignoble pack of jackals. But they ride at midday into the county seat, while court is sitting, take the cash out of the vault, and put the cashier in and ride out of town to the music of cracking pistols. These men are bad citizens but bad because they live out of their time. The 19th century with its Sybaric civilization is not the social soil for men who might have sat with Arthur at the Round Table, ridden at tourney with Sir Lancelot or won the colors of Guinevere....

Such as these are they who awed the multitude on Thursday.... It was as though three bandits had come to us from the storied Odenwald, with halo of medieval chivalry upon their garments and shown us how the things were done that poets sing of.

Not everyone shared this view. Rival papers felt the shooting of a child was not quite in the style of the knights of old, but Edwards was undaunted. And in the October 15 issue of the Kansas City Times he printed a letter allegedly written by the outlaws which mingled humor and politics:

As a great deal has been said in regard to the robbery which occurred at the Kansas City Exposition grounds, I will give a few lines to the public, as I am one of the party who perpetrated the deed. A great many say we, the robbers, deserve hanging. What have we done to be hung for? It is true that I shot a little girl, though it was not intentional, and I am very sorry that the girl was shot; and if the parents will give me their address through the columns of the Kansas City *Times*, I will send them money to pay her doctor's bill.... Just let a party of men commit a bold robbery, and the cry is to hang them, but Grant and his party can steal millions and it is all right. It is true we are robbers, but we always rob in the glare of the day and in the teeth of the multitude....

Some editors call us thieves. We are not thieves—we are bold robbers. It hurts me to be called a thief. It makes me feel like they were trying to put me on par with Grant and his party. We are bold robbers and I am proud of the name, for Alexander the Great was a bold robber, and Julius Caesar, and Napolean Bonaparte, and Sir William Wallace...and Robert Emmet. Please rank me with these and not with the Grantites. Grant's party has not respect for anyone. They rob the poor and rich, and we rob the rich and give to the poor. As to the author of the letter, the public will never know. I will close by hoping that Horace Greeley will defeat Grant, and then I can make an honest living, and then I will not have to rob, as taxes will not be so heavy.

Whether this letter was a fabrication of Edwards or whether it was penned by Jesse James is not known. The names signed to the communique were those of famous British highwaymen from the past whose biographies were in vogue at the time. At any rate, in Edwards' skilled hands the letter was instrumental in turning Frank and Jesse James into heroic figures. Edwards, who was described by William Vincent Byars (1920:70) as "perhaps better known and better loved than any other newspaperman in any generation of the century," was the prime force in creating a Robin Hood image for the James brothers. For some 17 years he was to alternately deny, justify, and glorify the criminal deeds of these former Confederate guerrillas. As historian William Settle (1966:46) has noted: "Many of the 'facts' of the lives of the members of the band were first made known by Edwards' pen, to be repeated by other writers unquestioningly." Edwards undoubtedly created many facts to suit his ideological purposes, and his message of noble Southerners driven to crime by unjust Republican rule was a popular one in many parts of Missouri and the South.

Edwards served as an able "campaign manager" for the James brothers, but these outlaws also had a shrewd sense of how to construct a good public image. Beside writing letters to newspapers claiming innocence and condemning the ruling Radical Republicans, the bandits dramatized their robberies in meaningful ways. At an 1874 train robbery they provided a written account of the event for passengers to give to newspapers, thoughtfully leaving a blank where the amount of loot could be recorded and also cleverly listing false descriptions of the robbers as "large men, none under six feet" (St. Louis Democrat of Feb. 1, 1874). Accounts of the robbery stated that the robbers also examined the hands of each male passenger because they "did not want to rob workingmen or ladies, but the money and valuables of plug-hat gentlemen were what they sought" (St. Louis Republican of Feb. 2, 1874). During a stage coach robbery the money and watches of a Confederate war veteran were returned. Through such actions, the gang fostered a Robin Hood image tinged with post-war politics.

The year 1874 was marked by a number of events important in the development of the James brothers as heroic criminals. In April, while posses searched in vain, Jesse James was captured at the altar by Zee Mimms. The St. Louis Dispatch (June 9, 1874) broke the news that the celebrated Jesse James had been snared at last, "his captor a woman, young, accomplished, beautiful." Jesse granted interviews and announced to readers, "you can say we married for love, and that there cannot be any doubt about our marriage being a happy one." Papers throughout the land trumpeted the news, and several papers praised the outlaw as being a man of style. With the appearance of this modern Maid Marian, the portrayal of Jesse as a Robin Hood rather than a cold-blooded killer was easier to believe.

1874 was also an election year, and the Missouri Republicans turned outlawry into a political issue, claiming that Missouri Democrats sympathized with the ex-Confederate guerrillas and contributed to a social climate that led to "insecurity of person and property, the prevention of immigration, the utter prostation of business, and the ruinous depreciation of all values of property" (Cf. Jefferson City People's Tribune of Sept. 30, 1874). Out-of-state newspapers also attacked Missouri Democrats for the "outlaw problem" and portrayed Missouri as a crime-ridden state, a view which conveniently fit into the arguments being presented to influence immigration patterns into these states, who were competing with Missouri for settlers (Cf. Settle, 1966:63-4). Thus, outlaws such as Jesse James received a lot of national publicity because of the political implications of their outlawry.

Coinciding with the development of Frank and Jesse James as topics of political conversation was the entrance of the Pinkerton Detective Agency as pursuers of the gang. This further contributed to the politicization of the outlaw issue. The detectives had served as hired guns of the railroads, express companies, and large labor-employing corporations. They also were not local constables trying to maintain law and order; they were bounty hunters who pursued wanted men for money rather than morality. And finally, Pinkertons had served the Union army as spies during the Civil War. They were widely disliked by rural, Southern, and working class people.

In March of 1874 Pinkertons invaded the soil of Clay county in search of outlaws. They were not well received. In fact, three of them were murdered. It was suspected that the detectives had been betrayed by prominent people in Clay country and that the James brothers were being protected by local residents. Residents who did not sympathize with the outlaws remained quiet out of fear (Cf. statements made in the St. Louis Globe of March 20, 1874 by Pinkerton operative L.E. Angell).

On the night of January 26, 1875, a drastic approach to resolving the outlaw problem was tried that, perhaps more than any other event, generated much popular sympathy for Frank and Jesse James. Pinkertons and local constables surrounded the home of the outlaws' parents and tossed two illuminating devices through the farmhouse window. One of the devices exploded, scattering iron fragments about the room. One ripped a gaping hole in the outlaws' nine year old half-brother and killed him. Another shattered their mother's right arm so badly that it had to be amputated. No substantial evidence existed that the outlaws were even present at the home, but a Pinkerton agency revolver left at the scene of the "crime of the century," as local residents referred to it, indicated that the Agency was responsible for the act.

The incident received national coverage, and a reporter for the Chicago Tribune (Feb. 2, 1875) even managed to spend some time at the home of the "so-called bandits" as he put it, and announced that he had been "received kindly." The press almost uniformly denounced the event, with several suggesting revenge as a motive. Elements of the Democratic press were the most vitriolic in their condemnations. The Kansas City Times (Jan. 28, 1875) declared; "There is no crime, however dastardly, which merits a retribution as savage and fiendish as the one which these men acting under a semblance of law have perpetrated." The St. Louis Dispatch (Jan. 27, 1875) described the event in headlines that read: "Making War Upon Plain Folk With Torch and Bomb" and issued a call for revenge with clear political overtones: "Men of Missouri, you who fought under [Confederate guerrillas] Anderson, Quantrill, Todd, Poole, and the balance of the borderers and guerrillas,...recall your woodscraft and give up these scoundrels to the Henry rifle and

Colt revolver. It is because like you [the James brothers] were at Lawrence and Centralia,...and wherever else the black flag floated."

Supporters of the outlaws chose a more practical course of action. Stilson Hutchins, owner of the St. Louis Dispatch and a prominent Missouri Democrat, introduced a resolution into the state's General Assembly calling for an investigation into the bombing. The resolution met no resistance in the House, but in the Senate, according to Settle (1966:78), "Republican members spoke through half a day, condemning the measure and its supporters for not demanding the capture of the James and Younger brothers." The Resolution passed the Senate eventually by a vote of 20 to 5, with all but one Democrat voting for it and all the Republicans voting against it. Indeed, political affiliation seemed to be strongly related to the public attitude one held of the James brothers at the time.

The Resolution that sparked such a political fury led to a fruitless investigation. A grand jury indicted eight men for murder, including Allen Pinkerton, and called former Missouri Governor Woodson as a witness. No record of the testimony has ever been found. The follow-up on the raid of the Samuel farmhouse remains a political mystery to this day, suggestive of a cover-up to protect high-ranking officials who were implicated in the raid (Settle, 1966:80).

The investigation of the bombing of the Samuel household was quickly replaced by another political issue, however: amnesty. The St. Louis Dispatch (March 8, 1875) presented a passionate plea for amnesty to ex-Confederate guerrillas to alleviate the outlaw problem:

> How much better it would be to amnesty those unfortunate men, to whom are attributed all the crimes bold and startling in their daring, and so far astounding for their impunity, which have for the past two years been committed from Iowa to Texas, and from Tennessee to Kansas. Give them an opportunity to come home and be honest and peaceful citizens, instead of being hunted like wolves by detectives who are willing to sell their blood for the gold of paltry reward.... Let them be assured that arson, murder, and assassination shall not be employed against them and their innocent ones, and it is more than probable they will make at least as good citizens as Pinkerton's midnight spies and house burners. We speak of all those who like the James and Younger brothers have been educated to desperation by cruelties perpetuated on them and their families during and since the war, and who are hunted only for suspicion.

Within two weeks an amnesty resolution was introduced before the Missouri House of Representatives, a remarkably expressed document which described the James gang as men who were driven "from the fields of honest industry, from their friends, their families, their homes, and their country" and into a life of crime by a government that "arms foreign mercenaries with power to capture and kill them." It continued:

Whereas, believing these men too brave to be mean, too generous to be revengeful, and too gallant and honorable to betray a friend or break a promise; and believing further that most if not all the offenses with which they are charged have been committed by others, and perhaps by those pretending to hunt them or by their confederates; that their names are and have been used to divert suspicion from and thereby relieve the actual perpetrators; that the return of these men to their homes and friends would have the effect of greatly lessening crime in our state by turning public attention to real criminals....

We find in this formal political declaration a set of rationalizations offered for not considering the James brothers as "real" criminals. The logic was a bit confusing, but it was argued that these men were being used for political ends and were not really guilty of any crimes; but if they were guilty of crime, it wasn't their fault because they were forced into it by an unjust political system controlling post-war Missouri. Furthermore, these men typified many cherished American values and were of fine moral fiber. As gang member Cole Younger had written (St. Louis Republican of November 30, 1874) about his poor brother who had been shot down by detectives on a Missouri back road, "there is a day coming when the secrets of all hearts will be laid open before that All seeing eye and every one of our lives will be scrutinized; then will his shirts be as white as the driven snow while those of his accusers will be dark, dark, doubly dark." Or as Jesse James noted in a passionate letter to Allen Pinkerton, published in the Nashville Banner;

Justice is slow but sure and there is a just God that will bring all to Justice. Pinkerton, I hope and pray our Heavenly Father may deliver you into my hands and I believe he will for his merciful and protecting arm has always been with me and Shielded me, and during all my persecution he has watched over me and protected me from workers of blood money who are trying to seek my life, and I have hope and faith in Him and believe he will protect me as long as I serve Him.

There was no doubt in the mind of these outlaws and their supporters whose side God was on.

It is worth noting that the rationalizations and legitimations being fashioned about the James brothers and their crimes were being constructed and accepted by a wide range of people, including influential editors and powerful politicians. According to Robertus Love (1940:157-8) many intelligent and open-minded Missourians sympathized with the outlaws and felt that "under a happier environment the same men might have developed into respectable preachers or respected plutocrats."

Unfortunately for the outlaws, in 1875 there were few "openminded" Republicans in the Missouri House of Representatives. The Amnesty Resolution was narrowly defeated. 56 Democrats and 2 Republicans supported it, while 20 Democrats and 19 Republicans opposed it. According to William Settle (1942:416-7), most of the Democrats who opposed amnesty were from parts of the state that supported the Union during the war. "This vote was indicative of the political distribution of attitude toward James boys. Nearly all of the sympathy for them was to be found in the Democratic party." More specifically, their support came from the Confederate wing of the party, as every ex-Confederate in the legislature voted for amnesty (cf. Jesse James's letter in the Nashville Banner of Aug. 4 1875).

The defeat of the Amnesty Bill did not kill the issue of amnesty; the death of a Clay county resident, Daniel Askew, who had employed a Pinkerton detective as a farmhand, however, did. According to Love (1940:161), the killing was viewed by the public as an act of vengeance done by the James brothers, and public opinion turned against them. Such a crime could not readily be excused on moral grounds. Supporters of the outlaws maintained that they were being convicted by gossip rather than facts. Some even claimed, as did the Liberty Tribune (April 16, 23, 1875) that Askew was assassinated by detectives in an attempt to frame the outlaws and sway public opinion. Others (Kansas City Times of April 18, 1875; Triplett, 1882:106-08) claimed that Askew was killed by detectives or neighbors because he knew too much about the bombing of the Samuel home. These attempts to vindicate the outlaws were unsuccessful, and the amnesty issue was never revived.

For the next year the Democratic and Republican presses criticized each other. Republicans blamed the Democrats for supporting outlawry, and the Democrats condemned the Republicans for accusing the James Brothers of every bank and train robbery that occurred in the region. Mrs. Samuel, through the Kansas City Daily Journal of Commerce (Aug. 30, 1876), denied her children's guilt to all who would listen and castigated those who tormented her and her family. Jesse James again took up the pen and denied his guilt while offering the usual set of alibis. In a note to the Kansas City Times (Aug. 23, 1876), the literate lawbreaker charged the son of a prominent railroad official with engineering a phony robbery, denounced the detectives, and pleaded for amnesty:

If we had been granted full amnesty I am sure we would of [sic] been at work, trying to be good, law-abiding citizens. If we have a wise Congress this winter,...they will grant us a full pardon. I will not say pardon for we have done nothing to be pardoned for. But they can pass a law to destroy all those bogus warrants sent out for us and let us live in peace. What sense is there in spending so much money to have us arrested? I am sure we have thousands of friends that can't be bought although the detectives think they are playing things very fine. Poor fools they are. If the express companies want to do a good act they can take all the money they are letting those thieving detectives beat them out of and give it to the poor.

But the political climate had changed in Missouri over the past several years. No longer were former guerrillas being hung by angry mobs. Eleven years had passed since the close of the war. The rule of the Radical Republicans was about to end in the South. Instead, a new social evil plagued the Missouri farmer: banks and railroads. During the depression years of the 1870s, banks only seemed to hold repossession papers and the finances of the "monied interests" that preyed upon the farmer. Railroads created boomtowns and then dominated their economies, or left other communities stranded when the tracks failed to appear. And railroad rates seemed outrageously high to the farmer. As the Kansas City Times (Aug. 23, 1876) observed with uncharacteristic understatement: "The bold highwayman who does not molest the poor or the ordinary traveller, but levies tribute on banks and railroad corporations and express monopolies, is not generally such an object of popular detestation that he cannot secure a fair trial in our courts." Certainly no mob would materialize to harm men accused of robbing banks and trains in these days. However, none of the outlaws followed up the suggestion to surrender. And within three weeks of the communiques issued by Jesse James, an event took place which once and for all removed any doubt that these men robbed banks and trains for a living: the Northfield Raid.

The Northfield Raid stands as a high water mark in Western outlawry. The attempted bank robbery and the events surrounding it provide a story of the rise and fall of American banditry with all the proper dramatic ingredients. There was daring, loyalty, stubborness, greed, betrayal, and death. It was the Waterloo of the James gang.

The Northfield bank robbery differed significantly from robberies previously attempted. The bank was located in Minnesota, far from familiar territory and friends who could provide aid. Why the bandits deviated from their usual pattern of success is unknown. An explanation offered by one of the surviving outlaws years after the raid was that the hated former Union General, Ben Butler, had a vast sum invested in the bank, and they felt no guilt about robbing an institution that held the funds of the "military dictator" of New Orleans, a man who insulted Southern Womenhood by treating them as common prostitutes (Younger, 1903:76-77). The sympathetic Missouri press portrayed it as a mission of vengeance related to the bombing of the Samuel farmhouse (Boonville Daily Advertiser, Oct. 17, 1876). It is more likely that one of bandits, a Minnesotan, convinced the band that there was ample cash to be had at little risk, since Northerners were unaccustomed to Missouri-style bank robberies. And his knowledge of the place and people would make escape a simple matter. Whatever the reason, the attack on the Northfield bank on the quiet afternoon of September 7, 1876 was a disaster. No one would open the safe. The cashier was killed and another bank officer was wounded when he ran out into the street and gave the alarm. Some Northfield residents tossed stones at the robbers, while others grabbed rifles and began shooting. Within minutes two robbers were

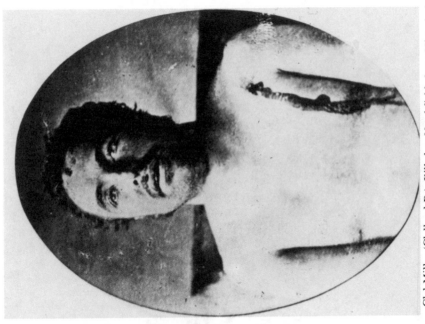

Clel Miller (Clelland D.). Killed at Northfield. State Historical Society of Missouri. Reprinted with permission.

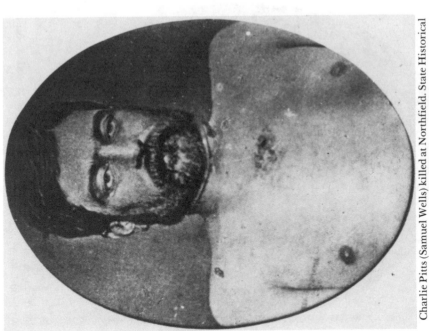

Charlie Pitts (Samuel Wells) killed at Northfield. State Historical Society of Missouri. Reprinted with permission.

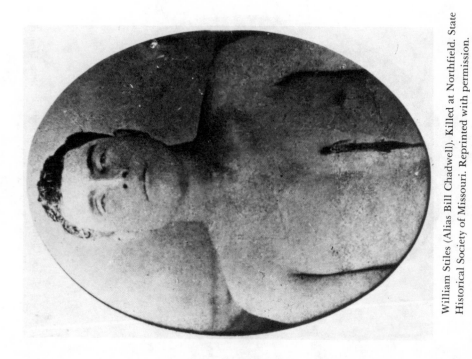

William Stiles (Alias Bill Chadwell). Killed at Northfield. State Historical Society of Missouri. Reprinted with permission.

Bob Younger. After capture at Northfield. State Historical Society of Missouri. Reprinted with permission.

Cole Younger. Shortly after capture Sept. 21, 1876. State Historical Society of Missouri. Reprinted with permission.

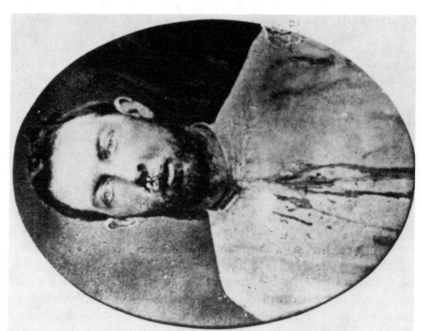

Jim Younger. After capture at Northfield. State Historical Society of Missouri. Reprinted with permission.

dead—including the important Minnesotan who knew the roads—and two were wounded. Not content with driving off the robbers empty-handed, and perhaps overflowing with enthusiasm at their newly discovered skill at gunplay, hundreds of local citizens and dozens of posses pursued the bandits. With two members wounded, short on food and horses, and lost in unfamiliar territory, one would have expected the band to be quickly captured. Such was not the case. Two weeks passed before the outlaws were finally trapped. Expecting only a rope when captured, the robbers tried to shoot their way out. The effort was a failure. One outlaw was killed. The other three—the Younger brothers—were severely wounded. But the remaining two outlaws were nowhere to be found.

Surprisingly, the captured bandits were treated kindly and regarded with curiosity more than with hatred. Numerous citizens took the opportunity to examine the celebrated outlaws and question them. A reporter from the St. Paul (Minn.) Pioneer Press (Sept. 22, 1876) interviewed the three brothers at length and recorded their testimonials:

> I told them I represented the Pioneer Press and asked them if they had anything to say to the public.
> Coleman (Younger) said that he was obliged and asked if I would kindly express their thanks to the citizens of Madelia who had treated them with such kindness. He expressed his surprise at the treatment and declared that he was grateful for it. . . .
> I found Bob—as he asked to be called for short—lying in bed shackled, suffering from wounds in the breast. He was 23 years old, and as fine a specimen of manhood as I ever saw. He has a kind expression and speaks in a low voice using the best of language. During our interview he did not use oaths or slang. He was willing to talk about himself but declined to say anything of the movements of the other men. . . . He said that he had tried a desperate game and had lost. He said that he and his brothers were rough boys and used to rough work and therefore must abide the consequences. . . .
> He said the shooting [of the cashier] was an impulse of passion on the part of the man who shot him. He said they all deeply regretted it. He declared that they could have picked off many citizens, as they were dead shots but did not desire to do murder.
> Bob Younger blamed himself for their capture, as he said he was overcome with drowsiness and insisted to the others on remaining in the field while the others pleaded to go on. He said they would not leave him; had they gone a half mile further they would not have been caught.

What kind of men were these bandits? The picture presented through the media was that of courageous men united by bonds of love, honor, and compassion. They were responsible citizens who were victims of circumstance rather than criminals at heart. Their personal characteristics and the form of their acts exemplified many American virtues, even if the content of their acts did not. The themes presented through the Democratic press of Missouri were reiterated in such Northern papers as the St. Paul Pioneer Press. Whatever the actual nature of these men, one thing was certain. They were quite adept at manipulating public sentiment. As William Settle (1966:93) notes:

Cole Younger shrewdly assessed the opportunity to win sympathy for himself and his brothers. He told of his family, spoke of his former interests in Sunday school and the Baptist church, quoted from the scriptures, expressed regret for his crimes, and asked for the prayers of Christians. He was able to touch some of his audience, and when they wept, he allowed tears to roll down his cheeks. Then the visitor would usually reach a 'wipe' through the bars for him to use in drying the tears.

Amazed that they had not been lynched, the prisoners appeared penitent and worked hard to earn popular sympathy. They cooperated in every way but one. They refused to identify their escaped comrades. There was little doubt about who they were, however. And while Frank and Jesse James returned to Missouri to resume their trade, the Younger brothers received life sentences.

The most important implication of the Northfield fiasco was that it destroyed years of carefully worded denials of guilt by the James gang and their backers. There was no doubt that the James and Younger brothers made a living from crime. This fact was eagerly seized upon by the Republican press. The men of Minnesota accomplished "what Missouri could have done—but to here shame—did not do—ten years ago," proclaimed the St. Louis Globe Democrat (Sept. 25, 1876). And a fawning Democratic party was held responsible for allowing outlawry to flourish.

The Democratic press found fuel for response with the capture and release of a man named John Goodwin, who was mistaken for Frank James by the St. Louis detectives hired by the railroads to apprehend the gang. The Kansas City Times (Oct. 17, 1876) described the seizure of the innocent Goodwin with headlines that read: "The Farmers of Jackson County Getting Up on Ear. Vigilance Committees Being Organized to Protect Their Homes and Firesides. A Third Attempt Made by St. Louis Outlaws to Hunt Down the James Boys. Who are a Thousand Miles Away, While Women and Children are Robbed in their Home." The articles which followed were equally vitriolic. The Times (Oct. 19, 1876) also had choice comments about the nature of the Republican press:

Some years ago when a venomous Radical majority controlled Missouri by means of proscription laws and legalized as well as lawless violence, their papers were forced to justify the high-handed usurpations and bloodshed of Radical rule by representing the people of Missouri as a set of robbers and bushwackers who deserved no better treatment than savages or hyenas. The course these papers then pursued, they still follow, partly from habit, but chiefly because the only way they can attack the Democratic government in Missouri, or aid their party in other states, is by bearing false witness against our people....

Attacks would fly back and forth between Republican and Democratic papers over the political implications of the James boys outlawry repeatedly for the next seven years.

Although the next few years were relatively quiet ones for the James gang, they certainly were not forgotten. John Newman Edwards made certain of that. He was not content with simply publishing editorials which extolled the virtues of these bandits. Instead, he produced a lengthy tome, *Noted Guerrillas*, which more fully developed the story of Frank and Jesse James. Here the justification for the outlaw trail taken by the bandits is described in detail. We find Jesse being shot and left for dead when he attempted to surrender to Union forces at the close of the war and then later being hunted by enemies who wished to kill him for his wartime prowess. Edwards (1877:451) expressed the feelings of many Southerners when he wrote: "[Jesse] is an outlaw, but he is not a criminal no matter what prejudiced public opinion may declare or malignant partisan dislike make noisy with reiter-ation." Jesse James, according to Edwards, was driven to crime by "robbers" and "cutthroats" who controlled Missouri politics after the war. It was only because he and his companions were "men who would not be bullied—who were too intrepid to be tyrannized over" that they broke the law. As Edwards eloquently explained, "They were hunted and they were human. They replied to proscription by defiance, ambushment by ambushment, musket shot by pistol shot, night attack by counter attack, charge by counter-charge, and so they will do, desperately and with splendid heroism, until the end." To Edwards and to many others these lawbreakers were not so much criminals as men who continued the fight for Southern honor and American ideals in the only way they knew how (cf. Love, 1940:298).

While Edwards' book was not a big seller and many of those who purchased it already shared his convictions, the book was given wide press coverage, with portions being published in many Missouri papers. Apparently it was well-received by both the public and by literary critics (Settle, 1966:183). Undoubtedly some readers previously unsympathetic to the outlaws were won over. More important, however, for the development of the legend was the indirect effect of the book. Later chroniclers of the James gang took many of Edwards' descriptions and interpretations as factual. In this way, Edwards shaped the views of many readers not just in his lifetime but for decades following. It is fair to say, as does Albert Castel in the introduction to the 1976 reprint of *Noted Guerrillas*, that this work did more than any other book "to establish and perpetuate the fame of the James boys."

For three years following the Northfield Raid, Frank and Jesse James had apparently retired from outlawry. But then, in October of 1879, somebody robbed the Glendale train, and Jesse James was recognized as one of the bandits. This time there was little public sympathy for them. Fifteen years had passed since the end of the Civil War, two years had passed since Edwards' book made such a sensation, and the populist sentiment against the banks and railroads had subsided somewhat. It was very hard to explain how these men could have been "driven" into outlawry again after three years of peace. Even major Democratic papers like the Kansas City Times (Oct. 15 and 28, 1879) and the St. Louis Post-Dispatch (Oct. 18, 1879) joined with the Republican press in denouncing the outlaws.

The Republicans again made use of the outlawry issue in the 1880 elections. Outlawry was linked with economic issues such as land values and immigration figures; and the Republican state platform contained a resolution (reported in the Missouri Statesman of Sept. 24, 1880) condemning the Democrats "for failure to prosecute notorious criminals of the state...." Historian William Settle (1942:414) suggests that the political pressure applied by the Republicans led the Democrats to nominate Thomas Crittenden for governor. Crittenden, a favorite of the railroad companies, was no friend of the Missouri bandits. He would prove to be instrumental in the final destruction of the James gang.

Crittenden was elected governor in 1880 and followed through on promises he made to the railroad interests who supported his candidacy. In his inaugural address, the new governor pledged to rid Missouri of the banditry that plagued the state for some fifteen years:

> We should let all know that Missouri cannot be the home and abiding place of lawlessness of any character. No political affiliations shall ever be evoked as the means of concealment of any class of lawbreakers, but when crime is committed, pursuit and punishment will be inflicted under the forms of the law without fear, favor, or affection (cited in Settle, 1966:107).

We find in this remarkable statement an acknowledgement of the political nature of Missouri banditry. Political affiliations, especially the Confederate wing of the Democratic party, were widely viewed as "being in the James boys camp." If individuals in the party were not physically sheltering the outlaws and informing them of efforts to capture them (as was rumored), they certainly were providing the bandits with protection through rationalizations and proclamations made in the press. We also find that the Governor addressed concerns Jesse James had expressed in letters to previous governors—the promise of a fair trial.

The James gang responded to Crittenden's message by robbing two trains within two months. The robberies, unlike previous ones, were marked by excessive brutality and indescriminate terror. A conductor and a passenger were murdered. In addition to stealing the money belonging to abstract institutions like banks and express companies, the outlaws also robbed the passengers of their personal belongings. In fact, because of the "unprofessional manner in which the entire affair was carried out," one conductor expressed doubts that he was victimized by the James gang (Kansas City Times of Sept. 8, 1881). But evidence would surface which clearly showed that Jesse James and his band were the culprits.

The violence of these crimes was symptomatic of problems developing within the James gang. There was now a large reward for the capture of Frank and Jesse James, creating a natural tension within the band. Furthermore, after the Northfield fiasco, Jesse James was forced to rely upon less skilled recruits to carry out the family trade. No longer was he working with men trained in the border war, united by blood and the ordeals of guerrilla life. One outlaw, Tucker Bassham, was arrested when he showed the poor judgement of bragging about his deeds to a new acquaintance, who turned out to be a detective. Another, William Ryan, was captured when he became intoxicated, announced that he was a famous bandit and brandished pistols at an unappreciative audience.

Tensions further increased when Bassham was offered immunity in exchange for testimony against Ryan in what one biographer (Love, 1940:321) considered "the most exciting [trial] that ever took place in a criminal court in the Middle West." Railroad officials refused to testify because of death threats. Rumors circulated that the bandits were massing to rescue Ryan from his cell. Fires burning in the woods were believed to be outlaw signals. Nevertheless, Ryan was convicted, Bassham fled the territory, and a cycle of betrayal and murder within the gang began. Within six months of the trial, Jesse James was assassinated by a fellow gang member—shot in the back of the head while unarmed—under circumstances that again politicized Missouri banditry.

On April 3, 1882 the news of Jesse James's death was trumpeted throughout the nation. For days large crowds gathered about the house in St. Joseph, Mo. where the killing occurred. In many major cities of the Midwest, crowds gathered and discussed the news. The Kansas City Journal (April 4, 1882) reported that "since the killing of President Garfield there has never been any one thing which has created such a tumult of excitement as the news of the killing of the notorious outlaw, Jesse James.... The response was almost unanimous that the whole thing was a gigantic hoax." Newspaper coverage was prominent and extensive; and for good reason. For many papers, only the issue covering the assassination of Garfield sold more copies (cf. Kansas City Evening Star of April 4, 1882).

Rumors were in abundance. Some papers reported that Frank James had taken an oath of vengeance. The Sedalia Democrat (April 5, 1882) published a message allegedly from Frank James which stated: "As to the Death of Jesse James it is a Dam lie. He is still alive Large and wishes you to Publish this Note and relieve the people." Many were convinced that the man killed was not Jesse James, and that the state was either covering up their error or participating in a conspiracy that would finally end attempts to pursue the outlaw (Cf. Kansas City Evening Star of April 5, 1882). But as Jesse James's family and friends came forward and identified the body, doubts disappeared. The outlaw's mother was particularly convincing. After identifying the body as that of her outlaw-son, she turned to one of the betrayers and cried: "Traitor! Traitor! Traitor! God will send vengeance on you for this.... Oh you villain; I would rather be in my boy's place than in yours" (St. Louis Missouri Republican of April 5, 1882)!

Public reaction to the assassination varied. Generally, however, there was widespread disapproval over the manner in which Jesse James was "brought to justice." The center of controversy was the Democratic Governor Crittenden. In an interview with the press (St. Louis Post-Dispatch, April 4, 1882), the Governor unwittingly implicated himself as an accessory to murder:

> People have no idea how much trouble I have had in getting my men to work together and keep at it. The result is I have succeeded in suppressing train robbery, and have broken up the gang of bandits. I tell you, my mysterious man, 'Bob,' as they call him, did the work.... My great point in this whole business has been secrecy. My success has been entirely brought about by keeping quiet and not revealing my information before I affected my purpose.

Crittenden's "mysterious man 'Bob' Ford and his brother Charles were found guilty of first degree murder, but were saved from a hanging by Crittenden's total pardon.

Crittenden's ill-advised boast and subsequent pardon of the Fords made him the target of Democrats sympathetic to the outlaws, Republicans hoping for political gain, and anyone who believed in Justice and due process. No one was more eloquent than John Newman Edwards in denouncing the Governor. According to Edwards, "there never was a more cowardly and unnecessary murder committed in all America than this murder of Jesse James." The death of Jesse James was an act of treachery in which the state of Missouri "leagued with a lot of self-confessed robbers, highwaymen, and prostitutes to have one of its citizens assassinated, before it was positively known that he had ever committed a single crime worthy of death." Justice was not represented by law in this case. For "here the law itself becomes a murderer. It leagues with murderers. It hires murderers. It borrows money to pay and reward murderers. It promises immunity and protection to murderers. It is itself a murderer—the most abject, the most infamous, and the most cowardly ever known to history. Therefore this so-called law is an outlaw, and these so-called executors of the law are outlaws." For Edwards, justice could only be satisfied by revenge, and he called for the outlaw's friends

Jesse James, dead. Photographer—Lozo.
Western History Collections, University of Oklahoma Library. Reprinted with permission.

to assassinate those who were responsible for the death of Jesse James. (Kansas City Times of April 3, 1882).

Other papers made the same points without calling for the murder of political officials. The Chicago News observed that "the murder of Jesse James doesn't reflect anything except disgrace upon the Governor of Missouri.... No life of outlawry can justify the means employed by Governor Crittenden to secure even a desperate criminal, and the plan, generally adopted, would lead to anarchy and lawlessness all over the country." The St. Joseph Herald, after observing the Governor's liberal use of the pardon to excuse murderers, noted that Crittenden might be indicted as an accomplice for murder. This raised an interesting question: "If convicted, who will pardon Crittenden" (papers cited in the Sedalia Democrat of April 15, 1882)?

The attack on Crittenden spilled over from the newspapers onto the floor of the Missouri House of Representatives, where the Republicans attempted to push various resolutions through that would embarrass the Democrats. Many of these resolutions contained inflammatory phrases which suggested that the assassination was either an indication of the inability of the Democrats to execute the law or another example of their inherent lawlessness. Resolutions were generally ruled out of order, rulings that were sustained often by straight party vote (Settle, 1966:122). Even in death, Jesse James was a tempestuous political issue.

With Jesse James dead and buried although certainly not forgotten, there remained just one more dramatic scene to be enacted. It was universally agreed that Frank James would be the leading actor in this drama, but no one was quite sure what the final script would be. Would he suddenly appear with guns blazing and avenge his brother's death? Would the world awaken some morning and read another tale of betrayal and death? Would he be gunned down or captured in the midst of a daring robbery? Or would he disappear forever, like a gray ghost, never apprehended but occasionally seen? The final scene was to be even more dramatic than any of these.

On October 5, 1882, Frank James and the redoubtable newspaperman, John Newman Edwards, strolled into Governor Crittenden's office, where a group of newsmen had assembled. The script, no doubt fashioned by Edwards and Crittenden, was perfect. The Governor had just finished showing the gathering a letter he had received from Frank James, and the assembly was busy commenting upon the style and penmanship of the noted bandit. A reporter for the St. Louis Missouri Republican (Oct. 6, 1882) was present and described what then occurred:

Major Edwards and his companion walked in and right over to where the governor sat in the midst of the row. The light shown in from the west, and as the outlaw walked that direction with his hat in his hand the most conspicuous feature about him were his eyes, which seemed unusually dark and shone like brilliants, and his face, being clean shaven, was unusually pale, but his walk and his manner were as easy and natural as though this occasion, which was one of life or death, was nothing unusual for him. The assembled company halted their laughing and joking merely out of respect to strangers, and when Maj. Edwards said: Gov. Crittenden, I want to introduce you to my friend Frank James, a death-like stillness took possession of the room, and the men sat like statues. Gov. Crittenden arose and stepping forward shook hands with the visitors. Meanwhile the spell which had come over the spectators held its sway. After shaking hands the outlaw stepped back two steps and unbuttoning his coat, reached to his waist and unbuckled a broad belt which had become visible. Giving it a swing he held out the belt heavy with cartridges and made bright by the polished revolver, but "Gov. Crittenden," said he, "I want to hand over to you that which no living man except myself has been permitted to touch since 1861, and to say that I am your prisoner."

Frank James, now safely removed from his weapons, was greeted in friendly fashion by all present, whom he informed that crime did not pay and that he looked forward to living a peaceful life.

The drama did not end that day, however. The next morning Frank James, under guard, boarded the train that would take him to the Independence, Mo. jail. News of his surrender spread rapidly through the state, and crowds swarmed the train at every stop hoping to get a glimpse of the famous outlaw. The highlight of the journey occurred at Independence. A journalist present recorded what took place when the train arrived at the station (cited in Crittenden, 1936:270-1):

Arriving at Independence, James was met by his old maimed mother, his wife and his little boy, Robert. The crowd fell back as he emerged from the car and hushed all its noisy muttering and whispering as the old mother fell upon her boy's neck and sobbed loud and pitifully. And yet by a single great effort she mastered her grief and turned to the masses behind her a calm and impenetrable face, fixed and set as though the beginning of the end had not arrived. But it was when Frank took his handsome little boy in his arms, and the child began to prattle and pat his father's cheeks, that the crowd broke down, and stout men and sympathetic women wept.

Surely a hero had appeared in their midst, albeit a tragic one.

Frank James was accorded royal treatment during his stay at Independence. The most prominent men of the community offered to pay his bond. Many leaders visited him, including the Governor and Mrs. Crittenden, prompting some Republican papers to ask caustically if it was not the State that was surrendering to Frank James rather than the other way around (cf. St. Louis Globe-Democrat of Oct. 10, 1882).

Finally on August 23, 1883 Frank James was brought to trial for the murder of a train passenger during an 1881 robbery. Crowds that attended daily were so large that the spectacle was moved appropriately to the spacious Gallatin, Mo. opera house. There the dramatic orations of his prominent attorneys filled the air. Numerous allusions were made to Frank James's war "service" and to the bitter period that followed the war in Missouri. Frank James was driven to outlawry by the Radical

Republicans who seized Missouri. His crime was to stand for his rights, and he was a victim more than a victimizer. Testifying in support of Frank James were General Joseph Shelby—a beloved Confederate hero who insisted on shaking the outlaw's hand—and Governor Crittenden, who contradicted key testimony offered by the prosecution's star witness, the former James gang member Dick Little. Frank James was a political criminal who had been persecuted unjustly. At least, this was the point that his lawyer, John Phillips, impressed upon the jury in his closing statements:

> To convict this man because some town politician or public clamor demands it, would not only be cowardice, but judicial murder. The men who cry out for the life of the so-called outlaw, no matter what the proof or the law, are themselves outlaws and demons. No, gentlemen, this court is the temple of justice. The voice of clamor, the breath of prejudice, must not enter here. You are sworn sentinels on guard at its portals. Do your duty.

The jury needed only four hours to determine that their duty was to find Frank James not guilty.

The acquittal was poorly received by the Republican press. The St. Louis Globe-Democrat (Sept. 6, 1883) reported that "there is loud talk of a packed jury." Indeed, rumors circulated that the jury had been obtained from a special list provided by Frank James's lawyers. Head prosecutor William Wallace (1914:287-89) in his autobiography years later claimed to have proof of jury rigging, but was informed by the judge that any protests would be refused "in order to prevent bloodshed." Also, the fact that prominent Democratic politicians like Shelby and Crittenden testified in James's behalf infuriated editors like Pulitzer of the St. Louis Dispatch (Sept. 7, 1883), who noted that "for fifteen years it had been the burning disgrace of Missouri that the bandit chief and his gang had so much political influence that they could rob and kill and terrorize" without fear of arrest. "Yet never was this political influence displayed with such bravado as at this trial...." The editor of the St. Joseph Herald (reprinted in Crittenden, 1936:331) went so far as to claim that Shelby and Edwards kept the outlaws posted about efforts to capture them. "There is little doubt that Shelby and others were in sympathy with the outlaws, if not actually in league with them."

Frank James was not free of prosecution, however, for other charges were still pending. But then the State Supreme Court ruled that the testimony of a convicted felon was inadmissible as evidence in court unless he had been pardoned. This put a crimp in the plans of the prosecution, because their star witness, Dick Little, was a convicted felon. The appeal for a pardon was inexplicably refused by Governor Crittenden. As a result, all charges against Frank James in Missouri were dropped.

He was however, in danger of being convicted of robberies in Alabama and Minnesota. Missouri officials granted extradition to Alabama, where Frank James was easily acquitted of charges against him. Immediately following the verdict, James was placed under arrest by Missouri authorities for a train robbery for which he would never be tried. As Settle (1966:153) astutely noted, "thus, no chances were taken of letting James fall into the hands of Minnesota officers if any were in Huntsville as rumored." The arrest was quickly recognized as a hoax. It was clear that the Democrats of Missouri were taking care of one of their favored sons. Crittenden was widely condemned in the Republican press for his actions, for it seemed that the Governor had saved himself the political embarrassment of pardoning Frank James by ensuring that he would never be convicted (Cf. Kansas City Journal of Feb. 12, 1884; St. Joseph Herald of Feb. 15, 1884). If that was the intent, then the Governor was successful. As the result of such political maneuvering, Frank James was to spend the rest of his life a free man. He was never found guilty of committing any crime by any court of law.

Even after the James gang had been completely destroyed, they continued to be of political importance. Three of Frank James's lawyers made noted political advances. Two were granted judgeships, and one was elected to Congress. The political fortunes of the opposition were less propitious. William Wallace, who headed Missouri's attempts to legally prosecute Frank James, had a long string of political failures afterward (Horan, 1977:3). The role Crittenden played in destroying the James gang also affected his political future. Placed in the difficult position of trying to appease both the Confederate and Union factions of his party, he managed to antagonize both while trying to rid Missouri of the stigma of being called the "outlaw state." The Southerners never forgave him for the part he played in murdering Jesse James, and the Northern faction condemned him for his handling of Frank James. Crittenden was even refused a diplomatic post by President Cleveland years later because, according to Settle (1966:159), Crittenden had arranged for the assassination of Jesse James, and Cleveland "could not 'shoulder public opinion of the subject.' "

How then did a pair of mass murderers and thieves become heroes? These criminals were the product of a violent internal conflict, the Civil War. The social conditions that produced their outlawry, according to many of their contemporaries, were the violent nature of the war in and around Missouri, where neighbor battled against neighbor in some of the bloodiest and most extreme atrocities ever witnessed; where families were persecuted and left destitute because of their political affiliation; and where 'no quarter' was taken literally.

When the war ended, as one sympathizer noted, the James boys "found themselves in the enemy's territory" and continued to be at war with the authorities. The feeling of being in the "enemy's territory" was a common one felt by many Missourians who fought for the ideals of the Confederacy, people who also felt like second-class citizens when paying the taxes imposed by Radical Republicans without being allowed any political representation of their own. Edwards (1877:450) may not have been exaggerating too much when he wrote that the James Boys "have more friends than the officers who hunt them, and more defenders than the armed men who seek to secure their bodies, dead or alive." After all, he noted after the surrender of Frank James (Sedalia Democrat of Oct. 14, 1882), "was it wrong for the Confederates of this state—when the war had closed—to look with some degree of gratitude upon men whose vigilance saved hundreds of homes from unmilitary desecration? With their history as defenders of the faith, how natural it was for a generous people to extenuate the crimes that for seventeen years have been charged to these men." These men were not lower class ruffians or psychologically depraved scum. They came from good middle-class homes where the Bible was read. The natural father of Frank and Jesse James, before his early death, had helped establish the Baptist William Jewell College, and served as one of its trustees. And gang members like Cole Younger and the James brothers quoted freely from scriptures in their epistles to the press. Being portrayed as "defenders of the [Confederate] faith" also added a religious hue to their actions, for these outlaws could be perceived as noble men who died for lofty principles that are supposed to be represented in law, but sometimes are not.

Like the legendary Robin Hood, these lawbreakers were morally superior to their enemies, who operated under protection of law, but who were in fact the "real criminals" because of their immoral conduct. While Jesse James robbed banks and trains, lawmen killed children and blew off the arm of the outlaws' mother. The image of the law as "criminal" and of Jesse James as an unfairly persecuted man was seemingly verified with his assassination by a paid killer working in the employ of Missouri's Governor.

The nature of their victims also contributed to Frank and Jesse James's Robin Hood image. Banks and railroads were vilified by many as corrupting forces responsible for the moral decay of the political order, as well as the cause of personal misery for many farmers and workers who fell into debt to these allegedly ruthless corporate monsters. Anyone who preyed upon the banks and railroads could easily be cast as modern Saint George out to slay the industrial dragons that tormented an innocent populace. When respected local citizens such as Daniel Askew were killed by the James gang, public opinion would swing against the outlaws. Supporters of the gang would then go to great lengths to construct rationalizations or alibis for the gang, in the case of Askew even arguing that he had been murdered by detectives to turn the public against the outlaws! So long as outlaws confined their predations to disliked institutions (even though these were composed of people and their possessions), the public would not identify with the victims of crime and condemn the criminals.

Social conditions were suitable for the emergence of American Robin Hoods in the border regions following the Civil War, where communities first fell under the rule of Radical Republicans and then under the grip of an economic depression for which monopolistic institutions like banks and railroads were blamed. But not every ex-Confederate bank robber became a social bandit. Only those who possessed personal attributes and the proper connections to ensure career success became national heroes. Obviously, some degree of business acumen was required on the part of Frank and Jesse James to make it to the pantheon of American heroes. Had they been gunned down in their first robbery or captured in a drunken stupor early in their outlaw career, their fame would have been at best short-lived. But of equal if not greater significance is the nature of support available to them. Those who counted themselves friends of the James gang were more than simple disenchanted rural peasants. They were powerful politicians and members of the press.

It was the Old Democrats of Missouri, those of Southern sympathies, who supported the outlaws. In 1875 this faction of the Democratic party almost passed an Amnesty Bill for the outlaws through the Missouri House of Representatives. Frank James at his trials was represented by brilliant legal counsel from several prominent Democrats. Joseph Shelby, a former Confederate general and powerful Missouri Democrat, was an unabashed supporter of the James gang. The sympathy given them by Missouri Democrats served to keep the James gang in the national limelight, because the Republican press and party persistently made Democratic "support" of the outlaws a political issue. Even out-of-state papers, especially those in Chicago and Cincinnati, were guilty of celebrating the outlaws by their loud condemnations. The notoriety of the bandits grew with the amount of attention they were given by enemies of Missouri Democrats and by those who competed with Missouri for trade and immigration.

However, the Democratic press of Missouri was primarily responsible for creating the Robin Hood images of the James brothers. Editors such as John Newman Edwards selected the James gang from the great pile of "common criminals," some of whom were former guerrillas, and transformed them into heroic figures. The Democrat-controlled press allowed Jesse James to publish letters in which he defined himself as a political criminal persecuted unjustly by Radical Republicans and railroad detectives. Jesse's "concern" for the indigent was expressed on several occasions, and he often quoted from the Bible to justify his actions. In at least one robbery the gang refused to rob the passengers and tried to foster a Robin Hood image, an idea they may have gotten from reading newspaper editorials. There is no doubt that Jesse James and his supporters consciously attempted to take advantage of the social context in which they lived by defining themselves as modern Robin Hoods. But John Newman Edwards, through his book, *Noted Guerrillas*, and by his incessant editorial support of the James gang (along with whatever other support he may have given them), stands out as the "father" of the James boys as creatures of legend.

Other writers have taken the names of Frank and Jesse James and fashioned new stories of their heroism, perpetuating their names and deeds for future generations to scrutinize. They literally were legends in their own time, as numerous writers rushed tales of the gang to an eager public. Writers of newspapers, biographies, and dime novels all capitalized on the public interest in the dramatic stories of these outlaws. Unlike Edwards, whose motivations were primarily ideological, these scribes were typically inspired by profit. Over the decades, members of the James gang have continued to be viable literary figures. New meanings and values have been given to their criminality, so that they have transcended the social context that originally provided meaning to who they were and what they did. Over 300 books and pamphlets, several movies, numerous ballads, and television dramas have expanded and fragmented the legend in countless directions, creating new meanings for an ever-expanding audience. And by this process, these outlaws have become popular figures to a larger social audience than the farmer, laborer, or ex-Confederate who initially found symbolic meaning in their social banditry. Frank and Jesse James—like George Washington, Daniel Boone, and Thomas Edison—have become true American heroes.

Chapter 4

Billy the Kid

Of all the legends of the American West, those surrounding the life of Billy the Kid are among the most confusing. According to one historian (Fishwick, 1954:85), "Billy the Kid is the 'No' to the great American 'Yes.' He was mean as hell, and killed 21 men before he was 21—not counting Indians and Mexicans." Dixon Wecter (1941:350-1) described the young outlaw as an "adenoidal farm-boy" who was "casual in his blood-lust... 'a dirty little killer.' " Dime novelists portrayed the bandit as a psychopathic killer and sex offender (cf. Jenardo, 1881; Doughty, 1890). Not surprisingly, the Kid's death was hailed by the New Mexico press as a major achievement in civilizing the territory.

Yet others viewed poor Billy Bonney somewhat differently. Edmund Fable (1881:5), in a "true history" printed shortly after the Kid's death, cast him as the "very incarnation of border civilization." It is a sad tale of a youth cursed with misfortune and unjustly accused of crime. In an early passage, Fable (1881:15) has the outlaw saying:

> I have tried to do right. Since I came to this country I have molested no man, and see where I am? Robbed of all my hard earnings, passing my time in this dingy prison, why should I strive any longer for that which in this country seems impossible? I'm done with it. After this, I'll hold my own with the best of them.

Walter Noble Burns (1925:16), in a stirring literary effort chosen for the Book-of-the-Month Club, described the youthful criminal as a man with many admirable qualities. He was loyal to friends, courteous to women and children, and possessed a personality "brimming over with light-hearted gaiety and good humor." A 1930 film, the first among many, showed the Kid to be a generous lad who killed only when justice or self-defense required it. Notables such as a former governor of New Mexico, Miguel Otero, and the man who killed Billy the Kid, Pat Garrett, cast the lawbreaker as a tragic hero—a good man who was led to crime by unfortunate circumstances.

The actual nature of Billy the Kid remains lost to history. Most writers have accepted the fact that William Bonney was born in New York City in 1859, although historian Kent Steckmesser (1983:79) suggests that the young desperado was born in Indiana and was known as Henry McCarty. Parts of his early life were spent in Indiana, Kansas, and New Mexico. His biological father died when Henry (Billy the Kid) was quite young, and his mother remarried to a William Antrim in 1873. Within two years, the Kid's mother died of consumption. Henry Antrim was a decent father, and the Kid's older brother Joseph became a respectable citizen. But Henry fell in with "bad company" and had trouble with the law. At age 16 he was jailed for stealing shirts, but escaped by climbing out a chimney. Within two years he had advanced from petty theft to murder, killing a man after a trivial argument. He then became an outsider, drifting from place to place looking for odd jobs—legal and illegal.

There is nothing in the Kid's early years to suggest that he was the stuff from which legends are made. How was it that such a common thief and murderer became one of the most prominent figures of the American West? The answer partly lies in the particular social conditions found in New Mexico and especially Lincoln County when Henry Antrim (not the kind of name that inspires terror) rode into that area in 1877. The constellation of events comprising what is known as the Lincoln County War provided the elements needed for the creation of a heroic criminal. The Lincoln County war provided the stage upon which Billy the Kid could enact his legend. And broader social conditions—a severe depression—made tales of criminals like Billy the Kid appealing to a larger social audience.

It has been customary for historians to portray New Mexico as a dark and bloody ground where order was precariously maintained. Such portrayals seem accurate. According to U.S. Census data (1880, Tables 4&5), at the time Billy the Kid was carving out a niche for himself in the folk-history of this country, the sparsely settled New Mexico Territory accounted for 15 percent of all homicides in the country. In 1880 the homicide rate was 47 times the national average, and gunshot wounds were a leading cause of death! Indians, of course, were not counted in these figures.

Part of the reason for the high rate of violent crime was the corrupt and inefficient legal system. Historian Eugene Hollon (1973:183) does not exaggerate when he claims that "it is doubtful whether there has ever been another place in the United States where so many men were indicted for murder and so few convicted. If a lawyer could not win a case by bribing the judge or jury, escape for the criminal was relatively easy." And these options were supplemented by the threat of force for outlaws often had violent friends. As Governor Lew Wallace observed to Secretary of Interior Carl Schurz in 1878, "courts must sit surrounded by bayonets, and juries deliberate in dread of assassination." Law

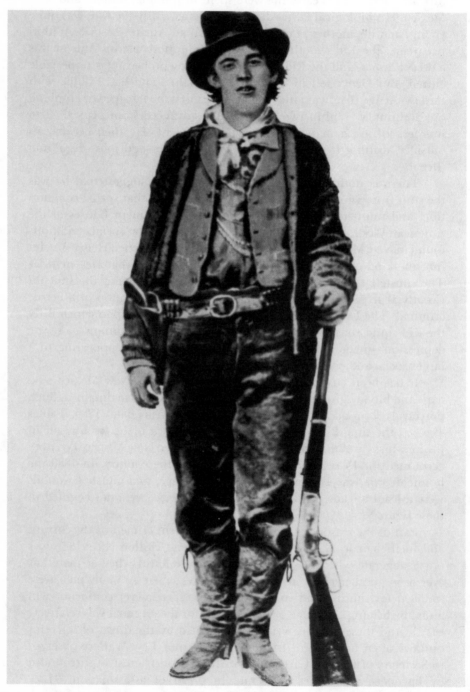

William H. Bonney or Billy the Kid. Rifle in the left hand. Western History Collections, University of Oklahoma Library. Reprinted with permission.

enforcement was as corrupt and inefficient as the courts. And by all accounts, Lincoln County was identified as the epitome of corruption.

Because of the failings of territorial law, many disputes were resolved by armed struggle between feuding families. In 1873 a conflict resulted when several Texans from the Harrell clan journeyed to the town of Lincoln and became drunk at the local saloon. A Mexican constable was killed by the boisterous Texans, but not before killing one of the clan in self-defense. This triggered a private ethnic war in which the Harrell clan managed to kill a number of Mexicans. Order was only restored with the arrival of Federal troops sent by President Grant. In 1876 the Pecos War began when John Chisum, one of the wealthiest men of the West, tried to extend his grazing territory while ridding the area of several small ranchers who were stealing his cattle. Private armies roamed back and forth between the Chisum brothers' ranch and the settlements of the accused cattle-thieves, but only a handful of men were killed.

Neither of these struggles produced a legendary figure like Billy the Kid was to become. These were essentially "private" affairs of short duration between small groups. And the law appeared impartial; it was used to restore order rather than to exploit others.

The Lincoln County War was unlike these previous struggles. It resulted from the systematic use of political office and law as tools wielded by a powerful group of men against the local population for a period of several years. The "establishment" consisted of Lawrence Murphy, James Dolan, and John Riley—all former army officers. They controlled the economy of Lincoln County by owning the only store, governing the only bank, and holding all government contracts to supply the Indian reservation and military outpost. In short, they regulated the flow of money and determined the standards for exchange. They were backed in these enterprises by the "Santa Fe Ring," described by one historian (Lamar, 1970:146-7) as "essentially a set of lawyers, politicians, and businessmen who united to run the territory and to make money out of this particular region." The operation not only included the local sheriff and district judge, but may have extended to Governor S.B. Axtell, U.S. District Attorney Thomas Catron, and Senator Stephen Elkins (cf. Klasner, 1972:98-9; Rasch, 1957:231; Steckmesser, 1983:83-88; Hinton, 1956:193-4).

For several years the Murphy-Dolan-Riley group was unchecked in its use of the political and legal system to further personal interests, even going so far as to arrange the murder of a grassroots leader, Robert Casey, who spoke out against Murphy & Co. on the floor of a political convention and influenced the defeat of the Murphy group's candidates for local office (Drago, 1970:53; Klasner, 1972:126-7; Fulton, 1968). But until 1877 the victimized were relatively powerless and not well-organized.

In 1877 three powerful men joined forces to wage an economic and political war against Murphy and the rest of the Santa Fe Ring. John Chisum, one of the wealthiest men in the West, provided financial support. Alexander McSween, a bright and ambitious lawyer, supplied legal tactics. And John Tunstall, son of a wealthy British family, provided leadership and direction. The Lincoln County War was not a battle between homesteaders and cattle barons, or poor Mexicans against the Anglo establishment. It differed from other regional conflicts in that both parties wielded considerable economic power and political influence. Consequently, the struggle was prolonged and attracted national attention. The Santa Fe Ring became known as just another example of Republican chicanery. The eventual assassination of Tunstall involved international politics. At the request of the British ambassador, Judge Frank Warner Angel was dispatched from Washington to investigate the situation in Lincoln County. While there, he interviewed the chief of military operations for the Tunstall-McSween-Chisum faction, a wiry, buck-toothed boy who called himself William Bonney—but who was better known by his nom de guerre, "Billy the Kid."

William Bonney did not become a hero by being a mass murderer who killed 21 men. It is doubtful that he killed even a third that number. His fame resulted from his role in the Lincoln County War as leader of "field operations" for the McSween-Tunstall-Chisum faction. As a man of action, he posed a serious threat to Murphy & Co. Consequently, the Murphy faction made use of the newspapers and courts they controlled to discredit the moral standing of their opposition. This in part involved presenting to the public an image of Billy the Kid as an evil, bloodthirsty killer. Later, after McSween and Tunstall had been murdered and the Kid began rustling Chisum's cattle, even the press that was sympathetic to his cause cast him in the role of a psychopathic criminal. But at least for awhile, there were those who viewed the Kid as a hero for the part he played in undermining the economic stranglehold Murphy & Co. held on Lincoln County (Stratton, 1969: 177-86).

So it was the political and economic situation in Lincoln County that led to William Bonney's heroic image. Because he served as military leader of the McSween-Tunstall-Chisum faction, his actions at least were tinged with legitimacy. He met personally with the governor of the territory and was interviewed at length by a special investigator from Washington. William Bonney was thus a most atypical murderer and robber. He was also a political figure whose criminality drew symbolic meaning from the social context in which his crimes occurred. Powerful promoters tapped young Bonney for the role of Robin Hood and paraded him before a national audience. It is to a detailed examination of the social conditions in Lincoln County and the influential figures who promoted the Kid's heroic image that we now turn.

The origins of the Lincoln County War might well be placed in November of 1876 when a young and a wealthy Britisher named John Tunstall chose Lincoln County as a place to build his fortune. In many interpretations of the War, Tunstall and his supporters are portrayed as friends to the poor and downtrodden. In some respects he and his allies—McSween and Chisum—were helpful to the disadvantaged of the region. They freed a number of small ranchers from the economic tyranny being exercised by Murphy and Company (cf. Fulton, 1968:64). With Tunstall opening a bank and store in Lincoln, the Murphy monopoly was in jeopardy—a situation that many residents found advantageous.

Tunstall was motivated by more than humanitarian impulses, however. As he explained to his father, New Mexico is run by "rings," and the way to succeed is to either join one or establish one. "I am at work at present making a ring and have succeeded admirably so far.... I propose to confine my operations to Lincoln County, but I intend to handle it in such a way as to get the half of every dollar that is made in the county by anyone."(in Nolan, 1965:282-3)Tunstall's plan was to undersell Murphy and Co. and expose any of their illegalities he could find in order to drive them from Lincoln. Naturally, he did not make his long-range intentions known to the residents of the community.

The intrusion of this Britisher into the economic affairs of the area did not please Murphy, Dolan, and Riley. With McSween providing legal guidance and Chisum providing capital, Tunstall had pieced together a formidable operation. Within a few months, however, a plan to destroy Tunstall's ring had been enacted. In 1874 Alexander McSween had been asked by Lawrence Murphy to collect the proceeds of a $10,000 life insurance policy taken out by a now deceased partner. After much effort, McSween was able to obtain a settlement from the insurance firm, which was claiming insolvency. A dispute arose over who was entitled to the sum, though, and McSween properly withheld the money until matters could be cleared. In December of 1877, however, Dolan had a warrant sworn out for McSween's arrest on charges of embezzlement. In February of the next year, McSween journeyed to Mesilla and faced a hostile district attorney and judge—both "friends" of the Santa Fe Ring (cf Fulton, 1968). Because important witnesses were absent, a continuance was granted with McSween still not cleared of the charges.

Accompanied by Tunstall and other friends, McSween started back to Lincoln. If the time in court seemed tense, the trip home was even more so. About sundown, the McSween-Tunstall party was confronted by a group of men led by Jesse Evans, a notorious New Mexican bandit. Evans had been receiving much attention in the local press and was even described in some circles as a local Robin Hood. The Mesilla

Independent (Oct. 6, 1877) referred to Jesse Evans and "The Boys" as the "pet banditti" and regularly chronicled their actions. In actuality, Jesse Evans and his band were extortionists who rustled herds from the large ranchers and then used intimidation to have charges dropped if by chance they were caught (cf. Mesilla Independent of Sept. 8, 1877). Evans had already done "business" with Tunstall, and the bandit had not gotten the best of the exchange. He and his men were actually captured by a posse and imprisoned in the Lincoln jail, from which it took three weeks to escape

McSween's and Tunstall's concern over how Evans might receive them took into consideration more than the fact that they had cost the bandits almost a month's worth of earnings by rendering them temporarily "unemployed." Rumor had it that Evans and his command had been hired out by Dolan, Murphy, and Riley to serve as a private army. Spending the night in a desolate area with bandits with a grudge did not make for ideal sleeping conditions. The night was relatively calm compared to what would transpire in the morning, however.

James Dolan had arrived at the bandits' camp during the night. The next morning, he and Evans interrupted Tunstall's and McSween's breakfast and challenged Tunstall to go for a gun. According to McSween, accompanying Deputy Sheriff Barrier placed himself between Tunstall and Dolan "and saved as I believe the lives of Tunstall and myself." More threats were exchanged, but little else. The remainder of the trip was uneventful.

More trouble was waiting back in Lincoln, however. Word had arrived that the District Attorney had refused McSween's bond, and McSween would be jailed in Lincoln until the money could be raised by levying on the lawyer's personal property. Sheriff Brady was waiting eagerly. He had a grudge against McSween and Tunstall because the Britisher had published a letter in the Mesilla Valley Independent (Jan. 26, 1878) in which he implied that the Sheriff was misappropriating public funds. This was just one in a string of embarrassments the sheriff had endured at the pen of Tunstall, who for several months had criticized the sheriff for incompetence and dishonesty. Tunstall and McSween felt that the sheriff was a tool of Murphy and Company, and they were probably correct.

Brady's revenge had to wait, however, because Deputy Sheriff Barrier, after taking in the scene at Lincoln, boldly decided to keep McSween in custody and allowed the lawyer to return home. Brady then found another way to settle his grievances. A writ of attachment had come from the Mesilla court authorizing the sheriff to levy on $8000 worth of McSween's property to cover bail. After levying on property in McSween's home, Brady began to attach on property in Tunstall's store. Since there was no legal partnership between Tunstall and McSween, it was questionable as to whether Tunstall's property could be seized to secure McSween's debt; but the sheriff decided to ignore this fine point of law since he had the blessing of the local district attorney, and proceeded to seize about $40,000 worth of goods (Fulton, 1968:110; Keleher, 1957:80).

Then, two days later, the sheriff sent a posse out to Tunstall's ranch to seize his cattle. In this action, Brady was clearly stepping outside the law, and the motives for this behavior obviously had little to do with the pursuit of justice. In fact, this remarkable posse may have been one of the most bizarre ever formed in the annals of the American West. Included among its members were Jesse Evans and two of his most trusted lieutenants, all wanted by the law. U.S. Deputy Marshall Robert Widenmann, a close friend of Tunstall who happened to be at the ranch when this assemblage of horsemen arrived, asked for help in arresting the outlaws, but he received no support from any members of the sheriff's posse. Support was offered only from other Tunstall employees, most notably Billy the Kid. As nervous hands felt for cold steel, it was decided by the visitors that perhaps another time would be more suitable to their interests, and they rode away.

Five days later, on February 18, the posse again visited the Tunstall ranch. The Englishman's cowboys urged armed resistance after hearing rumors of the posse's impending arrival, but Tunstall vetoed the plan and led a small party toward Lincoln to straighten the matter out. When the posse arrived at the ranch, they found all the livestock present except for a few horses which had been specifically exempted from attachment by the sheriff. But it was clear that livestock was not ..hat the party was after, and several set off in pursuit of Tunstall. Unaware of the danger, the Tunstall group slowly meandered toward town. Billy the Kid and another hand brought up the rear while Tunstall herded the horses. The Kid testifying before a special investigator sent from Washington, described what then happened:

> When we had travelled about 30 miles, John Middleton and I were riding in the rear of the party and just upon reaching the brow of a hill we saw a large party coming toward us from the rear at full speed. Middleton and I rode forward to warn the balance of the party. We had barely reached Brewer and Widenmann who were some 200 or 300 yards to the left of the trail when the attacking party cleared the hill and began firing at us....
>
> But the attacking party, undoubtedly seeing Tunstall, left off pursuing us to turn back to the canyon in which the trail was. Shortly afterwards we heard two separate and distinct shots. The remark was made by Middleton that they, the attacking party, must have killed Tunstall.

Middleton was right. The "sheriff's pose" had murdered Tunstall.

Tunstall had either lost his head or failed to understand the nature of law in Lincoln County, for he galloped toward the posse, ignoring the pleas of his companions to flee. Exactly what next transpired has never been determined, except that Tunstall was shot twice and killed. According to official reports, Tunstall had been shot while attacking the posse, but this version of reality seemed as ludicrous at the time as it does now. It was very hard to believe that Tunstall, with his British passion for law and order, would attack a troop of 20 men by himself and armed with only a pistol. Far more likely is the version offered by George Kitt, a member of the posse who did not witness the shooting but arrived almost immediately afterward. He was told that Tunstall had been shot by "the boys." They called the Brit over and promised his safety, but then William Morton (a Dolan foreman who had been placed in charge of the posse) shot Tunstall in the chest at close range. Jesse Evans or one of his band then shot Tunstall through the head as he lay on the ground and put a bullet through the head of Tunstall's horse. Tunstall's gun was then fired to support the claim that he had attacked the posse. Nolan (1965:273) described the ensuing ceremony:

> Hill had Tunstall's revolver, with two chambers empty, in his hand, and it was passed around the members of the posse and then replaced in the dead man's scabbard. His body was neatly covered with a blanket, and the bloody head was pillowed on his folded overcoat. As a wry and macabre joke on Tunstall's great affection for horses, the dead bay's head was then pillowed on his hat.

This posse more closely resembled the Manson Family than representatives of justice.

The killing of John Tunstall on February 18, 1878 marked the official beginning of the Lincoln County War. Over the next year, two private armies composed of paid killers would roam back and forth across the countryside leaving death and destruction in their path. Each would claim to be acting in the name of justice, and each would vilify its rival as evil incarnate. A young man by the name of William Bonney would carve a niche for himself in Western history and American folklore for the part he would play in this sagebrush passion play.

The news of Tunstall's murder quickly spread through Lincoln. Plans to bring the killers to justice were discussed by McSween and his friends. Going through proper legal procedures seemed questionable, given the fact that Tunstall had been murdered by a "sheriff's posse." The dubious nature of the legal system was further illustrated by a letter from the territory's District Attorney Rynerson to John Riley, one of the avowed foes of the Tunstall-McSween-Chisum faction. The note, which Riley accidentally gave to partisans of McSween, urged that the "McSween outfit" be shaken up. It also contained a promise by Rynerson to aid all he could in the "punishment of the scoundrels."

While the local legal and political system seemed rigged against McSween and his followers, there was hope that the events taking place in and around Lincoln might attract national attention and bring into play more powerful political resources. And it seemed that local opinion also favored McSween, since he was still conducting his business in an orderly fashion, while the Riley-Dolan faction was primarily responsible for whatever violence and disorder that was occurring. Many wondered how it came to be that men wanted by the law, men who only three months earlier had escaped from the Lincoln jail, were found riding with a sheriff's posse! Sheriff Brady attempted to satisfy such queries by making public a note he had written to the deputy in charge of the posse in which it was specifically commanded not to "call on or allow to travel with your posse any persons who are known to be outlaws." But the Mesilla Valley Independent (March 30, 1878), which published Brady's note, spoke for many when it asked:

Why did Sheriff Brady find it necessary to instruct his deputy not to select "known outlaws" as a posse? Why did he permit a man to act as his deputy to whom it was necessary to send such instructions? And how does it come that notwithstanding the sheriff's written order, we find these "known outlaws" not only travelling and acting with the posse, but brutally murdering Tunstall under cover of the Deputy Sheriff's authority?

To many, Brady's letter seemed nothing more than a poorly conceived alibi written to make him appear ignorant of events he knew would occur. After Tunstall's funeral, an angry committee interviewed the sheriff to find out what action would be taken against Tunstall's murderers. They were also indignant because William Bonney and two others had been arrested for attempting to serve warrants issued by the probate judge on members of the murderous posse. Brady appeared belligerent and noncommittal, which seemed further proof that he was more concerned with obstructing, rather than pursuing, justice.

While many of McSween's allies urged that justice be meted out quickly and privately, the lawyer refused and continued to place his hope in alternative legal and political avenues not controlled by his opposition. Thus, one week after Tunstall's death, McSween wrote the British ambassador to the United States and described the circumstances surrounding the Britisher's demise. Other prominent citizens of the community also wrote to express hope that the ambassador would investigate the situation, and the matter was soon placed before Secretary of Interior, Carl Schurz. By involving these more powerful political figures, it was McSween's hope that he would not only avenge Tunstall's murder but also cripple his rivals and take control of the county's economy.

However, there were certain "men of action" who were too impatient to wait for justice to find her way through long and complicated legal channels. These men, including Billy the Kid, formed an organization called the "Regulators." Tunstall's foreman Dick Brewer was appointed constable and nine others were deputized by a local Justice of the Peace.

With warrants in hand, they hunted for Tunstall's murderers. Within a few days, they managed to capture two men, William Morton and Frank Baker, who were present at the Britisher's slaying. Once the men were apprehended, there was some question as to what should be done with them. Turning them over to Sheriff Brady seemed ill-advised. And there were rumors that Dolan and Company had organized an army of gunmen. The simplest solution, according to Billy the Kid, was to execute the captives. And so they were shot down "while trying to escape."

On the same day that Baker and Morton were tried, convicted, and executed by Billy the Kid, Governor Axtell came to Lincoln to investigate matters. Apparently the governor had already made up his mind concerning the origins and nature of lawlessness in the county. He spent a scant three hours in town, and only in the company of James Dolan. A decree was shortly thereafter issued which, according to one historian, "must rank as one of the most extraordinary official acts ever performed by governor of state or territory" (Fulton, 1968:143). The proclamation essentially made supporters of the Dolan faction the only officials possessing legal authority and allowed the U.S. militia to aid the Dolan faction in suppressing McSween and his supporters. The Justice of the Peace who deputized the Regulators had his appointment declared invalid. Robert Widenmann's appointment as U.S. Marshall was revoked. Thus, the military wing of the McSween faction was stripped of legitimacy. By the stroke of the pen they had been transformed from lawmen to outlaws.

For many residents of Lincoln, Axtell's proclamation destroyed any hope that justice might be obtainable through the law. Many shared the view of the editor of the Cimmaron News and Press (March 21, 1878), who acidly commented that the Tunstall murder was a "most damnable and dastardly crime" which probably resulted from his publicizing the sheriff's misappropriation of public funds for personal use. It seemed that revenge led to his execution at the hands of "a sheriff's posse composed partly of notorious outlaws who had broken jail while in the custody of this sheriff." Then, when public opinion rose against Sheriff Brady, and "it began to look as though the locality would be made too hot for this sheriff and those in whose interest he seemed to be running his office," the governor went to the rescue and ordered the military ready to "suppress the indignation and assist the sheriff and his *Outlaw* deputies to administer the law." Men who held formal office broke the law with impunity and hired criminals to abet them in their selfish pursuits. Men who attempted to restore justice to Lincoln County, the Regulators, became outlaws for their efforts.

Instead of disbanding, the Regulators decided to take the law into their own hands. Rather than wait for Brady to find them, they determined to make Brady their first victim. On April 1, Billy the Kid and several other Regulators ambushed and killed Brady and one of his deputies as they strolled the streets of Lincoln. A few days later, another Dolan supporter was killed in a gunfight. The war was on in earnest, and Billy the Kid was named by the courts as a murderer of Brady. The Kid had also risen through the ranks and was now recognized as the leader of the McSween militia. He had become an important actor in this political drama, perhaps the most dangerous member of the McSween faction. For while the pen may have been mightier than the sword, it was no match for the Kid's gun in terms of immediate consequences.

While Billy the Kid was preparing the Regulators for armed conflict, McSween and Chisum had called upon other allies to bring Lincoln County affairs to the attention of powerful figures in Washington, D.C. One such supporter, Doctor Montague Leverson, sent details to Secretary of Interior Carl Schurz and to President Hayes. Leverson claimed that Tunstall's murder "was plotted and continued by the District Attorney [Rynerson] by whom the district Judge is used as a tool." He further added that the Governor "has illegally and despotically exerted his power to screen the murderers." Sheriff Brady was described as "the leader of the thieves and assassins of this region." Also indicted was U.S. District Attorney Thomas Catron, who was accused of misusing his office to serve "particular interests" in Santa Fe. Leverson's cries of conspiracy were met with ridicule by the Santa Fe New Mexican (March 17, 1878), mouthpiece of the Santa Fe ring. Leverson was labeled insane and the letter inane: "Plotting assassinations! Shielding murderers! Forging indictments! Buying testimony; embezzling public finds! Here's richness!" But apparently powerful friends in Washington did not share the paper's opinion of Leverson. Soon the events of Lincoln County would capture the attention of the national audience, and Billy the Kid—a boy desperado—would have a coast-to-coast reputation.

For the next three months minor skirmishes took place between McSween's Regulators—led by Billy the Kid, and Dolan's forces—a curious mixture of appointed law officers and wanted criminals. In April a grand jury had cleared McSween of embezzlement charges and then brought indictments against Dolan for being an accessory to murder and for cattle theft. Nevertheless, the new sheriff, George Peppin, thought it more proper to pursue the McSween crowd than to arrest his friend, James Dolan. On June 18 Peppin deputized a small army of cattle thieves, murderers, and Dolan supporters. To enhance his chances of success, he appealed for aid from the local military post. Rumors spread that a reward of $1000 was offered for the death of McSween (Fulton, 1968:233). News of Peppin's death squad reached Lincoln, and spurred a mass exodus of not only McSween and friends but also others who had spoken against Dolan and his friends.

McSween and his supporters fled to nearby San Patricio, where they remained for about a month. Finally tiring of the fugitive role, McSween decided to return to Lincoln and force matters toward some sort of conclusion. On July 14, McSween arrived back home and quickly turned three buildings into fortresses. McSween, Billy the Kid, and a dozen others barricaded themselves in McSween's home. Peppin, Dolan, and their assemblage of warriors did the same with the buildings they occupied. By the next day, Lincoln was abandoned except for the two opposing factions of about 60 men each, and the fighting began in earnest.

For four days the battle raged, with each side sustaining only minor casualties. It seemed that the battle of Lincoln could last weeks. Dolan, however, had used his influence to involve the U.S. militia. He convinced local post commander Dudley that the McSween faction had fired upon a soldier during the fighting and that the presence of the army was needed in Lincoln "for the preservation of the lives of women and children." In violation of law, Dudley marched to Lincoln with 35 men, a gatling gun, and a howitzer. Leaders of the warring parties were informed that if anyone fired in the direction of the militia, they would blow the offenders right out of Lincoln. Dudley then placed his troops strategically so that it was virtually impossible for the McSween faction to fire at the Dolan army. Thirty of McSween's band became frightened and fled the town. McSween, Billy the Kid, and others in the McSween house were essentially prisoners. To fire at the Dolan crowd would doubtless be interpreted as firing at the troops as well, giving Dudley an opportunity to use his howitzer and gatling gun. While Peppin and his gunslingers could not direct fire at the McSween house, they could wait. Eventually the men in the house would have to come out. They would then have to fight from less advantageous cover, being easy targets as they raced across open ground.

There was the possibility, however, that the men in the McSween house might try to escape under cover of darkness. Realizing this, Peppin directed some of his men to sneak up on the house and set it afire, even though there were women and children in the home. This they accomplished, and as smoke filled one room after another, panic seized McSween and some of his followers. It seemed they had the choice of burning to death or being shot down as they fled. A desperate appeal to Colonel Dudley to accept their surrender was brusquely rejected. The mood of the men in the burning house has been captured for history by Mrs. McSween, who remained with her husband almost to the end. By her account, Billy the Kid took charge of affairs since her husband was in a state of collapse. He proposed that he and two others would run out first; then, while Peppin's men fired at them, the others could make their dash to safety (in Fulton, 1968:267-8).

By nine in the evening, the men were forced to crowd into one room. Although darkness had settled over Lincoln, the glow from the fire made the area around the burning house as bright as day. The only hopes were the element of surprise and a good bit of luck. Suddenly from the burning building raced Billy the Kid and three companions. One was gunned down almost immediately, but the Kid and two comrades made it to the safety of the river bank and darkness.

But McSween and the others were not so lucky. They waited too long to make their break, and the element of surprise was gone. They were driven back repeatedly by withering fire. After several attempts, one of the McSween men asked to surrender. When four of Peppin's men started forward to accept the offer, someone—no one will ever know whom—opened fire. One of Peppin's men was killed. McSween and four of his companions were also killed; another was so seriously wounded that he was left for dead. In writing of the events to Tunstall's father, Mrs. McSween described her husband's last moments (in Fulton, 1968:270):

> In the evening my husband and his friends blinded with smoke, wearied by battling flames and the no less remorseless enemies outside, and driven from room to room as the fire increased in fury till the last room was consumed, at last sallied from the house and—oh God, my heart almost did fail me to write it—was shot down like a dog on his own threshold, and when he had fallen upon his knees, calling out "I surrender, oh, my God save me. Oh, Lord, Lord, save me."

First Tunstall, and then McSween had met death at the hands of a sheriff's posse.

With the elimination of Tunstall and McSween, the only principal actors remaining to stand in opposition to Dolan and Company were John Chisum and Billy the Kid. Chisum wisely had long since abandoned the field of battle, and Billy the Kid was on the run as an outlaw. No one remained in Lincoln to protect McSween's and Tunstall's interests. Consequently, Peppin's "posse" swarmed over the dead men's property like ants attacking a rotting carcass. The men crawled all over Tunstall's store. Bits and pieces of the dead men's belonging were carried away in wagons. In a letter to Tunstall's father (cited in Nolan, 1965:380-1), the store's proprietor reported that the sheriff refused to stop the looting, and that after his men "got everything they wanted, they invited their friends to come and help themselves while they guarded the store, and it was not long until nothing was left."

By this time law and order had completely collapsed. There could be no respect for law and political office when such had been used so blatantly to serve special interests rather than represent impartial justice. Special Agent Judge Frank Warner Angel, sent by Washington to investigate the Lincoln County situation, described the state of affairs when he arrived at about this time as a war between two factions, both guilty of breaking the law. McSween, he felt had acted conscientiously; while Murphy, Dolan and friends had acted "for private gain and revenge." A host of desperadoes had come from throughout the Southwest to Lincoln to serve as mercenaries in the employ of one faction or the other, thus turning the county into the "elysium for outlaws and murderers." And the situation appeared to be worsening. It was reported that there were over 200 desperadoes involved, and that men were shot down "on sight" because they were identified as a member of the opposing faction. The law, Angel felt, at this time was unenforceable "for the reason that if the Murphy party is in power, then the law is all Murphy and if the McSween party is in power, then the law is all McSween." The result, noted historian Philip Rasch (1957:233), was chaos as armies "roamed the country, rustling, stealing, burning property, abducting and raping women, and openly defying the sheriff to arrest them." Many citizens simply fled the region, whether they were participants in the war or not (Cf. the Las Vegas Gazette of Aug. 17, 1878). A legitimation crisis had settled over Lincoln County.

The popular view of Billy the Kid at this time is unclear. Since he was wanted for murder, he was forced to live the life of an outlaw. But because he was identified as an important member of the McSween faction, it became customary for popular historians to portray him as something of a hero. It was commonly assumed that many local residents viewed Tunstall and McSween as men who gave their lives trying to liberate the citizenry from the economic squeeze of Murphy, Dolan, and Riley. Perhaps the populace realized that Tunstall and McSween had plans to establish their own monopoly, but as things stood, the fallen warriors' interests at this time would have been to the benefit of most in the community. Neither martyr ever mentioned the Kid in letters to friends, which suggests he was really little more than an acquaintance. But presumably because of loyalty to the Britisher and his lawyer friend, the Kid was cast as an avenger, striking back at those who unjustly executed his friends, while at the same time making matters unpleasant for the real enemies of the people and corrupters of law. It was conveniently overlooked that he may have been paid for carrying on his work and that he already had developed a reputation as thief and murderer before arriving in Lincoln. The Lincoln County War provided the ideal context for the construction of a heroic criminal. It also provided a handy rationale for victimizing opponents, since self-interest could readily be transfigured into selfless politically-inspired motivation through the judicious use of the press and political sponsorship.

The five day battle at Lincoln had other far-reaching effects. Angel's report led to the resignation of U.S. District Attorney Catron, the removal from office of Governor Axtell, and the appointment of Lew Wallace

as the new governor. The removal of Axtell was decidedly in the best
interests of McSween supporters such as Billy the Kid.

Also recent to New Mexico was a one-armed lawyer named Houston
Chapman, a friend of McSween who was determined to continue the
fight through legal channels and the local press. His desire to fight in
the courtroom rather than the street was not to be realized, however.
On the night of February 18, 1879—exactly one year to the day of
Tunstall's assassination—another atrocity occurred which perhaps outdid
all others.

The evening began promisingly enough. Perhaps fearful of the
measures a new governor might take to combat outlawry, Jesse Evans
and Billy the Kid—the respective field leaders of the warring factions—
arranged a truce to see if an agreement "between thieves" could be worked
out. The Mesilla Independent (cited in Fulton 1968:324) carried the details
of the peace treaty:

I. That neither party would kill any member of the other party without first giving notice
of withdrawing from the agreement.
II. That all persons who had acted as "friends" were included in the agreement and were
not to be molested.
III. That no officers or soldiers were to be killed for any act previous to the date of this
agreement.
IV. That neither party should appear to give evidence against the other in any civil
prosecution.
V. That each party should give individual members of the other party every aid in their
power to resist arrests upon civil warrants, and, if necessary, they would try to secure
their release.
VI. That if any member of either party failed to carry out this compact, which was sworn
to by the respective leaders, he should be killed on sight.

Articles IV and V of this remarkable document provide insight not only
into the nature of these arbiters, but also suggest the motive for such
a conference. With the next session of district court due to convene and
with new and energetic administrators of law inspired by mandates from
Washington, it became very important that the outlaw fraternity exhibit
more brotherly love toward each other.

The mood surrounding the peace talks was tense, however. It began
with Evans threatening to kill the Kid. It ended even more bizarrely.
Chapman had arrived in town about ten in the evening and ran into
the negotiators of the treaty, who had been celebrating their diplomatic
skills with cheap drink. Upon meeting in the street, one of the Dolan
crowd attempted to intimidate the lawyer, who refused to be cowed and
promised he would extract legal revenge for McSween's death. According
to the Las Cruces Thirty Four (March 5, 1879), one of the Dolan men,
Bill Campbell, then replied: " 'I'll settle you,' and fired his pistol, the
ball going in the breast and coming out the back. Dolan shot him with

his Winchester. Then they set fire to his body. It is thought they soaked his clothes with whiskey to make them burn." The Kid was an unwilling witness to the brutal murder. When he saw what was coming, the paper reported, he tried to get away "but Evans held [him] fast and made him look on during the entire affair." The peace accord failed to last the night.

When news of Chapman's murder reached Governor Wallace, he moved with a swiftness uncharacteristic of his predecessor. Within two weeks he had visited Lincoln and found, to his utter amazement, that although everyone knew who did the killing, no arrests had been made. Immediately he ordered the military to seize not only Dolan, Evans, and Campbell, but some 34 others prominent for their lawlessness, including Billy the Kid.

Billy the Kid was no fool. He knew that the civil authorities and the public had grown tired of illegal acts, whatever the motivation for them. The only heroes of the moment would be those who would passionately pursue law and order. Furthermore, the Kid realized that it would not be wise to count on the Evans-Dolan contingent for protection from the law or from outlaws. John Chisum had long since abandoned both the McSween cause and the Kid. Consequently, the young desperado decided to align himself with the most powerful and impartial figure in the territory, Governor Lew Wallace. In mid-March, he wrote a letter to Wallace offering to testify against the murderers of Chapman in exchange for the annulment of murder indictments. The Kid claimed that the day of the murder, he was in Lincoln "at the request of Good Citizens to meet Mr. J.J. Dolan to meet as friends, as to be able to leave aside our arms and go to work." He concluded by noting:

I have no wish to fight anymore[,] indeed I have not raised an arm since your Proclamation. As to my character I refer to any of the Citizens for the Majority of them are my Friends and have been helping me all they could. I am called Kid Antrim but Antrim is my stepfather's name. [Rasch, 1966: 9]

Billy the Kid's carefully crafted letter, right down to its closing "your obedient servant," emphasized a concern for law and order that was eagerly received by the Governor. Wallace proposed a secret conference, at which time they could discuss plans for the Kid's surrender, amnesty, protection, and testimony.

On March 17, 1879 the Governor of New Mexico met alone with the young desperado in what must be considered one of the most dramatic moments in frontier history. Wallace was a prominent Civil War general who had served at such places as Shiloh, who had been on the jury that tried those accused of assassinating Lincoln, and who would yet achieve more prominence as the author of *Ben Hur*. Yet ironically his reputation would be eclipsed by the slip of a man, not quite 20, whose fame came from murdering and thieving. A hundred years later, few would remember Lew Wallace; but Billy the Kid would be a name almost everyone would know.

Billy the Kid listened quietly to offers of amnesty and protection in exchange for testimony against the murderers of Chapman. The plan set forth pleased the outlaw, who modified only the details of his "arrest" to include his close friend, Tom O'Folliard. By late March, the Kid was in protective custody. In April he informed a grand jury of the parties responsible for the Chapman killing. In May he testified on the Lincoln County War before a military board of inquiry trying Colonel Dudley for his part in the affair. Governor Wallace was surprised by the public reaction to the jailed mass murderer who was about to be tried for the killing of a lawman, for he noted in a letter to Secretary of Interior Carl Schurz that the "precious specimen nicknamed 'The Kid'...is an object of tender regard. I heard singing and music the other night; going to the door, I found the minstrels of the village actually serenading the fellow in his prison."[1]

But Billy the Kid was having second thoughts about the arrangement. His trial had been moved from Lincoln to less friendly Dona Ana County, where he would be charged for the murder of Sheriff Brady. In addition, District Attorney Rynerson—a member of the Santa Fe Ring and friend of James Dolan—was challenging the Governor's promise of immunity. At this point it certainly looked like the law was still favoring Dolan and his friends, for everyone in that faction had completely avoided punishment for misdeeds committed. But it seemed to the outlaw that he might be sacrificed to appease political interests, such as Rynerson, who wanted the Kid punished. Or he might be executed in his jail cell by friends of those whom his testimony would convict. So just prior to his scheduled trial in Dona Ana Country, Billy the Kid made his escape from custody.[2]

Once again outside the law, the young outlaw turned to John Chisum for financial aid, requesting $500 for services rendered for the Tunstall-McSween-Chisum faction during the Lincoln County conflict.[3] Chisum refused to pay, and the Kid reportedly attempted to change the cattle baron's mind by brandishing a revolver at him. Chisum refused to be intimidated and convinced Billy to put down the gun. After all, both knew that such a killing would effectively end any hopes the Kid might have of collecting any money. And Chisum was a powerful man with many friends. His murder would gain the Kid nothing but the wrath of the law and the displeasure of the populace. Certainly such a killing would not be viewed as justifiable (Santa Fe New Mexican, May 1, 1881).[4]

Instead, the Kid found another way to collect his debt: stealing Chisum's cattle. But times had changed. The press and the public had grown tired of outlawry. And the Kid and his followers no longer had a cause with which to justify their depredations. Worse, he had lost the backing of John Chisum. Without such support his outlaw days were numbered.

But Billy the Kid was no fool and, like Jesse James was doing about this time in Missouri, he took up the pen to defend himself. The Las Vegas Gazette (Dec. 3, 1880) had been blaming the Kid for numerous robberies in the region and described him as the "Captain of a Band of Outlaws." On December 12 the bandit sent a letter to Governor Wallace, hoping to smooth over the bad impressions the press was making of him. The letter was made public in the Las Vegas Gazette (Dec. 22, 1880). In it the Kid claimed that rather than being the head of a band of outlaws, he was in fact busy recovering stolen property "when there was no chance of getting an officer to do it." The Kid also fingered John Chisum as the man behind the smear campaign. "J.S. Chisum is the man who got me into trouble, and has benefited Thousands by it and is now doing all he can against me.... If some impartial Party were to investigate this matter they would find it far different from the impression put out by Chisum and his Tools."

Time and luck were running out on the Kid, though. Pat Garrett, a former friend of the desperado, was the newly elected sheriff. He probably knew the habits and patterns of the Kid better than anyone else. However, Garrett had some difficulty in rounding up a posse to help capture the Kid, since local residents were either sympathetic, apathetic, or intimidated when it came to the young mass murderer in their midst. Garrett's efforts were aided by the arrival of Texas cowboys hunting for stolen cattle. With such a formidable posse, the zealous sheriff quickly went to the Fort Sumner haunts of the Kid, and had Billy in custody within the week.

The captured Kid was quite a celebrity, the "best known man in New Mexico" according to the Las Vegas Gazette (Dec. 27, 1880). The local press took advantage of the bandit's stay in Las Vegas and conducted several lengthy interviews with the famous gunslinger. We read in these accounts that the Kid was something of an optimist who was somewhat surprised at his celebrity status and the big crowds that turned out to view him. They were undoubtedly curious to see a living legend, for Billy was the hero of the 'Forty Thieves' romance which the local paper had been running for some six weeks. The press went to great lengths to describe his appearance for the readers, noting that the outlaw "looked and acted like a mere boy...with the traditional silky fuzz on his upper lip, clear blue eyes, with a roguish snap about them, light hair and complexion. He is in all, quite a handsome looking fellow."

The Kid, the interviews show, was also very sensitive about his public image. As one reporter observed about the outlaw, "a cloud came over his face when he made some illusion to his being the hero of fabulous yarns." A positive image could sway the jury that would try him. Thrilling stories of his daring deeds might have unfortunate consequences, and there was always the possibility of a lynching sparked by inflamatory editorials. In an interview with the Mesilla News (Dec. 29, 1880), the Kid described the public relations problems he faced:

Well, I had intended at one time not to say a word in my own behalf, because persons would say, 'Oh, he lied.' Newman, editor of the Semi-Weekly gave me a rough deal; has created prejudice against me, and is trying to incite a mob to lynch me. He sent me a paper which shows it. I think it is a dirty mean advantage to take of me, considering my situation and knowing I could not defend myself by word or act. But I suppose he thought he would give me a kick down hill. Newman came by to see me the other day. But I refused to talk to him or tell him anything.

Billy the Kid had few influential friends by this time. The press was almost uniformly crying for his execution. Chisum had turned against the Kid. The population was tired of lawlessness and outlaws. In fact, major economic changes were occuring in the region. Gold had been discovered in late 1879, and immigration to the region suddenly increased. "Churches, schools, newspapers, and other marks of settled respectability took root" writes Robert Utley (1987: 160) and criminal violence and other forms of lawlessness were no longer easily tolerated. Ideally, the boy bandit would ride into the mythical sunset, the perpetual outsider looking for another community that could use his help in purging the law of injustice. But he had no such choice. He was to be tried for murder before Judge Warren Bristol, long considered an ardent foe of the Tunstall-McSween faction. Desperately, the Kid penned several notes to Governor Wallace, including one that smacked of blackmail:

Dear Sir: I wish you would come down to the jail and see me. It would be to your interest to come and see me. I have some letters which date back two years, and there are some parties very anxious to get them; but I will not dispose of them until I see you. That is, if you will come immediately.

The threats and pleas were to no avail. On April 13 Billy Bonney was found guilty of the murder of Sheriff Brady and sentenced to death by hanging.

But fate had a more dramatic ending in store for Billy the Kid. About the same time that Sheriff Pat Garrett was purchasing lumber for the Kid's gallows, the Kid managed to escape imprisonment by killing both of his guards with a pistol that probably had been hidden for him in a jailhouse privy (cf Fulton, 1968:393-4; Steckmesser, 1983:91).

At first the news of the Kid's escape was hailed by the press as but another example of his resourcefulness. The Santa Fe New Mexican (May 4, 1881), never before an admirer of young Bonney, went so far as to proclaim his jailbreak as "as bold a deed as those versed in the annals of crime can recall. It surpasses anything of which the Kid has been guilty so far that his past offenses lose much of their heinousness in comparison...."

Quickly the media changed its mind about the Kid, however. The Las Cruces Semi-Weekly, hostile Simeon Newman at the editor's helm, had been predicting the escape for weeks and warned that bloodshed would result afterwards, claiming that the Kid "has made his brags that he only wants to get free in order to kill three more men—one of them being Governor Wallace." In the months that followed, the press portrayed young Bonney as a maddened killer.

Rumors of the Kid's whereabouts were numerous, but law officials had little help in finding the young killer, even with the promise of a hefty reward. Some residents were sympathetic to the outlaw; many more were undoubtedly afraid of him and his gang. Pat Garrett had previously been glorified for his achievements, with one paper suggesting that he be "retained as deputy sheriff of Lincoln for 250 years, and at the expiration of that time his lease on life should be extended" (Las Vegas Daily Optic of Dec. 20, 1880). When the Governor refused to pay the $500 reward previously offered for the capture of the Kid, the local citizenry privately raised over $1000 to reward Garrett (Metz, 1974:75-6). But now he was chastised for failing to pursue the escaped Kid, and he became so frustrated with the lack of popular backing that he threatened to resign unless the citizenry showed "more readiness to support him in the execution of arduous duties" (Cimmaron News and Press of May 26, 1881).

The only help forthcoming was from the local press, which launched a spirited campaign to turn public opinion against Billy the Kid. The Las Vegas Daily Optic (May 4, 1881) led the attack, describing the outlaw in lurid language:

His name has long been the synonym of all that is malignant and cruel, and yet such is the inconsistency of human action, that his friends and admirers have been neither lacking in applause or weak in numbers. Urged by a spirit as hideous as hell, he has well nigh exhausted the boldness of courage and the ingenuity of cunning to inflict suffering upon all around him. With a heart untroubled to pity by misfortune, and with a character possessing the attributes of the damned, he has reveled in brutal murder and glorified in shame.

The Santa Fe Weekly Democrat (July 21, 1881) claimed that the Kid had killed 21 men, one for each of his 21 years; that the outlaw was constantly adding more names to his death list. The Las Vegas Daily

Optic (May 4, 1881) reported that its staff had been "entered on his death-roll." The Santa Fe New Mexican (May 1, 1881) falsely stated that the young desperado had ambushed and killed three of Chisum's cowboys, sparing the life of a fourth man "so that he could deliver a message to Chisum." The message was that the Kid would assassinate Chisum's cowboys at five dollars a head until the money owed for service in the Lincoln County War was settled. On May 5, the New Mexican announced that the Kid would not leave the territory until he paid his respects to U.S. Marshall Sherman and Governor Wallace.

Pat Garrett, in the meantime, had finally secured help in searching for Bonney from two men in the employ of a Texas cattle association—John Poe and T.L. McKinney. Hearing a rumor that the Kid had been staying on the Maxwell estate at Fort Sumner, Garrett and his two deputies journeyed there to investigate. For several days they found no sign of the Kid. They finally decided to ask Pete Maxwell, the wealthy estate-owner, what he knew of the Kid's whereabouts.

It was close to midnight when Garrett and his men approached the Maxwell house. The two deputies waited outside. Shortly after Garrett entered the room, the deputies observed a slender, bare-footed man approaching. They never considered the possibility that it was the Kid, and so remained motionless until the desperado almost tripped over them in the shadows. John Poe (1936:37-8) describes what then happened:

Upon seeing me he covered me with his six-shooter as quick as lightning, sprang onto the porch, calling out in Spanish, "Quien es?" (Who is it), at the time backing away from me toward a door through which Garrett only a few seconds before had passed, repeating his query, "Who is it?" in Spanish several times. At this I stood up and advanced toward him, telling him not to be alarmed; that he should not be hurt, and still without the least suspicion that this was the very man we were looking for. As I moved toward him, trying to reassure him, he backed up into the doorway of Maxwell's room.... An instant after the man left the door I heard a voice inquire in a sharp tone: "Pete, who are those fellows outside?"

Almost immediately shots were fired in the room. Pat Garrett came rushing out and said "That was the Kid that came in there onto me and I think I got him."

The trembling men standing outside the door were full of doubt and fear. Was it really the Kid who was in there? Garrett was sure he recognized the voice of his old friend, but still.... It was dark, and the shadowy figure had addressed the wealthy rancher, Pete Maxwell, on a first name basis. This suggested a friendship between the two men, which was not the kind of relationship one would expect between an extremely affluent land-owner and a mass murderer. And if it was the Kid, was he really dead or just waiting for a chance to add some more men to his death roll? Pete Maxwell was almost shot as he rushed from the room a few seconds after Garrett exited. Finally, a candle was obtained, and the light it provided as it was held by a window showed the prone form of Billy the Kid lying on his back in the middle of the floor, his life extinguished.

The Kid's death was international news. Even the London News (Aug. 18, 1881) carried a brief summary of the life and death of Billy Bonney. Although his earthly life had ended, the press would not let the image die. The White Oaks Golden Era (July 21, 1881) proclaimed: "those who are not familiar with the deceased's criminal record cannot comprehend the gladness that pervades the whole of New Mexico and especially this county. He was the worst of criminals." The New Southwest (July 23, 1881) greeted the news of the demise by stating: "The vulgar murderer and desperado known as 'Billy the Kid' has met his just desserts at last.... Despite the glamor of romance thrown around his life by sensation writers, the fact is he is a low-down vulgar cut-throat, with probably not one redeeming quality." The Eastern press quickly sensationalized the Kid's life and death by casting him as an evil being that drew pleasure from others' pain, building upon an image constructed by the Las Vegas Daily Optic (May 4, 1881), which described the Kid as a "Young demon... [to whom] the drooping forms of widows and the tear-stained eyes of orphans give no token of the anguish within."

Billy Bonney died with few friends in high places. With the backing of influentials and the context of the Lincoln County War, this mass murderer had the resources available to cast his criminality as politically motivated and socially acceptable. But with the end of the Lincoln County War, the demise of Tunstall and McSween, and the rejection of Wallace and Chisum; Billy the Kid became a rebel with no socially acceptable cause. Instead of a hero, he became a liability whom many blamed for attracting the criminal element to New Mexico and deterring the immigration of "good" settlers to the region.

Yet while some were vilifying the Kid, others were glorifying him, particularly after death had rendered him harmless. According to an eminent scholar of the Lincoln County War, William Keleher (1957:329), many people believed that the murders with which the Kid was charged were justifiable, even the assassination of Sheriff Brady. Lincoln County was in a state of war, and "in war, men who kill other men are not prosecuted, or questioned as to the how or why of the killing." Men on both sides committed murder. Many remembered how Tunstall and then McSween were murdered by a sheriff's posse, and how Deputy William Bonney had been arrested for attempting to serve warrants. Even the guard that escorted the convicted Kid to jail consisted of a wanted criminal, John Kinney, and other gunslingers of dubious reputation, including a man who had served in the posse that executed Tunstall. A few years later, James Dolan, who had participated in the murder of Chapman and several other atrocities of the Lincoln County War, would run for sheriff. Even Pat Garrett had been an acquaintance of the Kid and was rumored to have rustled a few cattle himself, and possibly even murdered a man or two, before turning lawman (Metz, 1974:8-10, 37). When criminals habitually rode with sheriff's posses, when lawful citizens were periodically executed by lawmen, and when outlaws occasionally tracked down and returned stolen property, it became difficult to determine who represented justice. So while the local press for the most part praised Garrett for his work in ridding the region of the Kid, many local residents considered the sheriff to be a kind of Judas and John Chisum a high priest of the Sanhedrin.

Pat Garrett was a man of political ambition. Being a lawman was dangerous and poor-paying. But if one was good at it, there was hope of higher political office and greater financial reward. But the role he played in terminating Billy the Kid's life became a political liability. Political rivals and the unfriendly press suggested that Garrett should be tried for murder; others accused him of hiding under Maxwell's bed and killing the Kid in a cowardly fashion. Garrett angrily denied such charges in the addenda to his *Authentic Life of Billy the Kid,* but he never succeeded in ridding himself of the Judas label. It must have come as a bitter surprise that in legend the Kid was to become the more famous and heroic figure.

Ironically, Pat Garrett, himself, played a significant role in establishing the written legend of Billy the Kid. His book, ghosted by Ash Upson, was one of the first of hundreds devoted to the life of outlaw. And since Garrett had the privilege of knowing the Kid and playing an integral part in events which helped build the legend, the book was frequently granted more authenticity than other attempts to make money by sensationalizing the exploits of the boy bandit. Many events and conversations first made public in Garrett's work were repeated without question in subsequent biographies of the Kid.

But Garrett was certainly not an objective and dispassionate historian in pursuit of truth. He hoped to make a great deal of money from the sale of the book, a hope that was not realized because of poor marketing (Metz, 1974; O'Connor, 1960). And since Garrett's political backing came from John Chisum, his view of the Lincoln County War was sympathetic to the Tunstall-McSween-Chisum faction and somewhat hostile to Dolan, Murphy and Riley. Garrett (1954:5) certainly helped fashion the Kid into a legendary hero, claiming, among other things, that Billy Bonney was "the peer of any fabled brigand on record, unequalled in desperate courage, presence of mind in danger, devotion to his allies, generosity to his foes, gallantry, and all the elements which appeal to the holier emotions...." Garrett wanted the nation to know that he had battled an outlaw of epic proportions, and thus deserved consideration as an epic figure himself.

From the multitude of murderers that populated the American West in the latter half of the 19th century, Billy the Kid has been chosen to wear the Robin Hood green. Powerful promoters fighting in the Lincoln County War ensured that the Kid would play before a national audience. These backers also enhanced the Kid's survival as an outlaw, offering him protection from the law in a number of ways. Not only did they enhance his physical escape from justice; they also provided him with a context in which his lawlessness could be justified. Journalists and popular writers, perhaps more interested in profits than politics, sifted through the events and characters of the Lincoln County War. Quickly they transformed Billy the Kid into a social metaphor expressing the discontent many felt over the manner in which law and politics were used to serve private rather than public interests, not just in Lincoln County, but throughout the United States during the bilious years of latter 19th century.

Over the years the legend grew. As in the case of Jesse James and other noted American Robin Hoods, rumors spread that Billy the Kid had never been killed by lawmen (cf. Sonnichsen and Morrison, 1955). The reports of his "non-death" were considered just another example of the malfeasance of justice, or perhaps on a deeper level suggested that the symbolic meaning of the heroic criminal—the idea of justice, or perhaps its ambivalent nature—still lived on. The original political context of the criminality lost its meaning and receded. The myth fragmented and scattered in numerous directions (cf Tatum, 1982). To some writers, the Kid became evil incarnate (Cf. Jenardo, 1881; Chapman, 1905; Adams, 1960; Steckmesser, 1965, 1983); to others he became a fabled brigand (Fable, 1881; Burns, 1926; Otero, 1936; Hamlin, 1959; Steckmesser, 1965, 1983). While to others he became the cosmic cowboy (Delany, 1967). But why and how Billy the Kid became a cultural icon can only be understood by considering the political context in which he played out his criminality, the powerful supporters who aided him in his performances, and a larger social audience that was amenable to the representation of a criminal as hero.

Chapter 5

Butch Cassidy

Jesse James and Billy the Kid achieved notoriety during the depression years of the 1870s; they were the most noted of an epidemic of American Robin hoods—such as Clay Allison, Sam Bass, "Black Bart" Bolton, John Wesley Hardin, Belle Starr, and Ben Thompson—that burst forth in those troubled times. For the next twenty odd years, no nationally prominent heroic criminals emerged. But then, in the 1890s, another depression gripped the Midwest, and criminals once again were cast in the role of hero. In Oklahoma, the Daltons and the Doolin gang rose to prominence. Tom Horn and King Fisher were lionized in other parts of the country. And John Wesley Hardin, after a long stint in prison, reappeared on the streets of Texas towns and quickly regained his outlaw stature. But none of these lawbreakers approached the eventual popular appeal of Butch Cassidy and his "Wild Bunch."

The 1890s were hard times for the Midwest, and large numbers turned to the Populist party in an effort to have their interests represented by elected officials. Great was the dissatisfaction with the manner in which political leaders were running the country, and the portrayal of political leaders as bandits who were robbing the people was not uncommon in the press. Headlines like the following in the Helena (Mont.) Democrat Independent (Sept. 14, 1900) were typical:

How Coal Trust Robbers Loot Their Miners
Hanna [President McKinley's close friend and advisor] and his friends pay miners less than a dollar a day for work.
HOLD THEM UP IN MANY WAYS.

A familiar cast of villains was again named as the cause of popular suffering and social injustice: banks, railroads, and other economic monopolies. These institutions were perceived as social cormorants that lived off the labor of "the people," and the law was viewed as a tool to make easier the exploitation of the common folk.

In this social and political context, certain criminals who successfully waged war against these "evil forces" could easily be cast as champions of the people, portrayed as men who were in the business of righting

99

social wrongs, figures who symbolically represented justice outside the law. Butch Cassidy and his criminal associates were just such men. For close to ten years they made a successful living from robbing banks, trains, and large cattle operations. Not only was Butch Cassidy a plausible candidate for heroism because of his success and the character of his victims; he apparently had no skeletons in his closet and left none behind during the course of his criminal career. There is absolutely no evidence of him ever killing a man, making him much more presentable as a Robin Hood figure.

It was not his success at business or regard for human life that led to this Robin Hood status, however. Rather, social conditions in the North country where Butch Cassidy and the Wild Bunch rode prepared such a role for him; in particular a series of events that took place in Johnson County, Wyoming—the location of Hole-in-the-Wall, an American Sherwood forest, which served as home for the Wild Bunch. These events, commonly described as the Johnson County War, assured local support and adulation for bandits such as Butch Cassidy. These episodes also provided a context in which the criminality of Butch Cassidy and the Wild Bunch could be infused with political meaning and justified to a larger national audience.

The Johnson County War of 1892 arguably stands out as the most blatant use of law and political office for the benefit of the rich and powerful against the common farmer and laborer that has been so far uncovered in the history of the United States. The acknowledged villain in this little-known chapter of history was the Wyoming Cattleman's Association, a fraternity of wealthy cattlemen, Wyoming's governor, and the state's two senators. Pitted against this group were many citizens of Johnson County, Wyoming.

The first account of the Johnson County War, Asa S. Mercer's *The Banditti of the Plains*, is a story in itself. Mercer, a Wyoming journalist, described the events of the so-called war and in the process accused some of Wyoming's leading business and political leaders of participating in obstruction of justice and being accomplices to murder. According to legend, the book was seized at the press, the plates were destroyed, and the author jailed on a charge of sending obscene material through the mail. Allegedly a few copies were smuggled out, including one which was sent to the librarian at Princeton University accompanied by a letter which warned of a conspiracy "united in an attempt to exterminate the book" and which described how the book would often disappear from library shelves (Kittrell, 1954). Unfortunately, recent historical research has discredited this imaginative tale (Hall, 1977). Instead it seems that an edition of a newspaper edited by Mercer was illegally suppressed. The paper contained a "confession" by one of the Texas gunslingers hired by the Association. The Republicans in power realized what effect

The Hole in the Wall Gang or the Wild Bunch. Left to right: Bill Carver and Harvy Logan. Left to right sitting: Harry Longabaugh, Ben Kilpatrick and George Parker, alias Butch Cassidy. Dec. 1900. Photographer—John Schwartz, Ft. Worth, TX. Western History Collections, University of Oklahoma Library. Reprinted with permission.

the story of their complicity in this incident would have on the upcoming election so they closed down the paper for two weeks and seized 24,000 copies of the "confession," which had been printed at the request of the Wyoming Democrats (Hall, 1977:59-60).

The story of Mercer's tome is a familiar one of economic conflict between the cattle barons who settled in Wyoming and the homesteaders who followed them to Wyoming and attempted to establish farms. For about ten years the cattle barons and homesteaders of Johnson County lived in harmony. However, by the mid-1880s a combination of poor weather and dropping cattle prices put the cattle barons in a bad economic situation. As the herds dwindled, the ranks of unemployed cowboys swelled, rustling increased, and the cattlemen grew increasingly militant.

To improve their situation, the Wyoming cattlemen made judicious use of the Wyoming legal system. A series of "maverick laws" were passed which gave the Wyoming Cattlemen's Association the right to control all cattle round-ups in the territory and the right to seize all unbranded cattle. These laws guaranteed a steady revenue to the members of the Association and kept the homesteader or small operator from expanding his herd. The laws were almost uniformly considered unfair, unethical, and probably unconstitutional. But they remained in effect primarily because the Wyoming Cattleman's Association "not only controlled the legislature, it had a friend in the governor's chair, friends on the bench, and a friend in the White House in Washington [Benjamin Harrison] who were subservient to its wishes" (Smith, 1966:85). It was a highly effective political machine.

The law was unjust, and it also proved to be unenforceable. Cowboys continued to brand mavericks and rustle cattle. The cowboys of Johnson County, where this activity was considered to be most out-of-hand, decided to hold their own "illegal" round-ups. The Association responded first by blacklisting recalcitrants, and then by systematic assassination of troublemakers. In July of 1889, two county residents, Ella Watson and Jim Averill, were found hanging side-by-side, their bodies discolored and swollen almost beyond recognition. A vigilante band of cattlemen had found them guilty of possessing stolen cattle. The identity of this "jury" was known since several people had witnessed the abduction. Six prominent ranchers were arrested but were eventually released because of "a lack of evidence." One witness, a young boy, had died mysteriously, possibly poisoned (Mercer, 1954:19). A second witness disappeared. No one else was willing to testify.

The death of these two citizens was widely discussed in the press, and the content of those discussions varied widely. The Cheyenne Sun, which was an organ of the cattlemen, busily constructed social identities of the murdered pair as thieves and cowards who terrorized honest cattlemen and decent citizens of Johnson County. The Casper Weekly

Mail, which had a history of opposition to the Association, portrayed the deceased as common citizens whose primary "crime" was opposition to the cattlemen. Several months before his death, in fact, Averill had published in the Casper Weekly Mail (April 7, 1889) a sharp condemnation of the cattle barons, a letter in which he suggested that the Association was more concerned about turning profits for "Eastern speculators" than benefitting the citizenry of Wyoming. The cattle barons were portrayed as monopolistic and hostile to the interests of the ordinary man. Thus, as the editor of the Casper Weekly Mail (Aug. 2, 1889) observed:

James Averell [sic] was not a cattle thief, and if this business is sifted to the bottom it will be found that his death was caused because he opposed the gobbling up of the public domain by individuals or corporations.... He held that a bona fide settler had a right to enter an enclosure fraudulently held or covered up by a large land owner. He favored the settling up of the rich valley of the Sweetwater with small ranches and the making of homes for hundreds of families, instead of having it owned or controlled by one or two. Averell (sic) stealing cattle—all bush and buncombe.

James Averill apparently was murdered because he was politically dangerous to the Wyoming Cattleman's Association. He was an activist who had the potential to mobilize organized opposition in Johnson County.

But revenge also may have been a contributing factor. According to O.H. Flagg, in an article written for the anti-Association Buffalo (Wyoming) Bulletin (June 9, 1892), Averill was assassinated as the result of a dispute with Association member Albert Bothwell "over some fine meadowland that Bothwell was holding illegally. Averill being a surveyor, had detected the fraud, and had contested Bothwell's right to the land, and the contest had been decided in [Averill's] favor only a short while before he was hung." Bothwell was one of the men arrested for the double murder and then released when witnesses disappeared. Bothwell then assumed title to both Watson's and Averill's land. This result, Asa Mercer (1954:20) caustically observed, "gave special encouragement to the stock growers and they determined to 'continue the good work.'"

For almost two years a relative peace settled over Johnson County. Then in the spring of 1891, the Association renewed its murderous attack upon the citizens of Johnson County. Within the year, three men were slain and two others were attacked, all in separate incidents. Each of the victims had in common a reputation of being vocal opponents of the cattle barons. Although the perpetrators were known, no witnesses would testify, and no arrests were made (Burt, 1938:287-8; Buffalo Bulletin of July 14, 1892).

The terrorist tactics of the Association failed to intimidate the citizenry of Johnson County. In fact, feeling ran so high against the cattlemen that it became virtually impossible to convict anyone of rustling cattle in the region, and rustling increased. To make matters worse, residents organized their own stock association and planned to hold their own illegal cattle round-up. As a result, "recriminations broke out anew against the damnable rustlers." It seemed to the cattlemen that the whole county was controlled by "rustlers"—that is, anyone who opposed the interests of the Association (Smith, 1966:160).

With this turn of events, it seemed that the legal system was an ineffective tool in furthering the Association's economic interests in Johnson County. There existed a legitimation crisis in that the populace refused to believe in the "rightness" of the maverick laws. Consequently, the powerful were forced to abandon the law and turn to naked coercion in order to "get their way." But episodic assassination only created more public antipathy toward the Association while rustling increased. Another method had to be employed and quickly, before other counties followed Johnson County's example. The solution: hire an army of mercenaries and declare war on the troublesome residents of Johnson County.

On the morning of April 5, 1892 a very unusual train pulled out of Cheyenne, Wyoming. On board were about 50 men, who had been recruited for this mission with the promise of $5 per day and a bonus for each man killed, plus expenses. Also among the troops were two reporters whose task was to chronicle the glorious expedition in a way that would reflect favorably upon the Association, and a surgeon just in case some difficulties were encountered. The plan, according to Hollon (1974:147-148), was simple: "They were to be deputized, furnished a list of approximately seventy rustlers, and given blank warrants that could be filled out with the dead man's name, whom they could then claim had been shot while resisting arrest." According to the Buffalo Bulletin (April 21, 1892), some 42 residents of the county were targeted for murder. The names on this list were a subject of wild rumor. Presumably, the death roll included the names of the local sheriff and his deputies, the three county commissioners, the editor of the Buffalo Bulletin, and a leading Buffalo merchant who had long been hostile to the cattle barons (Smith, 1966:194). According to A.S. Mercer (1954:47-8), after terrorizing the citizens of Johnson County, the army planned to march into adjacent counties and massacre opposition there, as well.

This "western mafia," as it was called by the Buffalo Bulletin (April 28, 1892), murdered two Johnson County men, but then its presence was quickly discovered. A long-time foe of the Association, Jack Flagg, stumbled upon the army while it was laying siege to the homestead of Nate Champion, a highly respected individual of the community and no friend of the cattlemen. Flagg escaped and alerted the town of Buffalo. Others also hurried to town to report gunfire. As one man after another rushed into Buffalo with tales of a roving army destroying everything in its path, the town was whipped into a frenzy. A leading merchant "mounted his celebrated black horse and, with his long white beard flying to the breeze, dashed up and down the streets calling the citizens to arms" (Mercer, 1954:83-4). As the Buffalo Bulletin (May 19, 1892) later observed:

[A] company of stockman with force of arms, invaded the county, bragging as they came, that every suspect shall be made a lead mine or an ornament to a halter and [that they would] deliberately kill and burn our fellow citizens. Should the people of Johnson county have quietly remained at home, not knowing who was to be the next victim? Could a law-abiding community do less than to rally around its sheriff to vindicate the law so grossly outraged?

By morning the community had organized itself under the command of the sheriff and set out to wage war with what the Buffalo Bulletin termed the army of the "Pope of Cheyenne and his consistory." Within a day, some 250 men had surrounded the invaders, who barricaded themselves at a ranch some 15 miles from town.

For two days, things were at an impasse. The band of mercenaries had constructed strong fortifications, and storming their position would have been costly. Supplies to the invaders had been cut off, but starving them out would take time and require a more disciplined and committed force than the sheriff of Johnson County could muster. Instead, an ingenious moveable breastwork was constructed. It would serve as a shield for the county forces, who could maneuver close enough to the entrenched men to toss dynamite into their midst and blow both the fortifications and the invaders to pieces. But just as the contraption was moving into range, as if in a Hollywood script, the 6th US Cavalry appeared on the scene. An urgent telegram describing the situation had reached the Wyoming governor, who in turn had sent a frantic message to President Benjamin Harrison asking for federal intervention. Harrison was roused from bed by one of Wyoming's Senators and acted just in time to save the lives of the invaders.

After meeting with the commander of the federal troops, the Johnson County posse agreed to permit the invaders to surrender to the military, with the stipulation that the mercenaries would be jailed and brought to trial for their murderous actions. But injustice would continue to follow injustice, and the people of Johnson County remained the big losers in the whole affair. The press controlled by the cattlemen, particularly the Cheyenne Sun and Laramie Sentinel, presented the public with sensational stories of mobs in Johnson County that were planning to attack the imprisoned cattlemen's army, that the residents of the region were terrorized by organized crime rings, or that most of the populace were rustlers (cf. the Buffalo Bulletin of May 18-20, 1892). These sordid tales of lawlessness, one historian claims, resulted in the railroads bypassing Buffalo (Smith, 1966:229). But perhaps the greatest blow was that not a single member of the cattlemen's army was ever punished by the courts. After a long delay, the prisoners were brought to trial. No witnesses were willing to testify. Two key witnesses for the state had been bribed by the Association (with bad checks!) and had disappeared from the region. All the defendants were acquitted, and the county was left with an enormous bill for the expenses of the trial and imprisonment.

Asa Mercer (1954:133), in his classic history of this "crowning infamy of the ages," claims that the public reacted with outrage to this injustice but "finally settled down to the common opinion that the ring had so many obstructions...that justice was not likely to be meted out in the event of a long and expensive suit, and perhaps it was as well to end the farce without further cost to Johnson County settlers." But the people of the region would long remember the lessons taught by the Johnson County War. As Burt (1938:271) observed:

> The implications widened as the causes receded into the past. Economic and social and political factors entered in. The fight became one between the man in possession and the newcomer wishing to possess. Between the man whose fortune was made and the man wishing to make a fortune. Between the small cattleman and the big cattleman. Between the ranchman who had a score of cowboys and the ranchman who had only himself and a son or two and maybe a hired hand. The fight, in short, became a class war....

And one lesson to be learned from this class war was that the legal system was structured to favor the interests of the wealthy and powerful few. Another was that in this episode, the affluent cattlemen made little distinction between homesteaders and rustlers. Vocal opponents of the Wyoming Stockgrowers Association were labeled as criminals and executed without due process of law, a theme expressed repeatedly in the local press. (cf Buffalo Bulletin of April 28 and May 19, 1892). Under these circumstances, many of the residents identified much more strongly with rustlers who victimized the wealthy cattlemen than with the representatives of the political and legal system. Social conceptions of justice were represented more in the actions of these cattle thieves than in the content and practice of law.

These same social conditions had given rise to popular criminals in Missouri and in New Mexico during the 1870s, as we have seen. So it is not surprising, then, that a band of heroic criminals could emerge in the Johnson County region in the 1890s. These were the bandits who made their home in Hole-in-the-Wall, a series of canyons some ten miles from the site of the only battle of the Johnson County War. They began as horse thieves and cattle rustlers, but by the late 1890s they turned to bank and train robbery. As Burt (1938:315) observed, these outlaws depended upon "the good will of the less clear-thinking residents of the Powder River country and the Big Horn Basin...[t]he Robin Hood tradition and the inherent dislike of the law on the part of law-abiding people." Sympathy promoted success, and with success came a national reputation as the "Wild Bunch."

Today the best known figure of the Wild Bunch is a young man born of Mormon stock named Robert Parker, better known as "Butch Cassidy." Cassidy, according to Burt (1938:318), "as much as anyone, came near to living up to the mythical Robin Hood tradition, and Wyoming and the Powder still remember him with tolerance and even affection."

Cassidy's rise to prominence followed a somewhat different route than that of Jesse James or Billy the Kid. For a major portion of his outlaw career he was cast as a supporting actor while other gang members received top billing. Some Western papers identified him as a key member of the Wild Bunch, but much confusion existed as to what part he played in many of the numerous bank and train robberies engineered by outlaws of the region. He did not really receive national recognition until his career was almost over, and he was certainly much better known decades after his life ended than during it.

Cassidy began his outlaw career, like so many others of his time and place, as a cattle rustler. But by the tender age of 21, he was already apprenticed in the business of desperados Warner and McCarty, robbing banks and trains. In 1892 Cassidy established a small ranch at Lander, Wyoming and went full time into the rustling business. In June of 1893 Cassidy was arrested for horse-theft but was acquitted. In 1894 he was again charged with horse theft, found guilty, and spent close to two years in prison.

Not much is known of Cassidy's activities for the months following his release from prison. Presumably he returned to the same activities he was engaged in prior to his arrest: stealing cattle, horses, and money.

The McCarty-Warner gang had become the Warner gang as the result of a disastrous bank robbery in which two of the McCarty brothers were killed. No doubt a skilled veteran like Cassidy would have been eagerly recruited, and since the gang was quite active (the Green River Star of Aug. 26, 1895 claiming that their "depredations are numbered by the hundreds"), it is very likely that Cassidy took employment there. He labored in relative anonymity, however. Matt Warner was recognized in the press as the leader of this "gang of Jack Shepards" (Green River Star, Aug. 26, 1895).

In September of 1896, Butch Cassidy became front page news, however. In May, Matt Warner had become involved in a shooting incident in which a number of people were killed. According to reports, Warner had been a member of a party planning to make a claim on a copper deposit. This group was followed by a number of armed men looking for the same reported vein of copper. Before the deposit was located, both parties first discovered each other and began shooting. Free enterprise! The gun battle ended in Warner's favor. Rather than fleeing, Warner tended to the wounded and summoned a doctor. Feeling the shooting was justified, Warner returned to town with the men he had just shot. When two of them died, the outlaw was jailed on a double murder charge.

Cassidy, upon hearing of Warner's plight, promptly robbed the bank at Montpelier, Idaho. The reason for this crime, according to the Salt Lake City Herald (Sept. 9, 1896), was "for the purpose of securing money with which to defend the notorious Matt Warner." The paper further noted that Cassidy and Warner "have been associated in many daring bank robberies. Either would lay down his life for the other if liberty was at stake and to secure it they would stop at nothing." The paper also claimed that $1000 of the stolen money had "already found its way into the pockets of an attorney associated in the case," presumably Douglas Preston, who had previously represented Cassidy in the Lander horse thief trials. Preston promptly claimed the accusation to be a "malicious falsehood" (Ogden Standard of Sept. 10, 1896). Preston was a prominent Wyoming lawyer with political aspirations. At this time he was a leader of the Wyoming Democrats, which undoubtedly explains in part why the Republican press paid so much attention to Warner's trial. Apparently Preston's association with Cassidy did not harm the lawyer's career, for he would serve in both chambers of the state legislature and as Wyoming's Attorney General (Betenson, 1975:93). For years he would also serve as chief counsel for the Wild Bunch.

Up to this point, Warner was identified as the "star" of the outlaw band, a natural leader who held "the unenviable distinction of having the most notorious record of any outlaw since the days of the James boys" (Salt Lake City Herald of Sept. 9, 1896). However, the Herald was doing a very good job of increasing Cassidy's fame. By September 10 they were spelling his name correctly and describing him as "perhaps no braver than the James boys, but certainly more daring and cruel." In addition, it provided the public with an interesting insight into Cassidy's character when it published a letter he allegedly had written to Matt Warner's wife shortly after the Montpelier robbery. Mrs. Warner, tired of her husband's outlaw ways, had decided to help authorities convict him and capture his accomplices. She had sent a letter to Cassidy asking to meet with him. Cassidy's astute reply was as follows:

Mrs. Rosa Warner, Salt Lake:

My Dear Friend—Through the kindness of Mrs._____ I received your letter last night. I am sorry that I can't comply with your request, but at present it is impossible for me to go see you, and I can't tell you just when I will get there. If you have got anything to tell me that will help you or Matt, write and tell me what it is, and I will be there

on time. I can't understand what it can be, for I have heard from reliable parties that
you did not want Matt to get out, and I can't see what benefit it could be to you unless
it was in his behalf. I may be misinformed, but I got it so straight that I would have
to be shown why you made this talk before I could think otherwise. But this is neither
here nor there, you are a lady, and I would do all I could do for you or any of the
sex that was in trouble. Of course I am foolish (which you have found out), but it is
my nature and I can't change it. I may be wrong in this, but if so, I hope you will
over look it and prove to me that you are all right, and I will ask forgiveness for writing
you as I have.... If I can do anything to help you out let me know and I will do it.
[Elza] Lay and I have got a good man to defend Matt and Wall, and put up plenty of
money, too, for Matt and Wall to defend themselves. Write me here in care of John Bluford,
and believe me to be a true friend to my kind of people.

George Cassidy

Here was a truly exemplary bandit—articulate, kind to women, and
faithful to his friends. Unfortunately for Warner, Cassidy's efforts were
in vain. Warner received a five year sentence, tempered undoubtedly by
the favorable testimony of a survivor of the shooting who was accused
by the prosecuting attorney of having "diarrhea of the jawbone" for
saying many kind things about Warner (Kelly, 1959:98). And Butch
Cassidy by default became the leader of what was once the Warner-
McCarty gang.

At this point in his promising outlaw career, Cassidy had not been
identified as a member, much less the leader, of the famed Wild Bunch.
Of course, at this time the Wild Bunch was far from famed. Under the
leadership of George Currie, their first major bank robbery netted less
than $100. One bandit was captured after his horse ran off and the mule
he attempted to mount unseated him. Within a month, all the robbers
had been captured. It appeared, as the banker who witnessed the crime
said, that "the entire gang were amateurs at the business" (cited in Kelly,
1959:120-121). Before long, however, all of the bandits escaped and
resumed their trade.

In the meantime, several Wyoming papers began to take Johnson
County to task for failing to do anything about the bandits who were
known residents of the region. The Douglas News (cited in Kelly, 1959:126)
commented:

A county that persistently tolerates a gang of outlaws in its midst; that even refuses or
neglects to protect property owners, will receive no support from the law-abiding citizens
of the rest of the state. If the Hole-in-the-Wall gang had been in any other county of
the state the whole outfit would have been in the penitentiary years ago for the full limit
of the law.

Horan (1949:205) suggests that the criminals of Hole-in-the-Wall
were an integral part of the Johnson County economy, and this had
a lot to do with their acceptance by not only the country folk but also
the country's merchants. The Buffalo Bulletin was often silent about

bandit deeds because the town's merchants counted on the outlaws for business. "Had the Bulletin openly defied the outlaw gang, the merchants would have undoubtedly pulled out their advertising" and put the paper out of business.

But it is hard to believe that the merchants of Buffalo depended for their livelihood on selling supplies to bandits. Historian Charles Kelly (1959:126-7) claims that some prominent businessmen in the county had more complex dealings with the outlaws. A number of merchants financed the shipments of stolen cattle out of the area. A few law officers would alert gang members of impending arrests and police ploys. Even fake robberies were arranged by bankers, "who would then collect from the stage or express company for losses of money which in reality had never been sent." That the Wild Bunch was supported by men of wealth was also claimed by the editor of the Basin City Herald (cited in Kelly, 1959:126), who marveled at the manner in which the gang "had defied the authorities for so long with such strange impunity." Justice demanded more than the death or capture of these bandits. "The moneyed scoundrels who aid and abet them, who take their stolen stock, who make their stealing possible and profitable, are far more guilty than O'Day and the rest of the gang." Thanks to the help of powerful men in high places, the nucleus of the Wild Bunch—George Currie, Tom O'Day, Harvey Logan, and Harry "Sundance Kid" Longbaugh—would enjoy years of prosperity.

For two years, from 1897-1899, not much is known of the activities of the Wild Bunch or Butch Cassidy. Apparently sometime during this period, Cassidy's gang merged with the members of the Wild Bunch, but exactly when and how remains a mystery. Unfortunately, outlaws tended to be insensitive to the needs of historians or sociologists who wished to piece together the incidents composing criminal careers. Instead of a chronicle of events and discussion of motives, one finds a mosaic of anecdotes and folktales about Butch Cassidy. We find, for instance, that Butch Cassidy and the Wild Bunch were seized with patriotic fervor at the onset of the Spanish-American War. Kelly (1959:212-3) relates:

When news reached Brown's Hole, Robber's Roost, and Hole-in-the-Wall that the Maine had been sunk, they forgot their old enemies—sheriffs and cattle barons—in their anxiety to fight the Spaniards.

Word went out on the underground telegraph that boys were to meet at Steamboat Springs, Colorado, to form a troop of cavalry to be known as the "Wild Bunch." On the appointed day, hard-riding, quick-shooting buckaroos began drifting in from all directions. It is not unlikely that Butch Cassidy himself passed the word, and it goes without saying that if a company had been formed he would have been leader.

Reportedly enthusiasm ran high at this meeting, but fear that the authorities might decide to have the volunteers serve in the penitentiary rather than in the military cooled the ardor of many of the bandits (Horan, 1949:220-222; Kelly, 1959:212-3).

We also find reports of a Train Robbers Syndicate forming, of which Butch Cassidy was the mastermind. One historian even goes so far as to state that George Currie and the Logan brothers were admitted as "bona fide members of the Wild Bunch under the leadership of Butch Cassidy" (Kelly, 1959:128). If this was true, it was apparently well hidden from the press. The first robbery pulled off by this "Syndicate" was at Wilcox, Wyoming on June 2, 1899. Butch Cassidy was rarely mentioned as a participant, much less a leader, of the gang to whom the crime was attributed (Chisum, 1983). Even as late as 1906, the press was identifying George Currie, not Cassidy, as the leader of the gang (Cf. New York Herald, Sept. 23, 1906). It was agreed upon, however, that all these desperate men made Hole-in-the-Wall their outlaw nest, a fortress "where only two men can enter abreast, and where three dead shots can defy hundreds" (Great Falls Daily Tribune, Sept. 3, 1900).

Unfortunately for members of the gang, in order to ply their trade it was necessary to leave the shelter of this American Sherwood Forest. Thus, in 1900 Lonny Logan and George Currie were killed, leaving the leadership of the gang open to speculation. Its next publicly proclaimed gathering was at Tipton, Wyoming on August 29, when the bandits robbed a Union Pacific train. The Denver Rocky Mountain News (Aug. 31, 1900) announced that the crime "Looks Like Work of Butch Cassidy Gang" in its headlines. The outlaws "did not attempt to molest the passengers. They only wanted what money there was in the safes, and all of it," proclaimed the paper. The bandits even refused the gold watch of the conductor, explaining "we want nothing from the railroad boys." Apparently this gang was well acquainted with the norms of social banditry.

Other papers described the band as being under the leadership of Harvey Logan at this time, however, although Cassidy was identified as an important gang member. Cassidy's fame was far from established except maybe in a scattering of communities. The Great Falls Daily Tribune (Sept. 30, 1900), for instance, in an article on the demise of the Hole-in-the-Wall outlaws, still referred to the gang as being under the commands of Harvey Logan. Butch Cassidy was described as "Buck Cassady, blood enemy of colonel Jay L. Torrey, train robber and cattle thief."

Indeed, it was Harvey Logan, sometimes called "Kid Curry," whom the press chose to cast as the heroic figure of the band. Undoubtedly this was partly because of the parallel that could be drawn between the James brothers and the Logans, kinship criminality. The Great Falls

Daily Tribune (July 21, 1900) even profiled the career of the Logans, referring to them in headlines as "kindly, genial men, not quarrelsome, and dead shots." It further exclaimed:

In these days when the Curry Gang of robbers is so prominently in the public eye, notwithstanding all but one are under the sod, it is a very slow Montana town which cannot turn some light upon the heroes of many a thrilling adventure or whose citizens cannot recall having seen these thieves in their midst but a few days ago.

Even the Eastern press, when discussing members of the gang, credited Harvey Logan with being mastermind of the Wild Bunch. According to the New York Herald (Dec. 7, 1902), Logan, a "gentlemanly assassin and train robber,...developed such daring in holding up overland trains that he became leader of the famous 'Wild Bunch' gang, of less than a dozen members, but equal to a whole regiment of ordinary desperados in terrorizing the Far West." But Logan did not make good Robin Hood material. He committed at least six murders, some in rage and others out of vengeance. He and his band were daring and successful, but usually only their "hometown" papers had anything kind to say about them.

While the leadership of the Wild Bunch was debated by the press, there was no question that the band was quite active and very successful. Three weeks after the Tipton robbery, the outlaws took $32,000 from a bank in Winnemucca, Nevada. They then journeyed to Texas where they spurred the economies of Fort Worth and San Antonio by engaging in wild spending sprees. It was here that the famous photograph of the Wild Bunch, attired in derby hats and expensive suits, was taken.

Another notable stop was in Wagner, Montana on July 3, 1901. Here the last great hold-up of the gang occurred. Using dynamite, the band blew open an express car and escaped with about $50,000. An interesting eyewitness account of the event was provided by the Great Falls Daily Tribune (July 4, 1901):

While the work of blowing up the safe was progressing, a horseman appeared and one of the robbers remarked, 'I don't like the looks of the ____ __ ____, and I guess I'll take a shot at him.'

'All right Billy,' said the boss of the gang, 'but don't hit him; hit the horse'; and thereupon the robber fired and the horseman wheeled and rode away and he was seen by the passengers at Malta, and there was a bullet wound in the fleshy part of the horse's hip, showing that the robber was a splendid shot.

Not only was he a splendid shot, but he was part of a gang that possessed an intuitive sense of what constituted good public relations. A train robbery in which no one was hurt but an impersonal express company would be viewed quite differently from a crime in which a local citizen was needlessly gunned down. Such a senseless murder would gain the band little, but it would lose a great deal of public sympathy. This would be the kind of victim with whom people could identify, and it would cast the outlaws as enemy, a threat to the well-being of the common man. It might also have had an effect on the amount of participation by local residents in the pursuit of the bandits, as the James-Younger gang found out at Northfield.

The Wagner robbery also added to the reputation of Butch Cassidy, for he was identified as a participant and described as "one of the most notorious criminals that ever worked behind a mask in the west" (Great Falls Daily Tribune of July 9, 1901). It was believed that the other members of the gang were the "Sundance Kid" Longbaugh and Harvey Logan. Even at this time there was confusion about Cassidy's role in the gang, however, because subsequent reports (and historians) failed to mention Cassidy as a participant in this crime (cf. Great Falls Daily Tribune of July 21, 1901; New York Herald of Sept. 23, 1901; Pointer, 1977:180-182).

The robbery of the Great Northern Railroad at Wagner was the last great episode of the gang. In November of 1901, one of the bandits and his girlfriend were discovered passing bank notes taken in the robbery. Pleading guilty to a reduced charge, Ben Kilpatrick received a 15 year sentence. Gang member "Deaf Charlie" Hanks was not so fortunate. In April of 1902 he was killed while resisting arrest.

Harvey Logan also encountered difficulties with the law following the Wagner robbery. In November of 1901 Logan was vacationing in Knoxville, Tennessee. A quiet game of pool turned into a heated argument, and Logan assaulted one of the players. The police were called in, and the bullets flew. Logan seriously wounded two law officers, robbed the proprietor, and escaped out a back door. The desperado leaped over a fence and fell thirty feet into a railroad cut. Logan walked 20 miles through the woods to the fringes of Jefferson City. Badly hurt by the fall and by a bullet wound, the outlaw was apparently in a state of shock. According to James Horan (1949:254), "the delirious outlaw staggered down the main street of Jefferson City" where he was quickly spotted. He fled back into the woods, "his blood leaving a crimson trail in the snow," and was quickly captured. In November of 1902, Logan was sentenced to prison for 130 years.

By the end of 1902, all members of the gang were either dead or jailed. Only Butch Cassidy and the Sundance Kid remained at large. According to Pinkerton files, the outlaws were living in New York City, and in February of 1901 Longbaugh and his wife, Etta Place, sailed for Argentina. Butch Cassidy did not depart with them, so it is possible that he remained in the United States and participated in the Great Northern Robbery in July of that year. One thing is certain, however.

By April of 1902, Butch Cassidy had joined the Sundance Kid and Etta Place in Argentina.

For many years, very little was heard of Butch Cassidy. Various rumors reached the United States of successful bank raids in the hinterlands of South America, pulled off by Yankee outlaws who refused to let certain frontier traditions die. But at this point, Cassidy seemed to be an outlaw with a limited "regional following," a bandit who was not even given top billing in his own gang. And the acclaim given to the gang seemed to be influenced more by its association with mythical Hole-in-the-Wall than by any string of successes or heroic deeds.

But in the depression days of 1930, Butch Cassidy was revived by the pen of Arthur Chapman. And by the time Chapman finished his tale of Butch Cassidy's life and times, an American Robin Hood had taken shape. As Pointer (1977:6) put it:

In the April, 1930 issue of Elks Magazine, Chapman immortalized Butch Cassidy as a swashbuckling Robin Hood of the West, jousting with cattle barons, dragon's in banker's clothing and the smoke-belching behemoths of land grabbing railroad tycoons. For more than a decade this flamboyant champion of small homesteaders sallied forth from that impregnable bastion of outlawry, the Hole-in-the-Wall, leading his famous Wild Bunch in guerrilla raids upon mercenary monsters of the West.

According to Chapman's opus, "the coolest, cleverest, and most dangerous outlaw of the age" was a sociable, trustworthy fellow who never betrayed a friend and was a champion of the oppressed.

Chapman's story provides numerous examples of Cassidy's noble character. On a visit to one Bolivian mine to check the feasibility of robbing the payroll, Cassidy was treated so kindly by mine owners that he decided not to victimize them. Between robberies, Cassidy worked for the Concordia Mine Company, we are told. On one occasion Cassidy learned of a plot to assassinate the cordial mine manager. According to Chapman, Cassidy "immediately mounted his mule and rode two nights and one day to give the manager warning." While Cassidy worked for the company, the life and property of every man was more secure. Once, when two neophyte bandits visited the mine, Cassidy ordered them to leave. When the robbers apologized and said they were driven to crime because they had no food, Cassidy gave them $100.

According to Chapman, Cassidy was admired by everyone who knew him. "Women who met him, without knowing anything of his history, invariably liked him." Cassidy also had the friendship of the native population. "As soon as he arrived at an Indian village he would be playing with the small children, and he usually had candies or other sweets in his pockets to give them. Because of this friendliness the natives looked upon him as a sort of Robin Hood." And after one robbery, a Bolivian army colonel in the area failed to give chase because "he knew Cassidy and had taken a liking to him." In Chapman's hands, Cassidy's image was shaped into that of a Robin Hood, a Santa Claus, a favorite uncle.

But Chapman's tale told of more than the life of Butch Cassidy. Here, for the first time, were the dramatic details of the deaths of Butch Cassidy and the Sundance Kid. In 1909 the Aramayo mines payroll had been seized by two heavily armed Americans—Butch Cassidy and Harry Longbaugh. The two bandits made their way to the village of San Vacente. As luck would have it, one of the mules in the outlaws' entourage was recognized by a local constable as belonging to a friend—a friend who was transporting the payroll. The lawman quickly summoned the Bolivian army. The Bolivian troops surrounded the residence in which the bandits were lodging, and the captain invited the outlaws to surrender. The offer was refused, and the battle began between the two robbers and the army. Badly outnumbered and running low on ammunition, the outlaws faced inevitable capture or death. For a day and night the troops were held off. Then, according to Chapman:

> The soldiers, about 9 or 10 o'clock in the morning, heard two shots fired in the bullet-riddled station. Then no more shots came.... The soldiers kept on firing all through the night and during the next morning.
>
> About noon an officer and a detachment of soldiers rushed through the patio and into the station. They found Longbaugh and Cassidy dead. Cassidy had fired a bullet into Longabaugh's head, and had used his last cartridge to kill himself.

Here was a dramatic death worthy of a heroic bandit: two men, holding off an army, each risking his life for the other, and choosing death at their own hands rather than surrendering. According to Pointer (1977:8-9), "Chapman's tale was picked up by the press, and in an item date-lined New York, April 23, 1930, the Washington (sic) Post proclaimed to the world, *Butch Cassidy is Dead*." And so began the formation of the Cassidy legend.[1]

The Cassidy legend was further embellished by an amateur historian named Charles Kelly, in a book entitled *The Outlaw Trail*. Kelly spent several years researching old newspaper files and talking with residents of Utah and Wyoming who knew Cassidy personally. Kelly provides the reader with several anecdotes of kindness that the outlaw had shown to local ranchers and reiterates a theme found in Chapman's article: that Cassidy never killed a man until that fateful day in Bolivia.

For the first time, however, the reader learns of Butch Cassidy's attempt to reform. According to Kelly (1959:266-273), Judge Orlando Powers, "Utah's most prominent criminal lawyer," was approached by Cassidy with a plea to persuade the governor of Utah to grant the outlaw a pardon. A local sheriff also interceded in Cassidy's behalf. According to Kelly (1959:269), the governor met personally with Cassidy and considered the request, but eventually determined that immunity could not be granted.

As in the case of Billy the Kid, Butch Cassidy's audience with the highest political figure of the area proved unsuccessful. In the meantime, however, Judge Powers had contacted officials of the Union Pacific Railroad and informed them of Cassidy's desire to retire from outlawry. According to Kelly, a deal was worked out whereby the railroad agreed to forget all of Cassidy's past transgressions against them. In return, Cassidy would serve, at a good salary, as an express guard for the railroad. Cassidy's lawyer, the noted Douglas Preston, was to serve as an intermediary between Cassidy and the railroad. A time and place for the meeting was established. But as fate would have it, Preston and the railroad representative were delayed by a storm, lost their way, and arrived 24 hours late. Cassidy already had left in anger. Kelly (1959:271) adds to this fantastic tale:

Just before they climbed into the buckboard, Preston, disgusted with his fruitless effort, savagely kicked at a flat stone lying under the lone cedar where the meeting was to have taken place. Underneath he found a piece of paper. On it Cassidy had written: 'Damn you Preston, you have double-crossed me. I waited all day but you didn't show up. Tell the U.P. to go to hell. And you can go with them.'

Kelly's account has been repeated unquestioningly by later biographers. Apparently no other attempt to strike a deal with the railroad was made (if such an attempt ever did occur), for within months the Wild Bunch was busily robbing the Union Pacific. The railroad suffered heavily at the hands of the bandits, and this colorful tale provided biographers with an interesting motive for Cassidy's choice of victim.

Kelly's research also yielded reports that Cassidy, like Billy the Kid and Jesse James in their day, had not been killed by lawmen but was still alive. Stories of Cassidy's visits to old Wyoming friends as late as 1934 circulated through the bandit's old haunts. Kelly discounted these tales, but in the late 1970s a television special was aired which repeated the claim that Cassidy had not been killed in South America. This version of Cassidy's non-death was developed even further in a 1977 book by Larry Pointer. According to Pointer, Cassidy had taken the identity of William Phillips and moved to Spokane, Washington. Five years of research yielded a mysterious manuscript, a biography of Butch Cassidy, written by Phillips. However, it is more likely that Phillips was a friend of Cassidy rather than the outlaw, himself. A letter from Mrs. Phillips which Kelly (1959:318-19) published seems to indicate that this was the case:

Wm. T. Phillips was born and raised in an eastern state until he reached the age of 14 years at which time, owing to dime novel influence, he ran away and headed for the Black Hills.... It was after that when he fell in with Cassidy. It was about the time of the Johnson County War, and I've heard him express himself entirely in sympathy with the 'little fellows' instead of the stock association. He thought he knew Cassidy very well and considered him as more sinned against than sinning.

And so the legend of Butch Cassidy continued.

In the late 1960s and early 1970s, a time when the country was again plunged into crises over an unpopular conflict in Viet Nam, urban riots, civil rights struggles, and Watergate; Butch Cassidy was resurrected. In 1967 a movie about two miscreants of the 1930s, Bonnie and Clyde, became a surprise movie hit. In an attempt to capitalize on the public's apparent willingness to spend money to see criminals glorified, Hollywood moguls paraded a variety of Western outlaws across theatre screens. The most popular of these cinema hoodlums were Butch Cassidy and the Sundance Kid. A 1969 movie featuring Paul Newman and Robert Redford in the title roles became the most popular Western of all time and is still one of the top 50 grossing films in Hollywood history (cf. Meyer, 1979; Parish and Pitts, 1976). A number of related television and theatre movies followed, a hit song emerged from the title track, and even clothing fashions showed the influence of the film versions of these dapper desperadoes. In the early to mid 1970s, Butch Cassidy, the Sundance Kid, and Etta Place (an early example of female liberation!) were multidimensional creatures in the pop culture of America.

Butch Cassidy had a background which made it easy to cast him a someone who was victimized unjustly by the legal system. He claimed as his victims those who were responsible for the perversion of law: banks, railroads, and large ranchers. His outlaw career was entwined with the careers of powerful political figures, most notably Douglas Preston. Finally, the kinds of social issues symbolized by his criminality were relevant to a large social audience. Many could relate to what they considered injustices at the hands of the powerful corporate interests of the West.

But Butch Cassidy differs from other famous outlaws of old in that he was not a national figure in his own day. Probably the major reason for this was that there was no entrepreneur at the time trying to turn Cassidy into an American Robin Hood. Lacking was a John Newman Edwards, a Pat Garrett. Instead, it seems that the location of the gang was the focus of attention. The magical Hole-in-the-Wall, located in troubled Johnson County, was the American Sherwood Forest. Various gang members who dwelled there were touted as notorious, if not heroic, figures. That Cassidy emerged finally as the most noted was because he and the Sundance Kid managed to outlive all the other members of this legendary band. His image was undoubtedly furthered by a well-acted, well-directed movie describing his career.

Cassidy stands as a truly romantic figure who, when the frontier age came to a close in the United States, kept the outlaw tradition alive by moving to the Wilds of South America. As the last of a dying breed, he was ideally suited for the Robin Hood role. And with the passage of time, the negative aspects of his criminality—the loss of life and property suffered by his victims—faded. Thus, during the Great Depression and again in the late 1960s, when social conditions were amenable to the marketing of heroic criminals, the legend of Butch Cassidy was revitalized.

Chapter 6

The Heroic Criminal of the 1930s

The economic depressions of the 1870s and 1890s were situations that were conducive to the formation of social bandits. Certain outlaws of those days were neatly fitted into the Robin Hood role; the frontier became an American Sherwood forest, and the banks and railroads played the part of the greedy clergy and wicked nobility. The evil sheriff of Nottingham was recreated in the guise of detectives and bounty hunters.

An even more severe depression than these was the depression of the 1930s, dubbed the "Great Depression" by historians. Once again social conditions favored the emergence of social bandits, outlaws who symbolized justice in a world perceived by many as being unjust. But gone were the romantic bandits of the frontier. In their place arose a new breed of heroic criminal: the gangster. This rogue made use of the auto rather than the horse, the machine gun instead of the Colt .45, and often lived in the urban jungle rather than the wide open prairie. John Dillinger, "Pretty Boy" Floyd, and Al Capone represent the most prominent of these lawbreakers and will be examined in this chapter, but there was a veritable epidemic of such figures during the 1930s who achieved fame and a public following.

During the 1930s the conditions which promote social discontent and loss of faith in the social system were quite in evidence. Even the conservative *Fortune* (Sept., 1932) magazine noted that about one fourth of the labor force was unemployed in the early 1930s and estimated that about 25 million people were facing severe economic hardship and in some cases, starvation. In large cities like New York City, over a third of the labor force was unemployed. The situation in Philadelphia was described as one of "slow starvation and progressive disintegration of family life" (p. 22). Conditions in Midwestern cities were even worse. Employment riots were common in Detroit; unemployment soared to 40 percent in cities like Chicago and Saint Louis; and in smaller urban areas like Toledo and Akron, 60-80 percent of the labor force was idled in the early 1930s (pp. 23-4).

The farmer also felt the brunt of depression. According to Lester Chandler (1970:62), during the first three years of the depression over 5000 banks collapsed, of which 75 percent were located in places with populations under 2500. Farmers not only lost their savings but also lost their farms. In Iowa from 1929-1933, a little more than one out of every ten farms was forcibly sold at foreclosure auctions (Bryson, 1934:369). Foreclosures were widespread throughout the Midwest, and by late 1932 farmers occasionally resorted to violence to prevent sales from occurring:

On December 28, a group of about 75 farmers tried to prevent an eviction in Ashland County, Wisconsin, but were thwarted by deputy sheriffs. On January 4, 1933, farmers in LeMars, Iowa were more successful: They overpowered the judge and sheriff and threatened the life of the attorney of the insurance company. Half a dozen sales were broken up during the next week. Another favorite device of the farmers was "to keep order" and bid in properties at new low prices. For example, in Shelby, Nebraska, a farm mortgaged to a bank for $4100 was bid in by friendly neighbors for $49.50 and turned back to the owner. In another case the price was $25. A house and automobile were purchased for a total of 20 cents (Chandler, 1970:64-5).

In Kansas, a sheriff was threatened with hanging by a group of farmers if he attempted to hold a foreclosure sale. The sale was not held as the lawman told the crowd that "he had just discovered that his attention was demanded by a safecracking case, and he 'regretted' that he could not 'entertain' them by holding the sale (Dewey, 1933). Throughout the Midwest, nooses decorated farms being foreclosed to discourage bidders.

Both in the countryside and in the city during the early 1930s, the quality of life for many hard-working Americans took a turn for the worse. The social welfare system was collapsing from the volume of people seeking relief. Sharing handouts with the indigent was a new welfare class. As a 1932 report by the California Employment Commission put it:

This study of the human cost of unemployment reveals that a new class of poor and dependents is rapidly rising among the ranks of young, sturdy, ambitious laborers, artisans, mechanics, and professionals, who until recently maintained a relatively high standard of living and were the stable self-respecting citizens and taxpayers of this state. Unemployment and loss of income have ravaged numerous homes. It has broken the spirits of their members, undermined their health, robbed them of self-respect, destroyed their efficiency and employability. Loss of income has created standards of living of which the country cannot be proud. Many households have been dissolved; little children parcelled out to friends, relatives, or charitable homes; husbands and wives, parents and children separated, temporarily or permanently.

During the depression years, a large number of individuals swelled the ranks of the discontented, a middle-class that found its American dream had turned into a nightmare.

Bonnie Parker and Clyde Barrow. Western History Collections, University of Oklahoma Library. Reprinted with permission.

Bonnie and Clyde's automobile. From the collection of the Texas/Dallas History and Archives Division, Dallas Public Library. Reprinted with permission.

Among the curious consequences of the economic collapse was the floating army of homeless who wandered the American landscape in search of opportunity. Estimates of this nomadic population approached one million (*Fortune*, 1932: 28), with many of them being "just average Americans of all ages, the older men with good work records, the younger who had come to working age in the past five years, with no experience in steady work" (Springer, 1934:420). Many of these young vagabonds were from once-affluent American families, and a considerable number had high school educations (McMillen, 1932:391). With no jobs in their home communities and with their families straining to make ends meet, these youths moved on in hopes of better luck elsewhere. But typically, in community after community they were turned away. These experiences made many of them cynical, turned some of them criminal, and left not a few of them dead.

The floating army of homeless was not the only army on the loose during the early years of the depression. A number of groups expressed their disenchantment with President Hoover's administration by marching on the nation's capital. Most important of these was a group of veterans from Portland, Oregon, who came to Washington, D.C. to petition the government for payment of a bonus promised to them for service during World War I. Although the bonus was not due until 1945, the small group decided to ask for immediate payment. They began their trek across country, taking any means of transportation available. On May 21, 1932 they reached Saint Louis. When the Bonus Expeditionary Force (BEF), as they amusingly called themselves, attempted to board an Eastern-bound freighter, they were set upon by railroad officials and the Illinois National Guard. Little harm came to person or property, but the incident attracted a great deal of media coverage and resulted in much publicity for the veterans and their cause.

As the veterans straggled through the towns and villages of America's heartland, news of their mission spread, and the BEF grew in number as others joined in. Veterans from Philadelphia and New York also mobilized and marched on the nation's capital. The Washington *Post* (May 25, 1932) cited reports of almost 100,000 unhappy ex-soldiers marching on the City, but the actual number who actually arrived in Washington was probably closer to 10,000.

For nearly two months this unique lobbying group camped on the outskirts of the capital, in a makeshift "Hooverville" known as Anacostia flats. In mid-June the bonus bill had been voted down by the Senate. This bad news had been greeted admirably by the veterans who had gathered outside the capitol. After a rousing chorus of "America," they had returned to their hovels. Most of the veterans, having little reason to return to their hometowns and enjoying the comraderie they were experiencing, had decided to remain in Washington. Some were joined by friends and family. Soon a little community was thriving on the banks of the Anacostia river in the summer of 1932, a community that according to eyewitness observers, "represented a cross-section of America," conservative in nature and middle-class in attitude. The vast majority were former servicemen, with only a handful of drifters in their midst. They came from all walks of life, from physicians to farmers, from conductors to clerks (*Nation*, Sept. 28, 1932:269).

The presence of these old warriors at the steps of the White House created some concern for President Hoover and members of his administration. Sporadic outbursts of mob violence had been reported throughout 1932 in cities, agricultural communities, and mining regions (cf. Piven and Cloward, 1979; *Fortune*, 1932). Then, in late July, a handful of alleged Communist agitators attacked police with bricks while some veterans were being removed from a vacant building. In the confusion, two veterans were killed. Panicked, the administration called out the army. As the Washington *Post* (July 29, 1932) described, "tear gas, bombs, and torches, unleashed by Federal troops in a sweeping offensive, routed the ragged bonus army.... In a relentless drive, infantrymen, cavalrymen, and tanks opened the drive against the veterans" and drove them from the city. Eyewitness accounts claimed that the army and the police turned their weaponry rather indiscriminately upon whoever happened to be in their way, including journalists, sympathetic bystanders, and community residents who wandered into their yards to observe the spectacle (Anderson, 1932). Remarkably, the casualties were quite low. Only two veterans were killed, an infant died from tear gas and shock, an eight year old boy was partly blinded, and an assortment of people received minor injuries.

Perhaps the greatest casualty of all, however, was the loss of faith in America's political leadership that resulted from this incident. As the *Nation* (August 10, 1932) editorialized:

> (N)o official statement can conceal the fact that the higher officials of the government lost their heads. And so, for the first time in our history, police and troops fired on and bombed their fellow-Americans in the streets of the capital. Indeed, if further proof of the state of nerves of the government is needed, we can cite the official statement of General MacArthur, Chief of Staff, who was so silly as to say that if President Hoover had not acted, "another week might have meant that the government was in peril."

The lesson was clear. A frightened leader would meet the cries of the dispossessed with bullets rather than with bread. The BEF was not a band of savage insurrectionists; they were a cross-section of Americana. They were not the shiftless or shifty; these men and their families espoused middle-class values. They were "good" people with whom many could identify and could sympathize. Attempts to justify the military action were ineffective and unconvincing. And the smouldering ruins of

Anacostia flats symbolized the hopes of the American people and the future of the Hoover administration.

The Bonus Expeditionary Force was actually the third army to march on Washington in a six month period. In December of 1931 the United States Communist Party organized an advance on the capital to protest hunger and demand unemployment insurance. Only 1600 converged on the city and abandoned their efforts after two days. In early January, however, Father James R. Cox led a band of 12,000 Pennsylvanians to Washington to protest hunger and unemployment. Unlike the Communists, who blamed the American political system for the economic plight of the country, Cox and his followers felt that the fault was with the traditional bogeymen of the conservatives of those days—Wall Street, the banks, and "moneyed interests." Cox also differed from the Communists in that his movement received legitimacy from his religious background. His actions were not seen as self-serving but were viewed as the inspired work of a man following moral convictions and representing a higher authority. Indeed, men who represented traditional religious authority or who wrapped themselves in Americanism, a form of civil religion (cf. Bellah, 1979)—men like Cox, Huey Long, Dr. Frances Townsend, and Father Charles Coughlin—became the spokesmen for grassroots discontent.

During the 1930s, historians tell us, the threat of violent revolution was seen as a real possibility (cf. Bernstein, 1960; Piven and Cloward, 1979; Schlesinger, 1957). Farmers, coal miners, and the unemployed all engaged in outbreaks of violence during the early 1930s, and a myriad of martyrs who were living outside the law existed, potential symbols of justice in an "unjust" world. One such example was Ella May Wiggins. In late 1929 she was busily involved in union activities in Gastonia, South Carolina. To help support her large family of nine children, she worked the night shift in the local textile mill. When several of her children came down with whooping cough, she requested a transfer to the day shift so that she might better care for her young ones. When her request was refused, she quit her job. Four of her children died because she was unable to afford proper medical care. Angered by the insensitivity of the mill owners, she helped organize a strike. Six months into the strike, Ella May Wiggins was murdered in an ambush. Sixteen men were indicted, most of them employers of the mill being struck. One was identified by several witnesses as the man who fired the fatal shot. Despite the evidence the jury found all defendants not guilty. And Ella May Wiggins, rather than being canonized, was vilified as yet another example of Communist insurgency. Indeed, the ruling elites went to great effort to label most expressions of hostility toward the policies of the administration and big business as "Communist-inspired." Even the Bonus Expeditionary Force, which like Cox and other conservative spokesmen wrapped their protests in the banners of patriotism, was branded by the Hoover administration as a conspiracy of radicals and troublemakers. And those who were so labelled often found the legitimacy of their claims undermined. They were seen as individuals who acted for selfish reasons rather than for the greater good; indeed, they were cast as villains attacking the American Way, and by implication, the best interests of the American people. However noble were their lives, however many injustices they suffered, no matter how twisted was the law used to persecute them, such men and women were not the stuff from which heroes were made.

Instead, the nation turned to Mid-western bank robbers and gangsters to find symbolic representations of justice at a time when the legal and political system seemed to be operating against the interests of the people. Criminals such as John Dillinger and "Pretty Boy" Floyd were cast in the role of social hero. After all, many people blamed the banks for the plight of the hard working man. Dewey (1933), in an article entitled "The Farmer Turns Gangster," captures the sense of desperation that afflicted many American farmers in the 1930s.

The apologetic bank robber has been caught. He is Ross Mundell, 51 year old Kearny County, Kansas, wheat farmer. Six years ago he was wealthy. Since then he suffered several crop failures; then, in 1931 wheat prices fell to the calamity price of $.25 per bushel. Recently foreclosure action was brought against his livestock and farm machinery. After leaving the bank, Mundell went to the farm home of a neighbor, Henry Walle.

I've just robbed the Garden City Bank,' he told Walle, 'and I want you to take this money and bury it. Later I want you to give it to Mrs. Mundell and the children. All of us are facing starvation and I couldn't bear to see the children go unhappy. I'm going down the road now and kill myself.'

Mundell had scarcely reached the road before he was overtaken by Sheriff Terwilliger of Garden City and taken into custody. He readily admitted the robbery. Dependable citizens of the vicinity appeared to sign bond for his appearance to stand trial almost before Mundell was locked up. What form justice will take in the case of Ross Mundell is not known, but his action is clearly indicative of the desperation of the farmer in Kansas and the Middle West.

Robbing a bank was something that may have crossed the mind of many men who found themselves facing unaccustomed hard times, especially those who believed populist claims that the banks were responsible for their economic hardship. It was easy to identify with bank robbers who were cast as victims of injustice and driven to crime. It was easy to sympathize with such figures. It was easy to see such criminals as symbolic champions whose exploits spoke for the discontented. It was easy to turn such lawbreakers into social heroes.

But how did certain lawbreakers become chosen as heroes? Malcolm Logan, writing in 1934, observed that the worship of glamorous criminals has a long history, but that during the depression years, "the supply of persons properly qualified for our veneration does not equal the demand." Thus, it became necessary to create supercriminals:

> In much the same way that a journeyman prizefighter is built up as a logical contender for the heavyweight championship, our supercriminal is fashioned by newspaper ballyhoo from the ordinary stick-up men or the gangster. There must of course be some basis for his reputation, at least one gaudy crime or sensational prison break. But once he has his reputation, he need never do anything more to justify it. Innumerable crimes of which he is entirely innocent will be credited to him until he is regarded as a local or even national menace.

The creation of such figures was beneficial to a number of different institutions. Newspapers found that stories about noted criminals helped to sell papers. Magazines, movies, and books found such criminals to be profitable topics.

As the depression deepened and the public mood turned increasingly sour, so did the content of media presentations of crime. Instead of portraying criminals as cardboard representations of evil, the media began to see some lawbreakers as complex and misunderstood. Movies began to present stars as criminals in films that treated representatives of law as incompetent, corrupt, and insensitive. As Richard Gid Powers (1983:13) notes in his excellent study of Hoover's FBI in American popular culture, in the early 1930s a series of popular prison films portrayed the hero as a prisoner who was wrongfully convicted, and the prison served as a metaphor for life in depression America. But as the depression deepened, the heroes of crime movies were no longer victims of mistaken justice. They were victims of social injustice, and "the authority of law had all but disappeared." The contents of these films were often amalgamations of newspaper accounts of actual criminals of the time, contributing even further to their veresimilitude. And in addition to the fictionalized presentation of crime in the media was a flood of biographies of contemporary criminals. In the early 1930s there were seven biographies of Al Capone, alone!

Also benefiting from the creation of supercriminals were police and the FBI. Any crime that was not easily solved could be attributed to the supercriminal. The failure to capture such masterminds could be chalked up to the brilliance of the outlaw or the lack of public support for the police rather than the ineptitude of the lawman. When such criminals were apprehended or killed, such an event would only add to the glory of the "G-Man" or whomever bested such lawbreakers. In addition, the threat of such dangerous men provided good reasons for increasing financial allocations and legal power of law enforcement agencies at both the local and national level. Certainly the FBI benefitted from the predations of criminals such as Dillinger and Floyd, as a series of crime control bills were passed in 1934 which greatly expanded the jurisdiction of the FBI, bills that were pushed through Congress as a direct response to the crimes of these lawbreakers (*New York Times*, April 24, 1934).

The social construction of heroic criminals through the efforts of the press is certainly exemplified in the case of John Herbert Dillinger, whom Jay R. Nash (1975:133) described as "America's classic bankrobber." Or as the Chicago *Tribune* (July 23, 1934) put it:

> No other criminal in American history ever so captured the imagination of the public. His insouciance, his cynical attitudes, his put-on good humor when bullets did not serve the immediate purpose he had in mind, were as much a part of the legend of this supercriminal as his uncanny ability to shoot his way out of traps or his unfaltering courage in battle.

But John Dillinger, when first brought to the nation's attention, was little more than a common bank robber who was not even leader of the gang he was in. John Toland (1963:134) observes that Matt Leach, an Indiana detective who was in charge of that state's police efforts to capture the Pierpont gang, felt that if the press began naming Dillinger as the mastermind, it might create jealousy within the gang and lead to its destruction. The local press agreed to the ploy, but in the course of singling out Dillinger as a prominent criminal, the press became somewhat overenthusiastic.

First, Dillinger was discovered to be a "misunderstood boy," the son of an "honest farmer father" (*Time*, May 7, 1934). The press quickly pieced together Dillinger's early life. It was discovered that he was a promising young baseball player who was led to his first robbery as a youth by an older companion who was, ironically, a local umpire! The robbery was bungled, and upon questioning, Dillinger confessed to his part in the crime. For this petty robbery he received a 10-20 year sentence while his companion received a two year sentence. This injustice and the bitter prison experience, the press explained, were what led young John to a life of crime (cf. Chicago *Tribune* of July 23, 1934). Indeed, the Dillinger story served as an exemplar for those who felt that the criminal justice system was too harsh to young first offenders and did more harm than good.

The press also dramatized Dillinger's exploits. His amazing ability to avoid capture led the press to compare him with other famous bandits of history. The Chicago *Tribune* (March 4, 1934) proclaimed that the desperado "is today what Dick Turpin, the English highwayman, and Jesse James, the American road agent, were to the public of their day." The staid *New York Times* (March 11, 1934) stated that Dillinger and his exploits were "true to the old frontier types" such as Jesse James and Black Bart. And *Time* magazine (May 7, 1934) devoted a four page spread to the bank robber, making comparisons to Jesse James and Robin Hood; quoting his father's description of his notorious son as a country boy who liked to return home once in a while for "good green vegetables and home-cooked meals;" and even providing its readers with a half page sketching of a *Dillinger Land* board game which mapped out the Dillinger episodes.

Dillinger could not help but read of the legend that was being created about him. And like others before him, he began deliberately to cultivate the image of a social bandit. Matt Leach, the Indiana detective in charge of that state's Dillinger hunt, told newsmen eager for information that the infamous bandit had been telephoning taunting messages to him. Then one Christmas, a book mysteriously appeared at Leach's door— an 1862 dime treatise entitled *"How to be a Detective."* When no one took credit for the caper, some papers reported that Dillinger was the practical joker (Toland, 1963:157).

During a robbery at Greencastle, Indiana, the Dillinger gang netted some $70,000 from the vault. More significant to the editors of the Chicago *Tribune* (Oct. 24, 1933), however, was that "for some reason the invaders ignored piles of silver and paper currency lying on counters within easy reach." For chroniclers of the Dillinger legend, this behavior was easily explained. Dillinger only wanted the bank's money (cf. Nash, 1975:151). A similar event occurred during the robbery of a Chicago bank in January of 1934:

Dillinger, raising his voice slightly, announced he was robbing the bank. It was like the carefree days before he joined Pierpont, and the wonder is that he didn't impetuously leap over the barrier. When a customer, who had just cashed a check, started backing away without picking up his money, Dillinger said airily, 'you go ahead and pick it up. We don't want your money. Just the bank's' (Toland, 1963:174-5).

Such stories made Dillinger appear as a Robin Hood of his time; he only stole from the rich, not the poor.

But the episode that was perhaps more instrumental in the development of the Dillinger legend was his dramatic escape from the "escape-proof" jail at Crown Point, Indiana in March of 1934. On March 4 the Chicago Tribune announced to its readers that Dillinger, "aided only by his own desperate courage and a little toy pistol he had made himself, escaped yesterday morning from the heavily guarded jail at Crown Point." Paper after paper heralded the story of how Dillinger had used a razor blade and some black shoe polish to fashion a wooden pistol, which he used to fool his captors and to make his escape. As Powers (1983:119) notes, Dillinger's wooden weapon "became an instant pop icon, a symbol of law enforcement idiocy and incompetence."

John Dillinger at Crown Point, Ind., Jail where he was returned after his capture in Tucson, Ariz. Jan. 1934. (L to R): Sheriff Lillian Holley; Prosecuting Atty. Robert G. Estell; Dillinger and Chief of Police Nicholas Maker. UPI/Bettmann Newsphotos. Reprinted with permission.

Dillinger, who by this time had become quite aware of his public image, gave his father a photo showing the bandit with wooden pistol in one hand and machine gun in the other. He wrote a letter to his sister bragging about the incident and mocking claims made by deputies that Dillinger had a real gun. Some months later evidence turned up which suggested that someone had smuggled Dillinger a real gun and that he was aided by someone within the prison administration, but the public clearly found this attempt at revisionism unconvincing (Toland, 1963:209-10).

Dillinger immediately assembled a gang upon his escape and pulled off several dramatic bank robberies, including one in Iowa where the gang also captured the town's entire police force. Swelled with success, Dillinger decided to visit his family and friends in hometown Mooresville, Indiana. The elder Dillinger took the occasion as an opportunity to hold a family reunion. The fact that the young Dillinger, although quite famous and very busy, would take time off from his work to visit his old hometown and family, made a very peculiar impression on the people of Mooresville. A petition was circulated requesting that the governor of Indiana pardon Dillinger if he surrendered. Toland (1963:258-9) has reprinted the petition, which included among its justifications for such an act the "precedent in the case of Governor Crittendon's pardon of Frank James in the state of Missouri" and "...that many of the financial institutions of the state have just as criminally robbed our citizens without any effort made to punish the perpetrators."

Indeed, Dillinger was considered widely as a heroic figure. Historian John Toland (1963:260) claims that "no bandit since Jesse James had won such widespread sympathy. He robbed banks—not people—and had become a sort of depression Robin Hood. The dash and derring-do of his escapes, his impudence to those in authority, and his occasional chivalry during a robbery made them see him as a folk hero." Dillinger's activities resulted in the deaths of a number of people, however, and a great deal of embarrassment to law enforcement and political officials. He was, as the New York Times (July 23, 1934) observed, a "political shibboleth." Assistant Attorney General Joseph R. Keenan wrathfully proclaimed to Time magazine (May 7, 1934), "I don't know where or when we will get Dillinger, but we will get him. And you can say for me that I hope we will get him under such circumstances that the Government won't have to stand the expense of a trial." And J. Edgar Hoover, as Powers (1983) skillfully describes, utilized the mass media as a propaganda instrument extolling the virtues of the "G-Man" while condemning the symbolic evil represented by gangsters such as Dillinger.

In fact, time was running out on Dillinger. He was pursued by the FBI, various state police units, and interested citizens whose appetites were whetted by the large sums of money being offered for his capture. The spring of 1934 found Dillinger leaping from one trap into and out of another. In late March the outlaw shot his way out of a police ambush in Saint Paul, Minnesota. In late April he escaped from the clutches of officers in Wisconsin. In desperation Dillinger underwent a series of operations to alter his appearance, used acid to obliterate his fingerprints, and dyed his hair.

But these efforts were in vain. On July 22, 1934 Dillinger was killed by FBI agents as he left a Chicago theater. The agency had been informed of Dillinger's whereabouts by the madame of a local whorehouse who had rented a room to him. Anna Sage, known in popular history as the infamous "Lady in Red," had hoped her information would cancel deportation proceedings against her. Being betrayed by a woman and shot down by lawmen who gave him no chance to surrender helped ensure John Dillinger a place in the pantheon of criminal folk heroes.

Public reaction to Dillinger's death took some unusual forms. Thousands of people flocked to the theater where Dillinger was killed. A car with Indiana license plates found near the theater was stripped by souvenir hunters who mistakenly thought it belonged to Dillinger. Others used handkerchiefs, pieces of paper, and even the hems of their skirts to soak up the blood that had leaked out of the fallen hero's body; turning the murder scene into some bizarre primitivistic ritual. Thousands more passed Dillinger's body, which was placed on display in the morgue, and purchased souvenirs celebrating the event.

Perhaps even more bizzare were the rumors that began to circulate. Dillinger, it was widely believed, was blessed with an abnormally large penis—presumably in keeping with his superhuman abilities in other areas! This organ had been removed by the FBI and was kept in a jar in the Smithsonian. Other rumors claimed that the FBI had killed the wrong man and were attempting to cover up their blunder. According to Toland (1963:331), some Mooresville residents who viewed the dead body claimed it was not Dillinger's. Others reported seeing him several years after his "death" in Chicago. Nash (1975:164-6) has proposed an elaborate theory which holds that the man killed in Chicago in 1934 assumed Dillinger's identity as part of "an underworld scheme to provide Dillinger with a permanent escape." Even today many people believe that Dillinger—like Jesse James, Billy the Kid, and Butch Cassidy—was never brought to justice, as the legal system of the time defined it.

While John Dillinger was busy robbing banks in the Indiana-Ohio-Michigan area, other criminals were making names for themselves further south. Ma Barker and her collection of criminal offspring presented the media with all sorts of interesting story lines, from inheritance theories of crime to value conflicts resulting from a misguided emphasis on following kinship norms over societal rules. There was the poor henpecked "Machine-Gun" Kelly who was nagged into kidnapping by his attractive wife. There were gangsters everywhere turning organized crime into a structure more resembling Standard Oil than an assemblage of small family businesses. There was the Barrow gang, featuring the literary Bonnie Parker, who helped propel this relatively inept group into notoriety primarily through her poem, *The Ballad of Bonnie and Clyde*. Like Dillinger, Bonnie Parker had become aware of the legend being fashioned about Bonnie and Clyde by the media and participated in the myth-making process herself, even going to the point of kidnapping a policeman and having him promise to tell "her public" that she did not smoke cigars, as had been widely portrayed in a newspaper photograph, "because nice girls don't smoke cigars" (Treherne, 1985:185). Despite such efforts to shape public opinion, the Barrow gang never quite achieved the notoriety that some of their contemporary criminal brethren did.

The one outlaw whose fame did approach that of John Dillinger's was Oklahoma's bandit king, Charles Arthur "Pretty Boy" Floyd. Dillinger and Floyd had a number of things in common aside from their interest in robbing banks. Both were farm boys who were easily cast as "God-fearing and with a Jesse James complex of imagined fair play about them" (Nash, 1975:180). Floyd spent his youth battling the Oklahoma soil for crops, soil that was battered by drought and erosion until the region became known as the "dust bowl" and families were torn apart by the harsh realities of geography, politics, and economics. In this context it was easy to cast Floyd as a victim of multidimensional injustices.

By the time he was 24, Charles Arthur Floyd realized that bank robbery was his vocation. Unfortunately, he was captured shortly after his first robbery and spent five years receiving further training in this skill at the Missouri State Penitentiary. After his release in 1930 until his death in 1934, Floyd was credited with over 30 bank robberies and the deaths of a half-dozen men. Many of these robberies and murders occurred in his native Oklahoma. Perhaps the most audacious of these robberies was that of his hometown bank in Sallisaw. A dispatch to the *Kansas City Star* (reprinted in *The Literary Digest* of Dec. 10, 1932) provides a detailed account:

> He was born and grew up in Sallisaw. He is known to everyone in town. His mother lives within two blocks of the bank. As Floyd's car stopped in front of the bank, he and his partner, George Birdwell, leapt quickly out and ran into the bank....
>
> Floyd and Birdwell wore no masks or other disguises. Entering the bank, both pulled out revolvers. Floyd was grinning at his acquaintances, the bankers and clerks, as he announced, 'It's a hold-up, all right,' and then, to Birdwell, who was standing everyone against the wall, 'Don't hurt 'em, Bird, they're friends of mine....'
>
> Within seconds Floyd had swept $2530 into a sack. He and Birdwell marched the bank cashier as hostage out to the car, bade him get on the running board and hang on, and then said to the boy at the wheel, 'All right, hike out,' and away they went out of town.
>
> A mile or so out they halted to let the man alight from the running board. Floyd shouted to him cheerfully: 'Good-by old man, take care o' yourself,' and their car sped on, down the highway, to oblivion, so far as the public was concerned.

Such a bold act, carried out in the middle of the day in a community where his face was known to practically everyone and with a large reward being offered for his capture, seemed to be a defiant mockery of authority.

In fact, Charles Arthur Floyd seemed to have little to fear from his native folk in the Cookson Hills. There, a long tradition of living outside the law existed. An attempt in 1933 by a force of more than 400 law officers who combed the region looking for wanted criminals was a dismal failure. Like the residents of Clay County, Missouri—the home turf of the James and Younger boys—or the inhabitants of faraway Sherwood Forest in the days of Robin Hood, many of the people of the Cookson hills felt themselves to be in an adversarial relationship with representatives of the law. Courtney Cooper (1934:9) described for the readers of the *Saturday Evening Post* the nature of the Ozark hills folk:

> [F]amilies have married into other families for years, scattering a train of relationships which envelop the whole region. Relationship among hill people is a fetish; it is not only undesirable to give information against a relative, but it is a disgrace to have even

a second cousin put in jail. For, after all, the law is, to a degree, an aggressor, from the warden who prohibits out-of-season fish and game repasts to the officer who seeks the illegal still. Rich persons are hated, a heritage of the old emnity between tenant and landlord. Bankers are reviled, and anyone who can get the better of one is a hero. This feeling has increased in the past few years, due to stories of misery created by bank failures.

And so outlaws such as "Pretty Boy" Floyd, who preyed upon the banks, were easily seen as heroes by the local folk. It was much easier to identify with these types of robbers than those working for the "establishment." Or as Woody Guthrie put it in his ballad, "Pretty Boy Floyd:"

> Now as through this world I ramble
> I see lots of funny men
> Some rob you with a six gun
> And some with a fountain pen.
> But as through this life you ramble
> But as through this life you roam
> You won't never see an outlaw
> Drive a family from their home.

Thus, when Charles Burns, superintendent of the Oklahoma Bureau of Criminal Investigation and Identification, was asked by newsmen why every one of his plans failed to produce the capture of Floyd, he replied that Floyd and his bandit associates "have a host of relatives and friends and sympathizers" who protect them from the reach of the law. In the Cookson hills of Oklahoma, Charles Arthur Floyd was a hero who struck back against the "real criminals" who robbed people by using the law as a weapon.

But Floyd had only a small following in the Oklahoma region until the Kansas City massacre on June 17, 1933. On that day five men, including an FBI agent, were gunned down by machine-gun wielding desperadoes who were attempting to either spring or assassinate Frank Nash, a noted gangster who was being taken to jail by the four lawmen. In short time Floyd's name was linked to this as well as a number of other sensational crimes—including the attempted kidnapping of a Hollywood movie star. The victims of these crimes were not hated social institutions, and these lawless deeds were not easily cast as morally inspired actions of a politically conscious criminal. The murder of a special agent of the Justice Department placed Floyd into the midst of a propaganda war waged by Attorney General Cummings, a battle "between the forces of law and order and the underworld army, heavily armed" (*New York Times*, July 14, 1933). Floyd began to develop a national reputation as a "public enemy," As Jay Nash (1975:180) observes, "where Dillinger was romanticized in the newspapers of the day, Pretty Boy got the worst press of any outlaw in the 1930s...."

Still, the press did take note of Floyd's reputation in Oklahoma as a Robin Hood figure. And with the death of John Dillinger, "Pretty Boy" earned the title of America's most notorious criminal. As the *New York Times* (Oct. 23, 1934) intoned:

Charles Arthur Floyd wore the mantle which slipped from John Dillinger's shoulders when he fell, bullet riddled, outside a Chicago movie theatre. Floyd, who had already become known as a twentieth century edition of Jesse James, was called the 'most dangerous man alive.'

For the FBI, Floyd became the new symbol of evil to be hunted down and killed. For newspapers, the outlaw emerged as a readily available story which would help sell copies. And for grassroots populists, the criminal was well suited for the role of social bandit.

For months the FBI searched for Floyd and his partner in crime, Adam Richetti. Finally, in mid-October of 1934, the police chief of a small Ohio hamlet received a call about suspicious-looking strangers loitering in some woods on the outskirts of town. An investigation led to gunfire and the capture of one of the strangers, who turned out to be Adam Richetti. The other man, who escaped, was believed to have been none other than Floyd. The FBI was called in, and a massive manhunt was begun. For nearly two weeks the nation's presses provided a day-by-day account of the search. Finally on October 22, Floyd was cornered by lawmen in a desolate Ohio cornfield. As the outlaw fled across the frozen field, through the broken brown corn stalks, he was cut down by bursts of withering machine gun fire.

Federal agent Melvin Purvis, the man who directed the operation which led to the death of John Dillinger, was the first to reach the side of the dying Floyd. The *New York Times* (Oct. 23, 1934) announced to the public what then took place:

Upon reaching him the agents found he held a .45 calibre automatic in his hand and had a second automatic in a shoulder holster. Neither one had been fired, though the magazines of both were full.

'Who the hell tipped you?' Floyd asked the officers. A moment later he said, 'Where is Eddie?' 'Eddie,' the officers judged, was Adam Richetti, who was captured near Wellsville Saturday, when he and Floyd fought a gun battle with police.

The officers carried the desperado into the farmhouse of Mrs. Ellen Conkle, where he had appeared earlier for food.

Purvis bent close to Floyd, questioning him about the machine gun massacre of five men at the Kansas City Union Station in June, 1933. 'I am Floyd,' the dying bandit admitted, but to the last he denied complicity in the Kansas City killings.

The body of the fallen Floyd was returned to his family in the hill country of Oklahoma. He was buried on a small plot of land in a spot he had chosen for himself in a reflective moment. An estimated gathering of over 20,000 came to the funeral home to pay their final respects to the bandit king of Oklahoma.

Although "Pretty Boy" Floyd was dead and buried, like other social bandits, his legend lived on. His role in the Kansas City murders was quickly forgotten or denied. After all, Floyd had written a letter to police denying that he had taken part in the slaying, and his dying words were that he had nothing to do with it. The main source of evidence suggesting that Floyd was there was the word of a "stool-pigeon" big city gangster. It was easier to believe Floyd.

Over time new versions accounting for Floyd's criminal career emerged. Nash (1975:181-2) relates that Floyd could not find any work in Oklahoma to support his wife and children and so, like thousands of Oklahomans, he moved from town to town seeking work. But Floyd could not find work. He grew bitter and angry, and in an act of desperation he robbed a payroll. "Then he raced for Oklahoma and his pregnant wife." Unfortunately, Floyd was captured and sent to prison. Upon his release, Floyd returned home to find that his father had been murdered. The killer had been captured, but justice was not forthcoming from the law:

Floyd sat quietly in the Sallisaw Court House and listened as Mills was acquitted of the murder. He went home, loaded his rifle and followed Mills to the nearby Cookson hills. Mills was never seen again.

'Chock done what he had to do' an Atkins resident said later. The Okies had their own way of handling things. But the law was looking for Floyd so he fled to Kansas City.

And of course, Floyd's amazing string of bad luck was to continue until his death.

Woody Guthrie, in his ballad "Pretty Boy Floyd," offers a somewhat different version, although a system of honor and justice linked to the kinship system again collides with these concepts as represented in the laws of the state. According to Guthrie, Floyd's wife encountered some 'vulgar words of language' from a deputy sheriff. A discussion between Floyd, the defender of the fair sex (a symbol of morality), and the crass lawman, took place. The chat ended with Floyd grabbing a log-chain and the deputy sheriff grabbing a gun. In the fight that followed, Floyd killed the lawman and became an outlaw.

Once he became an outlaw, however, he did not forget where his roots were, so the legend states. Newspaper accounts reporting Floyd's death took note of the fact that he had requested meals and transportation from the farm folk who harbored him unquestioningly. The fact that he paid Mrs. Conkle, who fed him his last meal, a dollar for supper and—according to his hostess—even praised her cooking, contributed to the tales of Floyd's generosity to the poor farmer. Woody Guthrie, in his ballad of the outlaw, has Floyd commenting:

> You say that I'm an outlaw
> You say that I'm a thief.
> Well here's a Christmas dinner
> For the families on relief.

And Nash (1975:184) describes how the bandit was given protection by the farm folk because "he was one of their own. They remembered how Chock in mad delight had ripped up first mortgages in banks he robbed, hoping they had not been recorded and thereby saving a fellow farmer's homestead." Tales like these embellished the Floyd legend and portrayed him as a true Robin Hood.

New tales have emerged about the death of Floyd, transforming him even further into a mythical outlaw. *Time* (Sept. 24, 1979:25) reported that Chester Smith, a retired police captain who was present when Floyd was killed, has offered to "set the record straight" concerning the death. According to Smith, the outlaw was at first not seriously wounded. When Melvin Purvis, the FBI agent who was in charge of the case, attempted to talk to the injured desperado, he was cursed. Purvis, enraged, had the bandit killed with a "burst from a tommy gun." The execution was covered up, according to Smith, "because they didn't want it to get out that he'd been killed that way." Other versions, even truer to the myth, hold that a cover-up occurred because—like in the case of Jesse James, Billy the Kid, Butch Cassidy, and John Dillinger—the police made a mistake and killed the wrong man. "Pretty Boy" Floyd, like other social bandits before him, was a symbol of social justice at a time when it was not represented by law, an idea that could not be killed.

The decade of the 1930s also produced another criminal of legendary proportions, the big city gangster who stood at the head of a large criminal organization. And Al Capone stood as the most infamous of this breed of criminal. As Richard Gid Powers (1983:4) observed, Capone's "wealth and political influence, his wide-open defiance of the law, and his highly publicized wars, lifestyle, and loutish personality combined to create the image of a criminal who was more than a match for anything law-abiding society could put against him." But although a lawbreaker, Capone did apparently have socially redeeming qualities—at least in some people's opinion. The *North American Review* (1935:2-3), for instance, after surveying noted criminals of the depression era, nominated Capone as its choice for the role of modern-day Robin Hood. Here was a man of "boldness and ingenuity," kind and moral "aside from his attitude toward other person's property;" but a man whose activities, they editorialized, were "directed against the rich" and had "at least a partial effect of aiding the poor." He was a curious blend of American virtue and noble outlaw.

Capone certainly had his detractors. After all, he was responsible for the deaths of perhaps 500 men. (Nash, 1975:79). His cruelty to foes was legendary. Yet the gangster seemed to have been a rather popular figure. "Scarface" was often described as a public benefactor who provided alcoholic beverages to a thirsty populace at great personal risk (and profit) during Prohibition. The fact that Capone mingled freely with celebrities and politicians gave an air of legitimacy to his extralegal power. He was part of Chicago's welcoming committee for Mussolini's goodwill ambassador. He was regularly quoted by the Chicago press, with whom he had a good working relationship. In fact, according to Powers (1983:6), Capone established personal relationships with several of Chicago's crime reporters "to get his side of a story out to the public before reformers could mobilize the city against him, and he fooled many Chicagoans into regarding him as a modern Robin Hood." Stories of his support for soup kitchens to feed the poor, of his providing tickets for boy scouts to attend football games, of his protection of show business personalities and common folk from the predations of street criminals, of his gifts of thousands of turkeys to the poor on holidays, all had a way of appearing in print and keeping the public informed of Capone's philanthropy.

Not just Chicagoans but all of America were kept up to date on Capone's civic service through the seven biographies that were published about him between 1929 and 1931. Fred Pasley's 1931 tribute to the Chicago warlord, subtitled "a self-made man," compared Capone to Abraham Lincoln, George Washington, and Henry Ford; and detailed the crime czar's "geniality, his boundless sympathy for the unfortunate and the underdog, and his munificence." More national publicity was provided at Capone's famous trial for tax evasion, where his lawyer portrayed him as a "modern, mythical Robin Hood, a creation of the newspapers," and called him a victim of "censorious agencies which had banded themselves together to run the country and now shouted 'Capone must be destroyed' " (Chicago Tribune, Oct. 17, 1931). This interesting interpretation of the battle between the representatives of law and those of crime probably did not gain Capone much support, although there was concern over the FBI as the harbinger of a police state. But Capone's conviction for income tax evasion certainly evoked public cynicism, if not sympathy. Capone had offered to pay back whatever money the government said was owed, but it was obvious to all but the most naive that justice was of secondary importance to political expediency. Capone had become a political embarrassment, a "mythical Robin Hood whose name was bandied all over the nation," said his lawyers. The machinery of "justice" was used as a tool to put Capone away. And as a result, Capone was easily cast as victim, a role with which many could identify.

Al Capone may be considered a type of heroic hood, but as the *New York Times* (July 27, 1934) editorialized, he was a different kind of criminal from the frontier bandits like Jesse James or even John Dillinger. While the bandit and the gangster may have shared a similar social class background, they often differed in their ethnic origins. Gangsters tended to be from "foreign" extraction, while bandits were of American stock. Furthermore, the victims of the legendary bandit were institutions responsible for the corruption of the American system. The victims of gangsters were often other gangsters, a kind of self-genocide that promoted indifference rather than sympathy. But unlike social bandits, gangsters were not portrayed as violating the law out of a sense of social justice. They were businessmen out to increase their power and profits, mirroring the corporate ethos in a perverted way. Indeed, crime barons like Capone were commonly identified as corrupters of the political and legal system, controlling judges and politicians to further illicit gain. While their success could perhaps be admired, they were far from symbols of justice. Finally, gangsters trafficked in goods that were often viewed as immoral and enslaving vices.

The gangster, then, does not readily fit into the Robin Hood role, however fascinating such a creature might be. Of all the noted Godfathers of American history, Capone comes closest to being an American Robin Hood, primarily because of the social context in which he emerged— the depression—and because he and his influential supporters attempted to create such an image. But his social identity as a foreigner and subverter of the political system, the identity of his victims as primarily other gangsters rather than sources of injustice, and the social meanings attributed to his lawlessness—personal profit—made him less than ideal for the position.

Bandits such as John Dillinger and "Pretty Boy" Floyd, however, fitted more comfortably into the guise of Robin Hood. They were bandits from rural backgrounds and good American stock. They claimed as their victims the banks that were identified as the unfeeling monsters responsible in part for the sorry state of America's hard-working farmers. It was simple to fashion justifications for the depredations of these desperados which rendered their lawless acts acceptable, if not admirable. The depression years provided a large sympathetic audience that would enjoy and support these kinds of criminals, and newspapers quickly realized that tales of these men would sell papers. Much of the notoriety was provided, however, by the FBI, which benefitted tremendously from the creation of supercriminals. By convincing the public and politicians that a horde of dangerous criminals was roaming the land, laws would be and were enacted which greatly increased the power of the Bureau to enable it to cope with the menace. In addition, any successes by the Bureau would appear all the greater because only the super lawman—the G-Man—would be able to subdue such a criminal. Notoriety was readily transformed into heroism for outlaws such as Dillinger and Floyd during the depression years of the 1930s—a time when the ranks of the disenchanted were swelled by a newly impoverished middle class, a time when law and politics were easily seen as a tool used by economic elites to oppress the disadvantaged, a time when those who victimized these elites were imputed with motives that transformed them into symbols of social justice representing the wishes of the people.

Chapter 7

American Social Bandits:
Identity, Power, and Structure

As we have seen in the preceding chapters, a number of American murderers and thieves have been fashioned into cultural heroes, Robin Hoods who have been glorified not only in their own lifetime but for following generations. Undoubtedly the psychological appeal such criminals have partly explains their existence. Through their lawlessness we may vicariously rebel against authority. By adorning them with cherished American values such as success, individualism, and courage, various writers also enhanced these lawbreakers' heroic status. But the primary force behind the phenomenon of the heroic criminal is a concept of social justice apart from that found in law. The American Robin Hood is a symbol of justice who emerges at times when the law fails to reflect popular conceptions of justice. The criminals who became American Robin Hoods were men who committed ordinary crimes which became infused with political meaning.

Of course, it is important to recognize that the heroic outlaw of the West is a mythological creature and that myths are by nature ambiguous and open-ended, "possessing an interminable diversity of sequences and themes so that they may have continued relevance in changing social climates and for diverse audiences" (Levi-Strauss, 1966:38-9). In order to achieve and maintain mythical power, the outlaw legends had to transcend the immediate political context which gave them meaning. But the political nature of the Robin Hood criminal is the fundamental reason for his existence. Seeing this figure as a political one helps us to understand why he appears at some times and not others, and provides us with insight into the shape of legends surrounding him.

These lawless men, outlaws such as Jesse James and Billy the Kid, Butch Cassidy and John Dillinger, undoubtedly were more interested in filling their pockets than in promoting social justice, but a number of critical aspects of their criminality led to a popular (mis)conception of them as symbols of populist dissent, men whose criminality was heroic and justifiable. In this chapter I will examine the factors that led to the portrayal of certain criminals as American Robin Hoods.

The outlaws we have examined in this work represent the most noted of the handful of criminals who might be called American Robin Hoods. We have no systematic way of determining why these criminals were chosen for such a role over other criminals of their day. Undoubtedly other criminals could have been molded into heroic figures as well. But we can note that in the case of each outlaw we examined there were common factors which accounted for his transformation into a symbol of extra-legal justice. As a way of explaining how these particular lawbreakers became cultural heroes, it is helpful to borrow a conceptual framework used in the sociological analysis of cultural products such as literature and art.

First, we may examine these American Robin Hoods as products— looking at their social identity, the identity of their victims, and the nature of their criminal acts. Of particular importance is the immediate social context that helped define the nature of their criminality. Second, we may examine the "authors" of this product. More specifically, who was instrumental in the initial portrayal of these criminals as Robin Hoods. Of particular importance here are the resources of power and influence that were put to use in shaping a social definition of these outlaws as heroes. Finally, we may consider the audience that might have found meaning in the social and political issues symbolized in the criminality of the American Robin Hoods. In order to emerge from obscurity and become a national figure, the heroic criminal must appeal to large numbers of people. These laudable lawbreakers seem to appear under certain structural conditions such as widespread depressions or other social conditions that give rise to what might be called legitimation crises. An implication of this is that heroic criminals may be widespread throughout societies at all times, but that only when large numbers of people feel outside the law or feel that the law is unjust do these criminals become national heroes.

The Criminal as cultural product

Who were these American Robin Hoods? What were they like? Such questions involve a determination of identity. A social identity is a socially constructed definition of who a person is. It has dynamic qualities and is always being negotiated and altered in some way. More important, a social identity lends itself to variations in interpretation. People will come to differing conclusions of who a person is.

Each of the lawbreakers who became American Robin Hoods had characteristics which made it possible to cast him as a morally upright man who had been the victim of legal injustice. Each came from a fairly large and respectable group that was widely viewed as exploited "victims" of the political and legal powers of the time. These criminals were coming from agrarian backbone-of-the-country roots, or from solid conservative middle class families. They were not radical political figures, poor white trash, or psychopaths. Consequently, law-abiding citizens who felt outside the interests of the law could easily identify with outlaws such as Jesse James, Billy the Kid, or "Pretty Boy" Floyd.

Jesse James was a symbol of the proud and unrepentent South following the Civil War. To his admirers, he was a Confederate soldier who had risked his life for a moral cause and who had been unjustly labeled a criminal by the Radical Republicans of Reconstruction Age Missouri for political reasons. He was the son of a preacher and a loving mother. His class standing was evident in his ability to use the pen and defend himself through the columns of the Democratic press. His moral upbringing was made obvious to many through his use of Biblical quotes and his marriage "for love." And certainly the fact that Pinkerton agents bombed his family home, murdering his step-brother and blowing off his mother's arm, contributed to a view of him perhaps as much a victim of the law as a violator of it.

Billy the Kid, because he worked for John Tunstall, a man who was brutally murdered by a "sheriff's posse," was also associated with the cause of popular justice. Rather than as a mass murderer, the young killer was portrayed as a vigilante whose criminality took on "the aura of a holy crusade" (Steckmesser, 1965:100). He was a key actor in a violent political struggle in which one group used the law as a tool for personal gain. The forces that the Kid opposed were seen as a monopolistic organization of wealthy men with political connections, men who exploited the citizens of Lincoln County. It was easy to show Billy the Kid as a champion of the oppressed, and the events surrounding his criminality made it appear that he suffered the loss of friends and supporters at the hands of his corrupt foes. Undoubtedly the young age of this outlaw made it somewhat easy to cast him as an innocent figure who suffered misfortune for which Fate or others, but not he, could be blamed.

Butch Cassidy was a farm boy born into a Mormon family. No doubt his identity as a man from a Mormon background made him amenable to presentation as a symbol of justice, for the history of the Mormons in the West is marked by persecution and acute struggles for political power. Wallace Stegner's (1942) history of Mormonism, for instance, includes a biographical sketch of Butch Cassidy, a Mormon boy whose father died a "good Saint to the last." It was Cassidy's affiliation with Hole-in-the-Wall, a series of box canyons located in Johnson County, though, that helped forge his identity as a champion of the common folk. The violent range war in which the Wyoming Cattlemen's Association used both legal and extra-legal means to secure profits for the wealthy ranchers of the region created a context in which a local rustler such Butch Cassidy could be considered a decent and respectable person. After all, the Wyoming Cattleman's Association failed to make any distinction between professional criminals and honest ranchers. So it was not difficult for local residents to blur the distinction and consider Cassidy as one of them.

In the 1930s, criminals such as John Dillinger and "Pretty Boy" Floyd emerged as Robin Hoods. These, too, were men from rural backgrounds who could be cast as symbols of agrarian dissent. Dillinger was described as a farm boy who was led into crime through the evil influence of an older man. As if to compound the symbolism, Dillinger's athletic prowess as a baseball player was often emphasized. This suggested that a truly All-American future could have been his if not for the evil influence of an older companion who was, quite fittingly, an umpire by trade. Authority figures in any uniform were suspect! And Dillinger's criminal contemporary, Charles Arthur Floyd, allegedly turned to crime out of desperation because he had no other way to support his family during the depression that ravaged his Oklahoma home, although other versions claimed that his assault on a sheriff who had insulted Floyd's wife also placed "Pretty Boy" forever on the wrong side of the law. Thus, he could be viewed as an honest, family man who turned to crime only because he was driven to it by harsh circumstances.

Besides being linked to a group that had been victimized by the legal system, these criminals shared another important characteristic. Each was killed by an agent of the law rather than captured and brought to trial. Jesse James was murdered by a gang member in the employ of the state's governor. Billy the Kid was shot by Sheriff Pat Garrett in a darkened room without being given a chance to surrender. Butch Cassidy was killed by Bolivian troops who denied him the opportunity to surrender and live. John Dillinger was gunned down by FBI agents as he left a movie theater. "Pretty Boy" Floyd was slain by the FBI as he ran across an open field. According to eyewitnesses, the wounded outlaw was murdered when he cursed the agents who surrounded him. The context surrounding their deaths made it appear that these men had been denied due process of law. This furthered their identity as victims of unjust persecution and seemingly verified the perception of the legal system as an instrument of corrupt men. Certainly in the cases of Dillinger and Floyd, the manner of their deaths contributed enormously to their image as American Robin Hoods in the tradition of Jesse James.

Of extreme importance in promoting the Robin Hood image of these criminals was the identity of their victims. The drama surrounding the lawlessness of these outlaws in the 19th century featured as victims the banks, railroads, and other institutions that were commonly viewed as "oppressors of the people." This view of these organizations may have been inaccurate but it was a perspective that was articulated repeatedly during the period by numerous populist political factions.

Charles A. "Pretty Boy" Floyd, about 1930. Archives and Manuscripts Division of the Oklahoma Historical Society. Reprinted with permission.

IDENTIFICATION
ORDER No. 1194
June 22, 1933

UNITED STATES BUREAU OF INVESTIGATION
DEPARTMENT OF JUSTICE
WASHINGTON, D. C.

Fingerprint Classification

23 L 1 U 000 19
L 1 U 000

WANTED

CHARLES ARTHUR FLOYD, aliases
FRANK MITCHELL, "PRETTY BOY SMITH"

DESCRIPTION

Age, 26 years
Height, 5 feet, 8¼ inches
Weight, 155 pounds
Hair, dark
Eyes, gray
Complexion, medium
Nationality, American
Scars and marks, 1 Vac. cic.
  1 tattoo (Nurse in Rose)

CRIMINAL RECORD

As Charles Arthur Floyd, No. 22318,
  arrested police department, St.
  Louis, Missouri, September 16,
  1925; charge, highway robbery.
As Charles Floyd, No. 29078,
  received S.P., Jefferson City,
  Missouri, December 18, 1925,
  from St. Louis; crime, robbery,
  first degree; sentence, 5 years.
As Charles A. Floyd, No. 16950,
  arrested police department,

Kansas City, Missouri, March 9, 1929; charge, investigation.
As Charles Floyd, No. 9999, arrested police department, Kansas City, Kansas, May 6, 1929; charge, vagrancy and sus-
  picion - highway robbery; released May 7, 1929.
As Charles Floyd, No. 667, arrested police department, Pueblo, Colorado, May 9, 1929; charge, vagrancy; fined $50 and
  sentenced to serve 60 days in jail.
As Frank Mitchell, No. 19985, arrested police department, Akron, Ohio, March 8, 1930; charge, investigation.
As Charles Arthur Floyd, No. 21458, arrested police department, Toledo, Ohio, May 20, 1930; charge, suspicion.
As Charles Arthur Floyd, sentenced November 24, 1930, to serve from 12 to 15 years in Ohio State Penitentiary [bank
  robbery, Sylvania, Ohio]; escaped enroute to penitentiary.

  Charles Arthur Floyd is wanted in connection with the murder of Otto Reed, Chief of Police of McAlester, Oklahoma, William J.
Grooms and Frank E. Hermanson, police officers of Kansas City, Missouri, Raymond J. Caffrey, Special Agent of the United States
Bureau of Investigation, and their prisoner, Frank Nash, at Kansas City, Missouri, on June 17, 1933.
  Law enforcement agencies kindly transmit any additional information or criminal record to nearest office, United States
Bureau of Investigation.
  If apprehended, please notify Special Agent in Charge, United States Bureau of Investigation, 905 Federal Reserve Bank Build-
ing, Kansas City, Missouri, and the Director, United States Bureau of Investigation, Department of Justice, Washington, D. C.

(over)   Issued by: J. Edgar Hoover, Director

Wanted poster for Charles A. "Pretty Boy" Floyd, 1933, sent to sheriff of Johnston County, OK in 1934. Archives and Manuscripts Division of the Oklahoma Historical Society. Reprinted with permission.

The banks, railroads and land monopolies subverted the legal and political order for their own nefarious purposes and were the cold-hearted enemies of the "common folk" (Cf. Fine, 1929; Merrill, 1967; Wiebe, 1967). During the 1930s, the list of evil organizations had dwindled primarily to banks, and the criminals who became heroes were exclusively bank robbers. Outlaws, then, in psychological terms were acting out the collective fantasies of a disenchanted populace. But the spirit of vicarious rebellion was shaped by a social context. By molesting these disfavored institutions, outlaws could be viewed as symbols of justice, and their crimes could be considered not only excusable but laudable.

When outlaws claimed as victims those who could not easily be seen as corrupting forces, public opinion would swing against them. When the death of Daniel Askew, a Clay County farmer who was suspected of aiding detectives, was attributed to Jesse James, the outlaw's image began to tarnish. Supporters of the Missouri bandit went so far as to claim that Askew was killed by railroad men to make Jesse James look bad. The murder of a banker in Minnesota during a robbery was attributed to a novice gang member by many biographers of the James brothers.

Similarly, when Billy the Kid was accused in the press of leading a band of thieves in the aftermath of the Lincoln County War, the outlaw wrote to the governor that he had not been rustling cattle; instead, he had managed to recover stolen property for its owners when the law was incapable of doing so. Naturally, the disclaimer was sent to the press in case the governor failed to pass on the information to the general public (Las Vegas *Gazette*, Dec. 22, 1880). Unfortunately, while trying to elude capture, the gang killed a highly liked local citizen who was serving on Pat Garrett's posse. While the death may have been somewhat accidental, the Kid "lost a lot of friends as a result of this episode" (Steckmesser, 1983:89). The local press no longer portrayed him as a romantic hero. Instead it urged that his lawless career be brought to a brutal end.

Likewise, the death of FBI agents in the "Kansas City Massacre" was a crime that plagued "Pretty Boy" Floyd to his dying day. Killing lawmen in cold blood was not part of the heroic formula, and the FBI through the press put the blame for this crime on Floyd. Interestingly, Floyd persistently denied playing a part in the killing. As he lay dying on a frozen Ohio field, the outlaw's last words were that he did not do it (*New York Times*, Oct. 23, 1934).

Aside from the identity of the criminal and the victim, the nature of the criminal act was also an important consideration in propelling certain lawbreakers to celebrity status. Involved were elements of justice and style. Criminal violence, to be considered just, had to be proportionate to the amount of social harm inflicted by the victims of the outlaw. The American Robin Hood should only kill in self-defense or when retributive justice required it. A banker who foreclosed on a farmer might be robbed, but executing him would be inappropriate. Ideally, crimes would also be conducted with a flair that would exemplify daring, courage, cleverness, and intelligence. A robbery in broad daylight was better than one furtively carried out at night. Crimes that were poorly carried out reflected badly on the image of a would-be heroic criminal. Acts of excessive violence would be public relations disasters.

Certainly the criminals who became American Robin Hoods had style, although it is difficult to determine how much of this was fabricated by writers who were fitting them into the Robin Hood formula. The James gang, for instance, was noted for its cleverness. Interrupting a lecture in Iowa to inform the crowd that the bank had been robbed, leaving a press release at the scene of a train robbery containing fictitious (and flattering) descriptions of the robbers, and examining the hands of passengers at one robbery so as to steal from only the idle rich were just a few examples of its flair. "Pretty Boy" Floyd robbing his hometown bank in broad daylight and waving to his friends as he drove away certainly was stylish. Billy the Kid's desperate dash to freedom from the burning McSween home and his daring escape from jail contributed to his legendary status. And certainly John Dillinger's dramatic jailbreak from the "escape-proof" cells at Crown Point helped shape his image as a criminal celebrity.

Where these American Robin Hoods persistently encountered difficulties in making reality match the myth that was evolving around them was in the area of excessive retribution. The crime business was a hazardous and somewhat unpredictable one. The authority of an outlaw to command others resided primarily through the coercive power of his gun. At times, it became necessary to use this weapon, and numerous individuals were killed who were not easily cast as villains deserving such a fate. In the course of robbing banks and trains, the James gang killed a number of employees of these institutions, such as cashier Sheets in the Gallatin bank robbery and conductor William Westfall in the Winston train robbery. Billy the Kid's execution of Sheriff Brady and several posse members who had been involved in the murder of John Tunstall was viewed as excessive retribution by some. Certainly these deaths provided a basis for the Kid's opponents who attempted to portray him as a mercenary and psychopathic killer; a desperado with 21 notches on his gun who had executed Chisum cowboys because he had not been paid for his services during the Lincoln County War. The deaths of jailers, police, and bank officials in the 1930s were not easily dismissed as punishments that were justly deserved, either. In the victimization of abstract institutions such as banks, outlaws would also inevitably victimize individuals with family and friends whose only "crime" was working in the wrong place at the wrong time. Consequently, architects of the outlaw legend, as well as the outlaws, inevitably had to contend with the fact that the "wild justice" dispensed by these heroic criminals might be seen as being more arbitrary and unfair than justice represented in law.

The role of entrepreneurs

Not every outlaw from a rural background who robbed banks and trains became transformed into a heroic figure. Such characteristics and actions could not assure bandits a place in the pantheon of folklore heroes. They needed assistance in informing the public of their qualities. The study of the historical circumstances surrounding the American Robin Hoods and an examination of those who were responsible for initiating their legendary status reveal that these men had powerful supporters and opponents, and the boundaries dividing their friends and enemies were often political in nature. Consequently, two diametrically opposed legends were fashioned about these outlaw figures. Those who felt the criminal to be a threat pieced together elements of his criminality and mythic formulas to present the outlaw as evil villain. But those who recognized the symbolic potential of a lawbreaker marketed him to the public as a heroic figure, selecting different aspects of his criminality and drawing on other mythic formulas to fit the outlaw into the Robin Hood green.

The resources of power and influence available to support a criminal plays a critical role in determining whether he will become a national celebrity. Without strong support, the bandit would not only have a short "reign," but the boundaries of his fame would be narrow. For instance, Chris Evans and John Sontag were successful train robbers in the 1880s. These bandits victimized the Southern Pacific, which in 1880 had hired an army of detectives to evict "squatters" from railroad land at Mussel Slough, California. In a gun battle started by the detectives, five settlers were killed. Rather than prosecute the detectives, the courts tried and convicted five settlers for the death of two detectives killed in the gunfight. According to O'Connor (1973:252), these events created "a railroad-hating climate in which a pair of hyperactive trainrobbers made themselves state-wide heroes and...achieved the status of Robin Hoods." According to legend, both men had been personally victimized by the railroad and turned to crime "out of principle, not for illicit gain, as avengers of the Mussel Slough affair." A play dramatizing the exploits of these bandits circulated throughout California and drew large crowds. But outside of California they were hardly known, and in a few years they had virtually disappeared from the public imagination. Even L.E. Sissman's (1971:45) plea for casting Sontag and Evans in the "next great Western movie" went unheard, even though he proposed that "a film about them, with all its implications for today, might carry the Western to new and higher ground."

What Evans and Sontag lacked was the presence of powerful and influential figures who could market them as national Robin Hood figures. The bandit, however charismatic he might be, could only come into contact with a limited number of individuals (and would often have to preserve his anonymity). In order for his fame to spread, he was dependent upon others. One way in which those criminals who became fashioned into American Robin Hoods attracted attention was their affiliation with powerful political figures. Jesse James, Billy the Kid, and Butch Cassidy each enjoyed the patronage of men involved in making and shaping political decisions. Jesse James benefitted from support given by the Confederate wing of the Missouri Democratic party. Billy the Kid sided with John Chisum, one of the most powerful ranchers of the American West. Butch Cassidy's interests were represented by Douglas Preston, one of the most influential lawyers of the American West and who later served as Wyoming's Attorney General. In addition, these outlaws had personal dealings with the highest ranking political official of the region, the governor. These political connections not only protected bandits in various ways; they also helped make them nationally known figures. And perhaps in some curious way, the political nature of their criminality was demonstrated, and this helped legitimate their deeds to the public.

On the other hand, criminals such as John Dillinger and "Pretty Boy" Floyd may not have had sponsors in high places, but they were "blessed," as were the heroic criminals in the nineteenth century, with powerful enemies. The detractors of the outlaw were almost as important as his defenders in making a large social audience aware of the significance of his criminality. The stature of the outlaw was raised by the amount of attention given to him by enemies. When the outlaw was challenged only by local law agents, his fame was minimal. When he became the topic of disparagement by state or national political parties, national crime fighting organizations such as the FBI, or by national celebrities, his fame was achieved. Perhaps the career of John Dillinger exemplifies this best, for he was not even the leader of his own gang. He was thrust into national prominence by the press, acting upon instructions from law enforcement officials who hoped to weaken the gang by making its members jealous of the attention Dillinger was getting. once he gained the status of a notorious criminal, which included the title of "Public Enemy Number One," Dillinger's bank robbing, his escapes from jail, his rural background, and other biographical data provided entrepreneurs with Robin Hood material (Toland, 1963:134). Likewise, as "Pretty Boy" Floyd became a national figure through the efforts of the FBI, populist protesters such as Woody Guthrie were able to reassemble the elements of Floyd's criminality and infuse a little mythic formula, thus transforming him from bad man to heroic figure. Similarly, Jesse James, Billy the Kid, and Butch Cassidy were marked out for the Robin Hood role partly through the efforts of powerful foes.

As the worth of the outlaw was determined to some extent by the quality of his enemies, so too did the "quality" of an outlaw reflect upon the worth of his opponents. Pat Garrett, who brought Billy the Kid's career to a close, is the cited author of one of the first detailed biographies of the outlaw. It was to Garrett's advantage to cast the Kid as a man possessing extraordinary qualities. Clearly such a tactic justified killing the Kid in a darkened room rather than giving him a chance to surrender; but it also suggested that only an extraordinary lawmen could vanquish so worthy a foe. Similarly, the creation of a host of supercriminals scampering across American landscape was quite advantageous to the FBI in the 1930s, at a time when it was struggling for recognition and power. Convincing the American public that an army of "public enemies" was out there was instrumental in expanding the jurisdiction of the FBI and creating the heroic image of the G-man, led by super hero J. Edgar Hoover (Cf. Powers, 1983, 1987).

It might also be noted that entrepreneurs who market certain criminals as Robin Hoods to the public do not have to be contemporaries of the lawbreakers. When social conditions favor the appearance of Robin Hood figures, criminals from both the present and the past may be found to fit the role. In all likelihood, Butch Cassidy was more widely known in the 1970s than at the turn of the century. A movie about Bonnie and Clyde, released in 1967, was one of the most popular films of all time (Halliwell, 1979:106). In the 1930s these two criminals were relatively unknown. At least press coverage of their crimes was nowhere near that of some of their contemporaries, and few positive comments about their deeds were made in the papers of their day. Indeed, it may be easier to resurrect figures from the past than to fit contemporary criminals into the Robin Hood myth. It is easier to depersonalize their victims since there will be no grieving widows and children to contend with. Also, it would be simpler to reconstruct their biography and convince audiences that these lawbreakers were heroic because conflicting evidence would not be immediately accessible and opposing viewpoints would be minimal. The political implications of their criminality would be latent and generalized. Jesse James may have upset the Missouri Republicans of the 1870s, but it is not likely that the Missouri Republicans of the 1970s would have found him a threatening symbol. Finally, the criminal would not have the capacity to invalidate the myth by acting "out of character." He would have long been retired from his career, if he were not already dead.

The heroic criminal and his audience

There are always criminals who are considered heroes for one reason or another by various segments of the population. The ghetto pimp or tough, for example might be a hero to some lower-class youth because he exemplifies "toughness" or "autonomy" (Miller, 1958. See also: Dance, 1978:224-246; Levine, 1977:407-420; Abrahams, 1970:61-85). He is a symbol of rebellion or success. But in order to emerge from obscurity and become a national figure, large numbers of people must find some symbolic meaning in his criminality and identify with him rather than with his victim. Even the most persuasive and powerful entrepreneur would find it difficult to transform Charles Manson into a national hero (although he appeared to have been a heroic figure for his "family" and others (Cf. Bugliosi, 1975:296-7).

Thus it was no coincidence that American Robin Hoods emerged in clusters at times when large numbers of people were touched by turmoil, found their daily routines shattered, and became dissatisfied with the representatives of the prevailing political order. As many felt that they were victims of social and economic injustice, and the political order failed to redress their grievances, symbols of justice who were outside the law were widely accepted by social audiences. Consequently, these heroic lawbreakers emerged as national figures at a time when society experienced upheavals such as the depressions of the 1870s, 1890s, and 1930s.

The geographic location of these heroic criminals was probably not coincidental, either. At the time that outlaws such as Jesse James, Billy the Kid, and Butch Cassidy worked their trade, there existed a national preoccupation with the American frontier. Many of America's cultural heroes—Daniel Boone, Davey Crockett, "Buffalo Bill" Cody, "Wild Bill: Hitchcock, and George Armstrong Custer—were inhabitants of the vast Western wilderness. There the individual, nature, and society acted out an age-old drama which captured such inherent tensions as those which existed between individuality and the need for order, between a desire for anarchy and hope for civilization. Heroic criminals lived on the edge of civilization both literally and symbolically.

In the years following the Civil War, furthermore, literacy expanded with the spread of education downward into the working and lower classes, perhaps to indoctrinate the waves of European immigrants into the meaning of America. The American frontier, then, was ideal ground for moral lessons, since it was possible to link the present colonizing of the West with the spirit of the country's founding fathers. The Puritan's city on a hill became a vast promised land of plenty. As a consequence of the growing literacy among the non-elites in America, popular culture expanded. A host of mass-circulation magazines and dime novels sprang up and spread the image of the outlaw to a national audience.

Constructing the heroic criminal

Undoubtedly many writers capitalized on the popular demand for Robin Hood criminals simply for profit. Public interest in the career of a brigand was sufficient motivation for the production of other heroic outlaws to be consumed by the popular appetite. Lawbreakers whose crimes could be easily politicized because of the immediate context of their criminality—their backgrounds, the identity of their victims, and pronouncements for or against them by influentials—were quickly fitted into the Robin Hood role. A criminal who victimized popular villains of the day—banks and railroads—and who possessed some personal characteristics that could be drawn upon to present him as a victim of injustice, was promoted to heroic status by zealous entrepreneurs.

Transforming these criminals into legendary heroes was not a complex process. First, a writer simply needed to adorn these lawbreakers with all sorts of cherished social values. As cultural explanations for the heroic criminal show, tales abounded with examples of courage, loyalty, individualism, success, innovativeness—in short, any ideal social trait imaginable. Thus, the moral character of the outlaw, when all was put in balance, was really quite positive. And the variation of ideal traits he exemplified assured that he would appeal to a wide audience which could find something worthy in his nature.

Second, the fabricator of outlaw legends only needed to insert these contemporary criminals into the basic Robin Hood myth. Outlaws such as Jesse James, Billy the Kid, and even John Dillinger appear very similar because their legendary reputations are based upon a set of stock concepts and anecdotes (cf. Klapp, 1962:13). Thus we find again and again that the lawbreaker is driven to a life of crime either because he is a victim of injustice or for committing an act which the state, but not the people, consider as criminal. He is viewed by lawful citizens of the community as a moral and honest man, and so many offer him support. He is a man who represents justice of a "higher" sort; he robs from the corrupt rich and gives to the deserving poor. He only harms others when "justice" demands it or in self-defense. He does not challenge the legitimacy of the state; he only opposes the evil opressors of the people who have debased justice. The context of his criminality is such that this lawbreaker may serve as a vehicle for vicarious rebellion, as psychological explanations for this figure suggest. But it may be more accurate to see these lawbreakers being fitted into the formula rather than exemplifying it by their own actions and motives.

Interestingly, these basic themes are parallel to the techniques of neutralization that Sykes and Matza (1957:664-670) suggest make it possible for juvenile delinquents to justify and commit illegal acts. According to Sykes and Matza, delinquents are not necessarily committed to the norms and values of a deviant subculture. These lawbreakers reveal guilt at their misdeeds and often express respect and admiration for model citizens. In fact, these delinquents generally show a firm commitment to conventional norms. But the normative system of society is flexible, sometimes ambiguous, and norms are qualified guides for conduct. Rules for proper moral behavior are variable and situational. Using "neutralization techniques," the delinquent is able to define the situation in such a manner that he excuses his violation of law.

In similar fashion, the Robin Hood criminal is not a member of a deviant subculture. He is seen as an individual who generally respects the basic moral precepts of society. In fact, his perceived commitment to ideals makes him appear to be a conservative political figure. As Hobsbawm (1969:21) points out, Robin Hoods are "activists and not ideologists or prophets from whom novel visions or plans of social and political organization are to be expected.... Insofar as bandits have a 'program,' it is the defense or restoration of the traditional order of things 'as it should be.' " The form of the Robin Hood legend surrounding certain criminals might best be seen as an attempt to neutralize the deviant identity of these lawbreakers and transform them into good men who represented morality and justice. Legends about heroic criminals evolved from what might be considered socially constructed rationalizations that excused and justified the lawlessness of these criminals and thus permitted people to glorify them. Sykes and Matza identified five neutralization techniques—denial of responsibility, denial of injury, denial of the victim, condemnation of the condemners, and appeal to higher loyalties. Each of the five neutralizations form an integral part of the Robin Hood myth. Each was utilized repeatedly by defenders of the outlaws (including the outlaws themselves) to justify their lawlessness.

The first neutralization technique identified by Sykes and Matza was "denial of responsibility," which enabled the lawbreaker to avoid feeling culpable for his actions by permitting him to view himself as a victim of the environment. In legend, we find this manifested by the idea that the outlaw was "driven to crime" by forces beyond his control. Thus, we find that Jesse James was wrongly labeled a criminal for his war-time service to the Confederacy. According to biographers, the outlaw was shot down in cold blood while trying to surrender at the close of the war. He miraculously recovered, only to be victimized by slanderous campaigns against him and other former Confederate guerillas. The Republican press in Missouri would identify these ex-soldiers as bank robbers, and they would be hunted down and sometimes hung without benefit of trial (Cf. Edwards, 1877; Settle, 1966; Triplett, 1970 repr.). As the amnesty resolution introduced in the Missouri House of Representatives in 1875 explained:

Whereas, under the outlawry pronounced against Jesse W. James, Frank James, Coleman Younger, James Younger, Robert Younger, and others, who gallantly periled their lives and their all in defense of their principles, they are of necessity made desperate, driven as they are from the fields of honest industry, from their friends, their families, and their country, they can know no law but the law of self-preservation, and can have no respect for and feel no allegiance to a government which forces them to the very acts it professes to deprecate...

Likewise, we find that Billy the Kid's career of crime "was not the outgrowth of an evil disposition, nor was it caused by unchecked youthful indescretions; it was the result of untoward, unfortunate circumstances..." (Garrett, 1954:5). According to legend, the young outlaw entered into his profession when as a boy he rushed to the aid of an older friend in distress, fighting three men at once, and killed one of the men, a man who had insulted Billy the Kid's mother. Having committed murder, "he went out into the night, an outcast and a wanderer. His hand was against every man, and every man's hand against him. He was out forever from the care, the love, and influence of a fond mother" (Garrett, 1954: 11; Cf. Burns, 1926:73-76). John Dillinger was seen as a farm boy who was led to crime through the evil influence of an older man. When Dillinger confessed to his part in a joint robbery, he was given a harsh and "unjust" prison sentence which led him to a life of crime (Chicago *Tribune*, July 23, 1934). "Pretty Boy" Floyd was forced into a life of crime out of desperation because he had no other way to support his pregnant wife according to some versions (Nash, 1975) or because a deputy sheriff had insulted Floyd's wife and in the ensuing "obligatory" fight which followed, the lawman was killed (Woody Guthrie: 1961). Similar justifications exist for all Robin Hood criminals.

A second neutralization technique described by Sykes and Matza which is also found in legends of the Robin Hood criminal is "denial of injury," which posits that no one is really harmed by the lawlessness of the criminal. While such actions may be illegal, they are not immoral. Thus, Robin Hood outlaws never harm the "common folk" and, in a sense, don't really steal because they are only taking property from the corrupt rich and distributing it to the poor to whom it rightfully belongs. A common tale told about outlaws such as Jesse James (Love 1926:282-3) and Butch Cassidy (Steckmesser, 1983:119) describes how after a hard day of riding away from posses, the bandit stops at the home of some poor widow for dinner. During the meal, tears appear, and the outlaw extracts from her the source of her unhappiness. She is about to lose her home to a local banker because she cannot pay her mortgage. The kindly outlaw immediately provides her with the necessary money, and after she pays the surprised banker, the outlaw robs him on the way back to town. Other stories tell how during the course of a robbery the bandit refuses to take the money of the customers because he is only after the bank's or railroad's money. In a bank robbery, Dillinger noticed a customer who had just cashed a check and then backed away from the counter without taking his money. "Go ahead and pick it up. We don't want your money. Just the bank's," Dillinger was reported to have said (Toland: 1963:174-5). Accounts of a train robbery conducted by the James gang stated that the bandits investigated the hands of each male passenger. The St. Louis *Republican* (Feb. 2, 1874) explained that the robbers "did not want to rob working men or ladies, but the money and valuables of plug-hat gentlemen were what they sought." And of course these Robin Hoods of legend never killed except in self-defense. In fact, we find that Butch Cassidy never killed a man in his life until his last stand, and this in some way makes him remarkable and excuses all the other crimes he committed (Kelly, 1959:3-4). We read that "Pretty Boy" Floyd would provide Christmas dinners for the families on relief and leave large bills under the plates of poor people who fed him (Guthrie, 1961; Steckmesser, 1983:130-37). In the hands of some writers, these murderers and robbers seemed to be more like fraternity boys out looking for a little fun, not really hurting anyone with their pranks, and doing all sorts of good for the community through their generous acts.

A third neutralization technique, "denial of the victim," makes a criminal deed morally acceptable by arguing that the victim of the crime deserved to be victimized. In legend, this theme is represented by the idea that those who lose life or property to the outlaw only received what they were due in much the same way a convicted criminal receives punishment from the court. Such a convict is not considered a "victim" of the court, and Robin Hood criminals are the personification of an effective court in which justice is swiftly administered. We find in the case of Billy the Kid that, according to legend anyway, his close friend John Tunstall was murdered in cold blood by a band of men in the employ of a corrupt land baron and a crooked sheriff. It seemed only right, then, that since the law was corrupt and ineffective, that the young outlaw took matters into his own hands and tracked down and killed those responsible for Tunstall's assassination. As Kent Steckmesser (1965:100) observers, "It seems only fitting that injustice should be punished, and so the Kid's pursuit of Tunstall's killers gives his biography the aura of a holy crusade. There appears to be an acceptable motive for his crimes." Thus, the murder of a sheriff and a number of other individuals is rendered justifiable. Similarly, the fact that outlaws like Butch Cassidy, Jesse James, John Dillinger, and "Pretty Boy" Floyd robbed banks and trains, institutions identified as corrupting forces responsible for the moral decay of the political order and the cause of suffering for farmers who could not pay back bank loans or make a decent living because of high railroad rates, made it possible to see these criminals as avengers of injustice.

Also typical in legends is what Sykes and Matza termed the "condemnation of the condemners." This posits that it is representatives of the law and political office who are the real "criminals" since they are immoral and unfaithful to valued principles such as justice. In a letter to the public, published by editor John Newman Edwards in the Kansas City *Times* (Oct. 15, 1872), Jesse James explained it this way:

Just let a party of men commit a bold robbery, and the cry is to hang them, but Grant and his party can steal millions and it is alright.... Some editors call us thieves. We are not thieves, we are bold robbers. It hurts me very much to be called a thief. It makes me feel like they were trying to put me on par with Grant and his party.

The life and times of Jesse James provided sympathizers with several opportunities to condemn the agents of the political establishment. Pinkerton agents hired by the railroads were responsible for the accidental death of the outlaw's young brother and the dismemberment of his mother. Local residents were periodically harassed by detectives, and on one occasion a citizen was seized and taken into custody because he was mistaken for one of the outlaws. Finally, Jesse James was murdered by wanted criminals who were working in the employ of the governor of Missouri (Settle, 1966). The situation surrounding the outlaw's death prompted men like John Newman Edwards to cry that "this so-called law is an outlaw, and these so-called executors of the law are outlaws. Therefore, let Jesse James' comrades...do unto them as they did unto him" (Kansas City *Times*, April 13, 1882).

Likewise, the assassination of John Tunstall a close friend of Billy the Kid, also provided an opportunity to condemn the political establishment. Tunstall, along with a local lawyer named McSween, planned to start a business enterprise which would undermine the existing economic monopoly that existed in Lincoln County. Through some very dubious legal maneuverings, warrants were obtained against McSween and Tunstall. The local sheriff, who was a close friend of the entrenched economic powers of Lincoln County, dispatched a posse to arrest Tunstall. Riding in this posse were men wanted for murder in Lincoln County. Tunstall was brutally murdered by the posse members when he surrendered. McSween was later gunned down by another sheriff's "posse." When outlaws rode with sheriff's posses and committed murder in the name of the law, it made fine material for a Robin Hood narrative in which the wicked sheriff of Nottingham could be resurrected in cowboy garb (Fulton, 1968; Keleher, 1957; Steckmesser, 1966).

Outlaws such as these, who preyed upon the banks and railroads and who were in the business of "righting wrongs," could be considered moral men when contrasted to the spectres of immorality that haunted political office and the halls of justice. As Woody Guthrie (1961) noted in his ballad of "Pretty Boy" Floyd:

As through this world I ramble,
I see lots of funny men,
Some will rob you with a six-gun,
And some with a fountain pen.

But as through your life you travel,
As through your life you roam,
You won't never see an outlaw
Drive a family from their home.

Emerging in the context of a depression that shattered the lives of millions of people, these criminals had an audience that was very receptive to negative portrayals of legal and political powers in society.

Finally, Sykes and Matza identify a fifth neutralization technique, "appeal to higher loyalties," which serves to legitimize deviant behavior when commitment to one social group takes priority to commitment to conventional society. Thus, in legend while the heroic criminal disobeys the laws of society, he is being faithful to higher moral duties which emphasize the contradiction existing between the law and the popular conception of morality. Outlaws are called upon to defend friends and family, but they are also seen as the representatives of a whole class of people—the oppressed. For instance, Pat Garrett (1954:5) informs the reader that Billy the Kid was "the peer of any fabled brigand on record, unequalled in desperate courage, presence of mind in danger, devotion to his allies, generosity to his foes, gallantry, and all the elements which appeal to the holier emotions...." He was, after all, a champion of the underdog and a man who turned to crime primarily because of the loyalty he felt to others, especially his murdered friend, John Tunstall (Burns, 1926:16, 49-52; Otero, 1935:215; Steckmesser, 1965:100). Outlaws like "Pretty Boy" Floyd not only robbed banks to "even the score" or to "provide Christmas dinners for the families on relief," as Woody Guthrie (1961) informs us; they also tore up foreclosure notices for people they didn't even know "out of principle." Jesse and Frank James, according to one biographer, "illustrated the American virtues of personal bravery and devotion to friends and to principle with such strong lights and with such gloomy shadows that their countrymen are patient with their follies and their faults" (Bradley, 1882:3). And in their ideal-typical form, the Robin Hood criminal became a political criminal who broke the law "for moral ideological purposes. The legendary hero's goal, for example, was not robbery, but aid to the poor" (Schafer, 1974:151).

Conclusion

These lawbreakers became social heroes because they were in the right place at the right time. They were foremost the product of particular social conditions. The social strains that existed at the time of their criminal careers created a market for symbols of extra-legal justice. Thus entrepreneurs rushed tales of Robin Hood figures to a receptive audience either by reviving traditional Robin Hood figures or by giving old tales new life by inserting contemporary actors into them. In the context of the time, criminals from rural backgrounds who victimized banks, railroads, or other "oppressors of the people" were prime candidates for the Robin Hood role. The political implications of their criminality earned certain criminals the privilege of appearing as social heroes, and by adorning them with cherished social values and providing rationalizations for their criminality, moral entrepreneurs fashioned good men out of bad ones. As Claude Levi-Strauss (1963:268) points out, there exists an "organic continuity apparent among mythology, legendary tradition, and what we must call politics." The Robin Hood criminal and his victims were simply the latest actors participating in an ancient morality play concerned with the relationship between law, justice, and the individual.

Over time, through "creative treason," new meanings and values are attached to the heroic criminal which transcend the social context that initially provided meaning to the criminality of the outlaw (Escarpit, 1968:424). The tales thus have continued relevance to various social audiences. But the heroic criminal is not a real outlaw. He is an image constructed by playwrights and poets; authors and songwriters; publishers and politicians; and also by the social audiences that select, interpret, and recall tales of the heroic criminal that blend into their particular understandings of reality. But these architects often are building upon an image that took life from social conditions and political issues.

Chapter 8

The Modern Heroic Criminal

Is the Robin Hood criminal an obsolete romantic figure of the American past, or is such a figure capable of emerging in a modern industrialized society? These glorified lawbreakers exemplify what Eric Hobsbawm (1959, 1969) has termed the social bandit. As we noted earlier (chapter two) an analysis of the appearance of such glorified lawbreakers in Europe and Asia led Hobsbawm to conclude that these criminals were the product of specific social conditions. The social bandit was a symbol of extra-legal justice who emerged "when a peasant society which knows no better means of self-defense is in a condition of abnormal tension and disruption" (Hobsbawm, 1959:5). These conditions included famines, wars, or periods of modernization which threatened to destroy or transform a traditional agricultural society. To Hobsbawm, the Robin Hood criminal was a rural phenomenon, a creature of traditional peasant societies, and above all the product of specific structural conditions.

These romantic figures are also judged to be relics of the past, for Hobsbawm feels that the social conditions which give life to them no longer exist in the modern world. First, modernization, with its improved police methods, efficient communication systems, and rapid transportation, deprives would-be Robin Hoods of the conditions necessary for criminal success (Hobsbawm, 1969:15). Second, and more important, modernization is accompanied by the politicization of the peasant. Armed with a political consciousness and an organization to articulate discontent effectively, the small farmer no longer needs the inefficient form of "pre-political" protest which the social bandit represents. Thus, the social bandit "appears only before the poor have reached political consciousness or acquired more effective methods of social agitation" (Hobsbawm, 1959:23). The days of the Robin Hood criminal are over, says Hobsbawm, for today's world no longer contains the structural conditions necessary for their emergence. Modernization in the form of industrial capitalism and political awareness in the form of Marxism or unionism have spread to all corners of the world.

160

Hobsbawm's (1959, 1969) work on social banditry is a brilliant attempt to link a cultural product—the heroic criminal—to particular structural conditions. However, it seems that social bandits have continued to emerge in modern industrialized societies populated by politically aware and efficiently organized rural-based politicial machines. Historian Richard White (1981:394), for instance, has argued that outlaws such as Jesse James, the Daltons, Billy the Kid, and John Wesley Hardin typify American social bandits but could not be considered simply the champions of peasants "because there were no American peasants to champion." Pat O'Malley's (1979, 1981) analysis of Australian bushrangers such as Ned Kelly has come to much the same conclusion. Even Hobsbawm (1981:150-2) has subsequently modified his position to allow that social banditry may have existed in the United States even as late as the 1930s because it was a recognized part of American popular culture, although such figures are "extinct, for all practical purposes."

There is, however, no reason to believe that social banditry cannot exist and even thrive in modern societies. For instance, there is no evidence to suggest that changes in technology, including a more elaborate bureaucratic criminal justice system, have any effect on the presence or absence of social banditry. As law enforcement becomes more technologically proficient, so also do criminals. Horses give way to automobiles, and six-shooters are replaced by machine guns. Improved transportation systems simply lead to faster getaways, make policing much more complicated, and lures more potential victims onto the thoroughfares. For instance, robbers could turn their criminal intentions to new forms of crime such as "skyjacking," as in the case of the "legendary" D.B. Cooper (Gunther, 1985). In some respects, it seems that the criminal justice system tends to lag behind criminals when it comes to utilizing the latest technology in the "war on crime," often reacting to criminal innovations in its struggle against crime. Furthermore, as highly developed military forces have discoverd again and again, modern weaponry and massive bureaucratic organization do not seem to be very effective against guerrilla warfare tactics, and the type of criminality represented by social banditry—with its community support, high mobility, low organizational profile, and political ramifications—resembles guerrilla warfare. There is no reason to believe that modernization would handicap the social bandit.

Indeed, in some ways certain bureaucratic and technological developments have greatly expanded the possibility for the existence of criminal celebrities. Of particular importance has been the development of the mass media. Prior to the 19th century, the credentials of a criminal could be presented to a rather small audience primarily through oral history. During the 19th century, newspapers, dime novels, cheap mass circulation magazines, and biographies spread the fame (or infamy) of criminals much further, making them known to a national audience (cf. Jones, 1978; Schudson, 1978; Smith, 1950). Today the exploits of a criminal may be sung on records that will be broadcast by thousands of radio stations, dramatized in movies that will be viewed by millions, reported by a news service that will ensure a worldwide audience, and possibly seen nationally on the evening news. Then, of course, there is the book contract and subsequent television features to develop further the mystique. Indeed, one unique aspect of modernization seems to be a steady need for the production of celebrities. There exists a vast celebrity industry involving the careers of thousands of individuals who make a living from the production and maintenance of such an unusual product. That they are proficient in what they do is obvious. Parents name their children after the characters represented by current media personalities, entire communities are plunged into despair or filled with euphoria depending upon the performance of local athletic celebrities. Even in death certain figures are treated with religious fervor, with shrines from Graceland to Cooperstown containing sacred relics to which the faithful make pilgrimages. In such a society, it would seem that the creation of American Robin Hoods by entrepreneurs sensing a market for such symbolic figures would be easier than ever. In fact, it is undoubtedly true that thanks to the media, outlaws such as Butch Cassidy and the Sundance Kid, or Bonnie and Clyde, were more popular in the 1970s than at the time they plied their lawless trades.

Nor is there any reason to believe that the development of more effective forms of political protest among agrarian poor would eliminate the appearance of the social bandit. As we have noted, Hobsbawm has argued that when agrarian groups have political machines to promote their interests, then crude expressions of political protest such as social banditry will not emerge. Likewise, Patrick O'Malley (1981:498), from his analysis of Australian bushranging, has concluded that social banditry may emerge as part of a chronic class struggle involving "direct producers" who have a sense of group identity but who lack effective political organization. Yet social bandits such as Jesse James in the 1870s, the Daltons in the 1890s, and "Pretty Boy" Floyd in the 1930s emerged concurrently with agrarian political organizations that were rather articulate and effective. By the 1890s, when Butch Cassidy and his Wild Bunch busied themselves with train and bank robberies, the Populists were powerful enough to elect six governors, control the legislatures of eight states, and bring to office some 50 Congressmen. In 1896 the populist cause was represented by William Jennings Bryan, arguably one of America's most skilled orators, who was influential enough to be nominated for the Presidency by the Democratic party. While the populists never succeeded in placing a candidate in the White House, it would be an error to consider them as an ineffective political force at the time when social banditry was present in this country.

It seems then that social bandits are quite capable of appearing in advanced societies and may exist concurrently with more organized and effective forms of agrarian political protest. However, an examination of American Robin Hoods leads to the conclusion that social banditry has, at best, a very indirect and somewhat confusing relationship with agrarian politics. First, although these heroic criminals claimed as victims those institutions that were widely perceived by Populist groups as the "enemies" of the common folk, the outlaws themselves appealed to a much broader constituency and were supported by a much more diffuse power base than "direct producers." Second, Populist parties typically deplored lawlessness from below, including social banditry, although occasionally a social bandit could be coopted into more formalized and effective political protest. The case of Pancho Villa is an example (Katz, 1981). Regardless of the relationship social banditry has with agrarian politics, these figures have emerged alongside more articulate forms of protest. And there is no reason to assume that even more effective political organization would hinder the appearance of social banditry. There is no reason to assume that political protest is a zero-sum phenomenon; if organized expressions of popular disenchantment exist, informal and less articulate modes such as social banditry will not necessarily be silenced.

Indeed, as I have suggested, the basis for the existence of the American Robin Hood is the symbolic quality of his criminality. He is at his origins a political figure who represents social justice. At a time when a widespread popular conception of justice exists which is not synonymous with legal justice, heroic criminals will exist. In fact, to understand the nature of the heroic criminal more fully, it is more important to consider *for whom* a criminal is a hero than to debate *whether* a particular lawbreaker is a heroic figure. Heroic criminals, to some extent are with us always. It is simply that at certain times, specific types of lawbreakers appeal to a wide social audience and achieve national reknown. In some respects, then, the question is not one of whether social banditry can exist in modern societies, but rather whether such lawbreakers might appeal to a broader constituency than the oppressed ghetto resident, the aggrieved consumer, or the disenchanted inhabitant of any number of different subcultures.

In recent years there have been a number of convicted criminals who symbolized extra-legal justice, but whose criminality had such relevance for only a small and relatively inarticulate audience. Gene Leroy Hart became front page news in 1979 when he was tried for the rape and murder of three Girl Scouts in Oklahoma. On the surface Gene Hart seemed an unlikely candidate for hero. He had been previously convicted of rape, kidnapping and burglary, and at the time of the girl scout murders, he was an escaped prisoner. But other elements of his biography were more amenable to shaping Hart into a hero. He was an Oklahoma high school football star and a full-blooded American Indian. As one chronicler (Wilkerson and Wilkerson, 1981:76) of the Hart tale observed:

It makes a great story—an Indian who has eluded the white gestapo pigs for over four years, and an even better story to intimate that he is an innocent young Indian football star who once again has been made a scapegoat. This little rural state has three things it can brag about: Indians, football, and oil. Boy, when you got a football playing Indian, he makes the greatest hero since Jim Thorpe.

The key to Hart's notoriety was the widespread sentiment that he was being tried "as much because he was a full-blooded Cherokee as because of the evidence against him" (*New York Times*, June 5, 1979). Hart was harbored from the law for years by many otherwise lawful citizens, many of whom were related to him.

At a time when the country was being sensitized to the treatment that the American Indian had unjustly received historically in this country (cf Brown, 1976), Gene Leroy Hart was an excellent criminal to transform into a contemporary symbol of legal injustice. The American Indian Movement (AIM) rushed to his defense, and at one time rumors circulated that members of the movement were going to break Hart out of jail (Wilkerson, 1981:155). A special church service was held in his honor, and several fund-raising events took place to raise money for Hart's legal defense. Local citizens who knew Hart were interviewed and generally had nothing but kind words for him.

Unfortunately for the development of the legend, Hart was found not guilty for the murder of the Girl Scouts, amidst controversy that the prosecution had planted evidence against him (*New York Times*, June 6, 1979), and claims that the defense had bribed witnesses to perjure themselves in court for Hart's benefit (Wilkerson, 1981). Hart was returned to prison to serve the 305 years he had been sentenced to for previous crimes. Within three months, he died while exercising in the prison yard. Over 1500 came to Hart's funeral, and rumors spread that he had been assassinated, although an autopsy revealed he had died of a heart attack (Wilkerson, 1981:246-7).

Such social reaction is not limited to the rural Midwest; it may also be found in the large cities of the East. In February of 1980, Bruce Wazon Griffith, a Washington drug dealer who was accused of murdering a policeman became an unlikely hero. The *Washington Post* chronicled Griffith's meteoric rise to fame over a two week period. Griffith's first noble achievement, according to the *Post* (February 15, 1980), was the killing of D.C. police officer Arthur Snyder: "Hundreds of junkies, drug dealers, and street people had gathered at the scene expressing jubilation over the death of Snyder," who was considered a racist and unduly aggressive cop.

Griffith's second step toward heroism was the manner in which he conducted himself while the police searched for him:

For three days he eluded police and became a legend on the streets. According to family members and friends who saw or said they spoke to him during those days, he would pop up on playgrounds near his home in an inner city Shaw neighborhood with candy for the children of his friends, then go jogging with his head down through Rock Creek Park, smiling tensely as he passed U.S. Park policemen (*Washington Post*, Feb. 20, 1980).

While hundreds of police were searching for him, Griffith presumably was out jogging, playing basketball, and befriending drunks.

The final step toward ensuring heroic status was taken when Griffith was killed in a gun battle with police just three days after he murdered a cop. In the eyes of the community, Griffith was assassinated. Although evidence existed that Griffith refused to surrender and began shooting when he was stopped by police, this was discounted as police propaganda. Many were much more willing to believe that Griffith was gunned down in cold blood. Over 4000 came to the funeral to pay their respects to this drug dealer and cop killer. The *Washington Post* (February 20, 1980) covered the funeral as well and observed that emotions reached a peak as the soloist began singing:

First, the congregation, which included garbage men, mechanics, day laborers, school teachers, preachers, cabdrivers and a cadre of street dudes, began to sob and weep. Then, voice by voice, they joined in the singing, drowning out the soloist as he sang the last refrain:

'Everybody's searching for a hero; people need someone to look up to... I decided long ago never to walk in anyone's shadow... No matter what they take from me, they can't take away my dignity.'

In the space of a few short days, a common criminal became a community hero. His major contribution to this transformation was probably getting himself killed.

Why did this small-time hoodlum evoke such sentiment? According to some Griffith became a hero to the black community because the events surrounding his criminality symbolized black relations with the police. Noted one inner-city resident, "Most of the D.C. cops live in the suburbs anyway, hunting deer and rabbits; then they come into the district to hunt niggers" (*Washington Post*, February 22, 1980). Others suggested that Griffith's heroic status was a reflection of the dissatisfaction with the general social conditions blacks faced in Washington. The Rev. Ray Kemp, who attended Griffith's wake, viewed Griffith's "sudden elevation to folk hero" as a natural consequence in a community with little hope for a better life, and observed that Griffith "probably became a sacrament of a lot of people's hopes and fears" (*Washington Post*, February 22, 1980).

Washington Post (February 25, 1980) editorialist Dorothy Gilliam, however, felt that something more lay behind the outpouring of public sentiment for this criminal:

> It is more than joblessness and hopelessness felt in some parts of the community. If you listen closely, you will hear that many people in Washington did not believe the alleged killer of D.C. police officer Arthur P. Snyder would ever come to trial. The feeling may vary from neighborhood to neighborhood, but what's being communicated here is that many solid citizens in this town no longer believe due process exists.

And as one well-respected and politically influential black minister quoted by Gilliam noted, "When we are at our thoughtful best, we know that's where we belong, at Griffith's funeral. Why? A nigger is a nigger is a nigger and we know that. We all get lumped together." It was an easy matter for blacks in Washington to identify with the treatment that Bruce Griffith received at the hands of the law.

Yet Griffith's emergence as a folk hero was very local and short-lived. Like Joan Little, the black woman who murdered her jailer because he allegedly raped her, the symbolic power of the criminality was relevant to a small minority. Even Charles Manson, the California commune leader who was linked to the murders of a number of celebrities and who was sensationalized by the press and district attorney who engineered Manson's conviction, had his fans. The underground paper, Tuesday's Child, named Manson its Man of the Year and showed him being crucified on one of its covers. Manson posters, buttons, and sweatshirts became novelty items. Friends and acquaintances of this habitual criminal appeared on radio talk shows, where they denounced his "persecution." Jerry Rubin, the noted political activist, visited Manson in jail and reportedly was "inspired" by the meeting (Bugliosi, 1975:296-7; Emmons, 1986).

But criminals like Manson, Griffith, and Hart did not have broad enough appeal to make them national folk heroes. They lacked a social identity that would enable large numbers of people to identify with them. These criminals were not seen as "common folk." Furthermore, the victims of these criminals were not easily cast as impersonal and evil institutions. These lawbreakers were not dispensing anyone's version of popular justice. Few people could find anything admirable about cop killers, sex offenders, or murderers of movie stars. Although these criminals may have been treated unjustly by the criminal justice system, and their criminality thus could serve as an example of the injustice many may have felt permeated the legal system, they were certainly not

Kansas Collection. University of Kansas Libraries. Reprinted with permission.

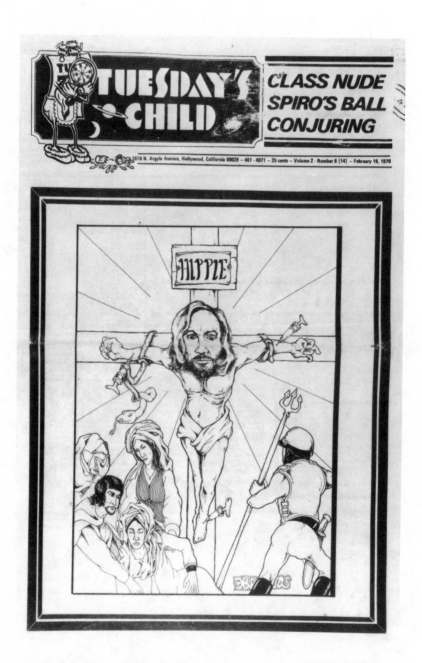

Kansas Collection. University of Kansas Libraries. Reprinted with permission.

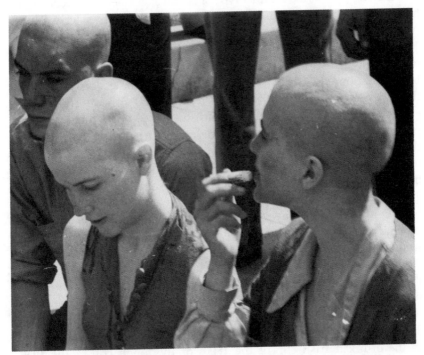

Charles Manson. UPI/Bettmann Newsphotos. Reprinted with permission.

good material for American Robin Hoods. Even the most skilled moral entrepreneurs could not transform these hoodlums and countless others like them into national heroes.

Yet the social conditions conducive to the emergence of American Robin Hoods certainly seemed present in the turbulent decades of the 1960s and 1970s. Racial injustice produced riots in many American cities, political figures were assassinated with shocking regularity, and students were massacred on college campuses for protesting what many considered to be an unjust and perhaps illegal military action in Indo-China. Perhaps most troublesome was the unprecedented resignation of a President of the United States, in the face of impeachment proceedings, for immoral and illegal behavior. This was a time, Jonathan Schell (1976:5) rightfully observed, tortured by events that "embittered every aspect of public life, and finally brought the American Constitutional system to the edge of a breakdown." It certainly seemed a time when symbolic representatives of extra-legal justice, such as social bandits, would be widely embraced.

During this period another type of lawbreaker emerged who achieved heroic status: the political dissident. Individuals such as Jerry Rubin, Abbie Hoffman, Mark Rudd, Bobby Seale, Eldridge Cleaver, George Jackson, Malcolm X, and Angela Davis achieved notoriety for their criminal deeds or for their advocacy of criminal acts. None of these figures became national folk-heroes, however. Like the labor leaders of the 1930s, they were more often cast as threats to the social structure rather than enemies of corrupt individuals or institutions. Rather than viewed as prophets calling for a return to the moral order represented by the past, they were seen as radicals espousing immoral and dangerous ideas— or publicity seekers more intent on glorifying themselves than promoting beneficial social change. Many individuals sympathized with the issues embodied in the criminal acts of these dissidents—opposition to the Viet Nam conflict, racism, and sexism, for instance. Other sympathized when the machinery of justice was employed against them in a manner which seemed unjust. But these lawbreakers were certainly not seen as American Robin Hoods in the tradition of Jesse James or "Pretty Boy" Floyd.

Also rising to prominence during this period was another key actor in the criminal justice system who was transformed into a symbol of the tension that apparently existed between law and justice: the "cop." The bad cop of the 1960s and 1970s was not on the same plane of evil as the drunken Irish cop of the 1800s or the tough cop of the 1930s. The bad cop of the 1960s was unmistakenly evil, and the distinction between cop and criminal faded in the writings of popular writers like Joseph Wambaugh. "Officer Friendly," who helped children across busy streets and retrieved family pets from trees, was replaced by another type of law enforcer—often caricatured as a racist bully who broke the law with impunity when it suited his needs. Or in some cases, these men in blue were shown as "street monsters" who were even more vile than the criminals they hunted. In Wambaugh's (1981:57) best-seller, the Glitterdome, the reader is confronted with a scene in which two street cops retrieve the dismembered corpse of an eighteen-year old-cheerleader from a trash bin:

Buckmore Phipps leaned inside and lifted the alabaster torso out of the bin, and holding the bloodless torso under the armpits with those hands as big as shovels—the cadaver's head lolling, tongue distended and blue as Buckmore Phipps' uniform—the giant street monster did a spritely Yul Brynner polka in the headlights of the patrol car, singing: "Shaaaall we dance? (do do do) On a bright cloud of music shall we fly? (do do do)..."

Psychopathic cops dancing with legless corpses made bigoted Southern sheriffs seem like country gentlemen in comparison.

Standing alongside the "bad cop" was the vigilante law enforcer. In the 1920s and 1930s, this role in literature was admirably filled by the "hard-boiled" detectives of Raymond Chandler and Dashiell

Hammett, shadowy figures of ambiguous moral standing. (cf. Knight, 1980; Porter, 1981; Symons, 1985) These detectives were unfettered by legal constraints. They did not have to worry about the constitutionality of illegal searches, coerced confessions, entrapments, and other fine points of law in the pursuit of justice. By the 1970s, a shift had occurred in the content of American crime fiction. These representatives of vigilante justice left private practice and entered the police organizations found in American popular culture. Gone were the days of careful policework typified by the officers of popular shows like Dragnet. In their place sprang the police detectives of Hawaii Five-O, Miami Vice, and of course "Dirty Harry" (cf Klockars, 1980).

These vigilantes were more a product of media fiction than the everyday police world. Life, however, has an occasional tendency to imitate art. And on a late December afternoon in 1984, the media and the American public found a most unlikely symbol of vigilante justice beneath the streets of New York City. On the afternoon of December 22, 1984, an ordinary-looking electronics engineer boarded a subway train. There, in the darkened tunnel somewhere between mid-town Manhattan and Wall Street, four black youths and Bernhard Goetz acted out a crime drama that would have national repercussions. Goetz seated himself in the midst of the youths and exchanged pleasantries. Shortly, one of them asked him for five dollars. Goetz then stood up, pulled out an illegally possessed handgun, and fired four shots, wounding each of the four youths. Three of them lay on the floor, and the fourth one was slumped over on the subway seat. Noticing no blood on the wounded youth who was sitting, Goetz then remarked, "You seem to be doing all right, here's another," and fired a bullet that would leave Darrell Cabey paralyzed from the waist down and permanently brain-damaged.

The public response to this mass execution was stunning. The wounded were vilified and the gunman was glorified, for this was an episode staged on the shadowy fringes where law and justice were not easily discerned. Bernie Goetz was a person with whom many could identify. Here was an ordinary man—white, blond, sensitive, hard-working, middle class; a man *Time* magazine (April 8, 1985) called "an Everyman"—who was driven to crime because of past experiences. He had been mugged before and the legal system had failed him. He had lost faith in the capacity of law to preserve order and security. This was a feeling that was widespread in New York City, and in many places outside the city. In the days following the shooting, the media were filled with testimonials of people who had been victimized by muggers (cf Tucker, 1985:19-24; Rubin, 1986). As one New Yorker commented (*Village Voice* of March 12, 1985):

When I first heard about the shooting, I was glad. I thought it served them right. I was actually happy for a few days, and the mood in the subway cars was a kind of camaraderie I had never felt before. It was like we all had won one.... Everybody was in agreement. Goetz had done something for all of us.

Goetz, although he pulled the trigger, was cast as the victim in this crime drama. He, like many other citizens, lived a life of desperate fear which drove him to purchase a gun and to use it.

While Goetz was being transformed into a victim, the wounded youths were transformed into offenders. Being black and young, they fit nicely into the stereotyped image of the criminal. The press quickly provided additional biographical material. As Lillian Rubin (1986:58) notes, "about them we read only the same bare story over and over again: They're eighteen and nineteen, high-school drop-outs, unemployed, live in South Bronx, have long criminal records." And to enhance this transformation, a persistent rumor circulated that the four youths possessed sharpened screwdrivers and planned to mug Goetz. On two of the teenagers the police found flat-head screwdrivers which admittedly were to be used to break into video machines. They certainly would have served well as stilettos without any sharpening, but the myth that these tools were sharpened contributed to the belief that these youths were malevolent creatures with murder unequivocally on their minds. Goetz never saw any type of weapon when he began shooting, but this was an easily overlooked fact. Also overlooked was the fact that Goetz loaded his illegally-owned gun with illegal hollow-point bullets designed to leave gaping holes in the flesh of their targets. Or that two of the youths were shot in the back. The props used in this crime drama were easily rearranged by a public with a strong will to see Goetz as the victim and the black youths as the offenders.

Comparing Goetz's gunplay to the "first shot fired at Lexington and Concord," columnists like Lars-Erik Nelson (*New York Daily News* of January 18, 1985) proclaimed the subway vigilante a hero for showing "that people are not prepared to live as constant cringers before daily, petty, bullying assaults by rowdies, toughs, skylarking hoodlums." Widespread public fear of crime and anger at the justice system provided a social context for the emergence of a populist hero, regardless of the fact that this hero gunned down four teenagers in blatant violation of law. A bullet in the back and a lifetime of paralysis was somehow considered justice for asking five dollars from a stranger. Through this 37-year-old electrical engineer-gunman, the public vicariously retaliated against the criminal and exorcised some of its uneasiness over crime. Bernie Goetz became a cultural icon whose criminality dramatized in a bizarre and twisted fashion public dissatisfaction with a criminal justice system that seemed unjust.

Subway gunman Bernard Goetz. UPI/
Bettmann Newsphotos. Reprinted with
permission.

What we observe, then, is that over the past twenty years there has
emerged a host of characters who have acted out crime dramas in the
gray borderland between law and justice. We have had romanticized
convicts, political criminals, criminal cops, and vigilantes. The
criminality of each has illuminated a concept of social justice which
has deviated from definitions of legal justice. An outbreak of such
symbolic figures was a natural result of the widespread disenchantment
with law and politics in modern America. The moral ambiguity embedded
in the identity of these characters reflect a perceived tension between
social and legal justice, between communal and political morality.

None of these lawbreakers exemplifies the Robin Hood criminal,
however. Indeed, it seems that practically every possible symbol of extra-
legal justice or legal injustice emerged during this period except a social
bandit!

While no new American Robin Hoods appeared during this period,
it does not mean that these other symbolic representations of extra-legal
injustice exhausted the demand for this type of criminal. Certain
traditional Robin Hoods were revived and enthusiastically received by

the public. During these years, virtually every American social bandit from the past was given a chance by the movie industry to capture the public's interest. Even lesser known criminals like Bonnie and Clyde and Butch Cassidy were cast successfully as celluloid heroes.

The fascination with social bandits also manifested itself in the music industry. Rock groups such as the Outlaws and the James Gang celebrated the outlaw image. Bob Dylan released an album entitled "John Wesley Harding" (sic) and performed in a movie about Billy the Kid. The Eagles' Desperado album recounted the the life and times of the Doolin-Dalton gang. Warren Zevon sang of Frank and Jesse James, the Byrds covered Woodie Guthrie's ballad of "Pretty Boy" Floyd, James Taylor recorded a tune about Machine-Gun Kelly, and both the Charlie Daniels Band and Ry Cooder released songs in honor of Billy the Kid. The New Riders of the Purple Sage and Bad Company reminded their followers of the trial and tribulations of the outlaw life. Numerous other examples exist, from the "outlaw" music of Waylon Jennings and Willie Nelson to the "hard-rock" of groups like Molly Hatchett and Bon Jovi. Guitars had replaced six-shooters, and hotel rooms rather than saloons were trashed, but many rock bands cast themselves as modern "primitive rebels."

It seems, though, that in the past twenty years we have looked exclusively to the past for our Robin Hoods. In some respects, this should not be surprising. A key aspect of the Robin Hood legend is the idea of redistributive justice, of robbing from the rich and giving to the poor. In the past, as we have noted, American Robin Hoods have emerged concurrently with a massive depression. While recent years have certainly had their share of political corruption and legal scandal, making extra-legal symbols of justice socially revelant, there has been no economic catastrophe that would make outlaws symbolically pursuing redistributive justice especially appealing to a wide audience.

This does not preclude the possibility that in the not-to-distant future, certain contemporary lawbreakers may yet attain the status of an American Robin Hood. Perhaps there will come a time when social conditions will again create a market for such criminals, and some opportunistic entrepreneur will retrieve a recent criminal and shape the meanings and content of his (or her) criminality to fit the Robin Hood myth.

Perhaps the most promising of recent lawbreakers is Patty Hearst. On February 4, 1974, the granddaughter of William Randolph Hearst was kidnapped by two black men and a white woman. The Symbionese Liberation Army presumably carried out the abduction as a form of political terrorism, and Patty Hearst was kept captive in a small closet for three weeks, raped by her abductors, and "brainwashed" into accepting the ideological views of the SLA (Hearst, 1982). When she emerged from incarceration, Patty Hearst was no longer the white daughter of affluent parents. She was "Tanya the Revolutionary." Apparently the

Patricia Hearst. UPI/Bettmann Newsphotos.
Reprinted with permission.

Patricia Hearst. UPI/Bettmann Archive. Reprinted
with permission.

intense psychological strain to which Patty was subjected made her a "willing" accomplice of the SLA, and she participated in a number of robberies. The fact that she was the granddaughter of an American legend made her and the SLA newsworthy. The media directed much attention to the story, and President Nixon, FBI Director Kelley and Attorney General William Saxbe made several controversial pronouncements on the case as uncertainty developed as to whether Patty Hearst was a kidnap victim or a willing accomplice of a terrorist band (cf. Alix, 1978). The members of the SLA attempted to cast themselves as modern Robin Hoods by demanding that the Hearst family distribute several million dollars worth of food free to the poor in California, but they were viewed more as political extremists extorting money unjustly rather than as noble criminals pursuing a worthy cause. Not surprisingly, Patty Hearst seemed to be the most appealing political symbol, as shirts with a picture of "Tanya the Revolutionary" sold very well for a time. However, she was not so popular with the general public, as opinion polls revealed that most favored no clemency for her when captured, and almost half believed she had engineered her own kidnapping (Hearst, 1982:404). The interest in the SLA probably peaked on May 17, as the result of a televised shoot-out between the Los Angeles police and five members of the SLA. The house in which the SLA was entrenched burst into flames during the battle, and the fugitives perished in flames, their bodies burnt beyond recognition. Patty Hearst, initially believed to be one of the charred bodies, remained at large until September of 1975, when she and other SLA members were captured by the FBI. She was tried and convicted of armed robbery and served almost two years in prison before having her sentence commuted by President Carter on February 1, 1979. Ironically, she then married one of her guardians.

Quite possibly some future legend will cast Patty and her Symbionese Liberation Army companions as a band of idealistic youth who turned to bank robbery and extortion from her wealthy corrupt family (Undoubtedly they would have viewed Citizen Kane) to provide for the indigent of Watts and other poverty-stricken areas. Patty may be transformed into a non-threatening feminist heading a racially integrated band of good-spirited rebels, with the legends noting at the same time that Patty was "driven" to crime because of her "brainwashing" by the SLA. The Patty Hearst of legend would not be a political extremist; indeed, she could be "anyone's daughter" as the title of Shana Alexander's 1979 biography states. In its pure form, such a future tale will have Patty perishing with the rest of her companions in a burning building following the shootout with the Los Angeles police. Indeed, because she was not killed while avoiding capture may be the only factor that has kept her from already joining such figures as Jesse James and Butch Cassidy as an American Robin Hood.

Conclusion

It is quite possible, then, for the American Robin Hood to emerge in modern times. At the heart of his criminality are issues that may be quite relevant to modern industrial societies, matters that probably have been relevant since the emergence of state societies. At times when broad segments of the populace become disenchanted with the legal and political order, the perception that law and justice are at odds may become common. At such times, a market exists for symbolic figures who represent extra-legal justice. Such figures are endemic to state societies, although often appealing to small and powerless audiences. At times when economic dislocations or other structural strains occur that effect the daily lives and routines of large numbers of people, social bandits may emerge as national figures of epic proportions. During periods of legitimation crisis, when the "rightness" of legal and political order is questioned by significant portions of the public, symbols of extra-legal justice may emerge in clusters. Certainly modern societies are not immune to structural strains that have given rise to these figures.

During such times of social crisis, entrepreneurs may construct heroic criminals by either inserting contemporary lawbreakers into the Robin Hood myth or by revitalizing previous American Robin Hoods. By drawing upon the Robin Hood formula and selected elements of a criminal's biography, promoters (including the criminal) construct for the brigand a social identity with which many may identify. The form of the myth remains the same. The glorified lawbreaker is endowed with noble attributes reflecting admirable cultural traits that negate the less desirable aspects of his criminality. His lawlessness is rationalized and justified, for he is "driven" to crime. Furthermore, he only claims as victims those institutions that are seen as the "actual" perverters of legal justice; thus, in addition to legitimizing his lawlessness by transforming him into an agent of justice, it becomes possible for his admirers to vicariously rebel through him against unjust authority. Altering the content of the myth by inserting new heroes and villains into it makes it relevant to new situations and new social audiences. Just as the deposed nobleman of early England was replaced in 19th century America by Western outlaws, so may modernized Robin Hoods emerge in the future. Villains may also be transformed. The wicked sheriff of Nottingham and the corrupt clergy were replaced in 19th century America by "thieving detectives" (as Jesse James put it), banks and railroads. Perhaps multinationals may eventually fitted with the villain's garb in future accounts. The social bandit thus serves as a powerful metaphor of social justice, and the flexibility of the mythic structure makes it viable even in advanced industrial societies.

Certainly the mass media has played an important part in the development of the heroic criminal in 19th century America. These social bandits first appeared before the public on the pages of newspapers. Clearly the narratives about such brigands served as entertainment for the readership of the time, but these criminals were also politicized by a press that often seemed little more than the mouthpiece of regional political interests. The media functioned not so much as an opiate that satiated an audience, but rather as an amphetamine that stimulated and provoked people. Consider, for example, the vitriolic style of John Newman Edwards and his journalistic efforts on behalf of the James gang. And since, as we have seen, social bandits like Jesse James and Billy the Kid emerged in a context of economic and political turmoil, the public image of these lawbreakers in the press was also marked by conflicting interpretations. Pluralistic accounts of the moral nature and political implications of criminality, and not ideological hegemony, seemed to be the rule.[1]

Currently, in modern societies such as the United States, the mass media have developed far beyond the dime novels and pulp magazines of the 19th century. The organizational apparatus necessary for the production and dissemination of heroic criminals to large and diverse audiences exists. The consequences this may have for the heroic criminal are profound. The mass media is basically a collection of bureaucratic organizations that must constantly be "producing" new cultural products in order to survive (Cf. Dimaggio, 1977; McKendrick, et. al., 1982; Peterson, 1976). Ideal cultural products are ones that appeal to the public, are easily reproduced, yet may be made to appear significantly different from previous presentations by introducing a few minor changes. The drama inherent in criminality and the formulaic nature of the Robin Hood myth thus make it ideal for mass media, although often in a depoliticized form so as to minimize the chances of offending potential audiences. The organizational needs of the media make the production of heroic criminals very likely (cf. Gitlin, 1983, 1987; Manoff and Schudson, 1987; Schudson, 1978). And if public interest in such presentations exists, there will undoubtedly be a veritable army of such figures unleashed upon the public. Indeed, the appearance of such figures in clusters during depressions in the 19th and 20th centuries is probably best explained by the response of the media to the popular appeal of these figures than by a sudden surge in idealistic and virtuous criminals.

But there exists not only a mass media represented by television networks, but also media addressed to more specialized audiences that may still reach large subgroups of the population. In other words, there is not just the *New York Times*; there is also the *National Enquirer*. This also has implications for the public image of notorious criminals.

Writers may present portrayals of lawbreakers to the public for a variety of reasons, and such figures may be presented in vastly different ways to audiences with widely differing views, needs, and interests. Consequently, the image of such lawbreakers may vary widely. He may be portrayed as an inspired political criminal, a self-serving psychopath, a fantasy figure with child-like qualities. But the fundamental basis for the existence of the heroic criminal was and still is the political implications of his lawlessness. The issues and social actors entangled in his criminality initially give him symbolic power, make him eligible for heroic status and separate him from other lawbreakers. So long as there exists a concept of justice that is not synonymous with Law, the idea of a heroic criminal remains. So long as a way exists to articulate his virtues to others, the lawbreaker may become a social hero.

There is another important lesson to be learned from this work aside from the possibility of future heroic criminals, however. What we may observe in the pages that preceded are the forces that shape what Richard Quinney (1970) has termed the "social reality of crime." A relationship exists between popular perceptions of crime, media portrayals of criminality, and politics. Each of these elements influences the others, bound together in cyclical fashion. The media are sensitive to economic pressures from both above and below. The ideological perspectives of the more powerful members and organizations of a community may be reflected in media content, or at least contrary positions may be avoided in the name of neutrality. Political figures, major corporations, and crime-fighting organizations have a decided edge in identifying to the public the nature, extent, and meaning of crime. The ideas of the dominant class, in other words, are more likely to be reflected in the media. Yet the media may develop images of crime that are in direct contrast to the ideas of the powerful if a market for these ideas may be found. The inspiration for these images, moreover, are not drawn from "above" but from "below," an interpretation of what the public wishes to hear and see. It is the organizational interests of the media, not simply the interests of the more powerful, that lead to the production of sensationalistic, formulaic, and overly simplistic perspectives of crime. These media images then shape social understandings of criminality. But this process unfolds in a social context that helps shape a demand for certain cultural products—such as a Robin Hood criminal. The consequences are conceptualizations of crime that are little more than caricatures, dramatized and even politicized almost beyond recognition.

Thus we find mass murderers and habitual criminals such as Jesse James and Butch Cassidy are transformed from offender to hero, while their victims—the banks and railroads—are transformed from victim to offender. The process and the results are not so different from what may be observed concerning more recent figures such as Bernie Goetz or Oliver North.

But we may also find gross distortions of criminality in another direction. The media and politicians present a world of crime inhabited by perverted murderers and rapists who are much different from ourselves. Consequently, it becomes a simple matter to make distinctions between us—the "normal" population, and "them"—the subhuman criminal forces that deserve to be treated inhumanely. Furthermore, we are warned again and again through the media of the evils inherent in drugs such as heroin or cocaine. Sellers of such substances are cast as "dealers of death," and we are urged to "just say no" to those who would urge us to consume such hazardous products. Yet the same media present to the public other drugs which are physically harmful, addictive, and may be objectively considered to be serious social problems—alcohol and tobacco products—and essentially urges us to "say yes" to these substances. And perhaps more important, certain forms of social evil— corporate violence (cf. Geis, 1973; Coleman, 1985; Clinard and Yeager, 1980; Monahan, et. al., 1979) and certain forms of sexual assault (cf. Russell, 1982; Cate, 1982; Makepeace, 1981), for instance, that do not fit our crude stereotypes of criminality—fail to be considered as criminal acts even by the victims of such offenses. It is hoped that by examining the process by which criminals such as the American social bandits were fashioned into heroes, we may be more aware of the role that politics, structural conditions, and the media play in shaping our understandings of crime. By recognizing the way in which our conceptions of crime may be distorted, we may take a small step to better understanding the true nature and origins of crime.

Notes

Note
Chapter 1

[1]See Ramon Adams (1954, 1979) for an excellent annotated bibliography of works on Western outlaws. Nash (1975) provides extremely interesting, although not always accurate, biographies of noted American criminals. For biographies of these criminals, consult the bibliography at the end of this chapter.

Bibliography

Adams, Ramon. 1954. *Six Guns and Saddle Leather*. Norman: University of Oklahoma Press.
_____ 1979. *More Burrs under the Saddle*. Norman: University of Oklahoma Press.
Becker, Howard S. 1963. *Outsiders*; NY: Free Press.
Betenson, Lula. 1975. *Butch Cassidy, My Brother*. Provo: Brigham Young University Press.
Cavender, Gray. 1981. " 'Scared Straight': Ideology and the Media." *Journal of Criminal Justice* 9:431-39.
Dalton, Emmett. 1931. *When the Daltons Rode*. Garden City, NY: Doubleday.
Fishman, Mark. 1978. "Crime Waves as Ideology." *Social Problems* 25/5 (June): 531-43.
Fortune, Jan I. 1968. *The True Story of Bonnie and Clyde*. NY: Signet Books.
Gard, Wayne. 1964. *Sam Bass*. Lincoln: University of Nebraska Press.
Garofalo, James. 1981. "Crime and the Mass Media: A Selective View of Research." *Journal of Research in Crime and Delinquency* 18/2 (July): 319-50.
Garrett, Pat. 1954. *The Authentic Life of Billy the Kid*. Norman: University of Oklahoma Press, repr.
Graber, Doris. 1980. *Crime News and the Public*. NY: Praeger.
Guthrie, Woody. 1961. "Pretty Boy Floyd." Fall River Music, Inc.
Hanes, Bailey. 1968. *Bill Doolin, Outlaw O.T.* Norman: University of Oklahoma Press.
Hardin, John W. 1961. *The Life of John Wesley Hardin*. Norman: University of Oklahoma Press, repr.
Hobsbawm, Eric. 1959. *Primitive Rebels*. NY: Norton.
_____ 1969. *Bandits*. NY: Dell Books.
Horan, James and Paul Sann. 1954. *Pictorial History of the Wild West*. NY: Bonanza Books.
Kelly, Charles. 1938. *The Outlaw Trail*. NY: Bonanza Books.
Kennerly, Paul. 1980. "The Legend of Jesse James." Rondor Music Ltd.
Kobler, John. 1971. *Capone*. NY: Putnam.
Martin, Charles. 1956. *A Sketch of Sam Bass, The Bandit*. Norman: University of Oklahoma Press.
Nash, Jay R. 1975. *Bloodletters and Badmen*. Vols. 1-3. NY: Warner Books.
Otero, Miguel. 1935. *My Life on the Frontier*. NY: Press of the Pioneers.

Rossi, Peter; Waite, Rose C. and R. Berle. 1974. "The Seriousness of Crimes: Normative Structure and Individual Differences." *American Sociological Review* 39 (April): 227-44.

Schur, Edwin. 1969. *Our Criminal Society*. Englewood Cliffs, NJ: Prentice-Hall.

Toland, John. 1963. *Dillinger Days*. NY: Random House.

Wellman, Paul I. 1961. *A Dynasty of Western Outlaws*. Garden City, NY: Doubleday.

Winick, Charles. 1978. *Deviance and Mass Media*. Beverly Hills, CA: Sage Publications.

Zevon, Warren. 1976. "Frank and Jesse James." Warner-Tamerlane Publishing Company and Dark Room Music, BMI.

Newspapers:

New York *Daily Graphic*

Sedalia (Mo.) *Democrat*

Notes
Chapter 2

[1]Gould (1966:42), in an analysis of Indian and white settlers' accounts of a massacre, noted that each side selected the happenings and impressions that had meaning in light of the values and believes of their respective cultures, and thus two quite different versions of the event were produced. Similarly, Leach (1968:185-98), in a classic study of myth and political systems in highland Burma, found that "every traditional tale will occur in several different versions, each tending to uphold the claims of a different vested interest." A more recent example is provided by differing interpretations of terrorism in various parts of the world. Depending on one's political perspective, the terrorist may be seen as a "freedom fighter" (i.e., ennobled political criminal) or a "terrorist" (i.e., immoral psychopath). See Klapper (1960) and Tunstall (1970) for explanations of these concepts and how they apply to mass media theory.

[2]James Clarke's (1982) excellent analysis of American assassins provides a number of fine examples of this, as does Austin Turk's (1982) discussion of political criminality. Actual motivations for crime may be denied by social audiences and may differ significantly from those that are imputed to lawbreakers. See also Marvin Olsen (1965) and Ralph Turner (1975) for empirical support of this statement.

[3]Recent work on the public perception of the seriousness of crime provides useful insights in this regard. See Rossi, et. al. (1974); Sellin and Wolfgang (1964); Sebba (1984).

Bibliography

Abrahams, Rogers. 1970. *Deep Down in the Jungle...*, (2nd ed.) NY: Aldine.

Becker, Howard S. 1963. *Outsiders*. NY: Free Press.

Bell, Daniel. 1962. *The End of Ideology*. NY: Free Press.

Bellah, Robert. 1970. *Beyond Belief* NY: Harper and Row.

Blok, Anton. 1972. "The Peasant and the Brigand: Social Banditry Reconsidered." *Comparative Studies in Society and History*, 14.

Buel, James. 1893. *The Border Bandits*. Chicago: Donohue, Heneberry and Company.

Bugliosi, Vincent. 1975. *Helter Skelter*. NY: Bantam books.

Campbell, Joseph. 1968. *The Hero With a Thousand Faces*. Princeton: Princeton University Press.

Cavender, Gray. 1981. " 'Scared Straight': Ideology and the Media." *Journal of Criminal Justice* 9: 431-39.

Cawelti, John. 1975. *The Six-Gun Mystique*. Bowling Green: Bowling Green University Popular Press.

Chandler, Lester. 1970. *America's Greatest Depression, 1929-39*. NY: Harper and Row.

Clarke, James. 1982. *American Assassins*. Princeton: Princeton University Press.

Cooper, Courtney. 1934. "Bandit Land." *The Saturday Evening Post 207* (Aug. 4): 879.

Dance, Daryl. 1978 *Shuckin' and Jivin'*. Bloomington: Indiana University Press.

Davis, David. 1968. "Ten Gallon Hero." in Henning Cohen (ed) *The American Experience*. Boston: Houghton-Mifflin.

Defleur, Melvin. 1966. *Theories of Mass Communication*. NY: David McKay Company.

Douglas, Mary.1967."The Meaning of Myth, with special reference to 'La Geste d'Asdiwal.' " In *The Structural Study of Myth and Totemism,* edited by Edmund Leach. NY: Tavistock.

Elkin, Frederick. 1967. "The Psychological Appeal of the Hollywood Western." *Journal of Educational Psychology* (October) 24:72-86.

Emmons, Nuel. 1986. *Manson in His Own Words*. NY: Grove Press.

Escarpit, Robert. 1972. *The Sociology of Literature*. Painesville, Ohio: Lake Erie College Studies.

Faulk, Odie. 1972. *Tombstone: Myth and Reality*. NY: Oxford Press.

Fine, Nathan. 1929. *Labor and Farmer Parties in the United States: 1828-1928.*, NY: Rand School of Social Science.

Fishman, Mark. 1978. "Crime Waves as Ideology." *Social Problems* 25, (June): 531-543.

Fishwick, Marshall. 1969. *The Hero: American Style*. NY: David McKay Company.

Folsom, James. 1974. *The American Western Novel*. New Haven: College and University Press.

Fulton, Maurice. 1968. *The Lincoln County War*. Tucson: University of Arizona Press.

Garofalo, James. 1981. "Crime and the Mass Media: A Selective Review of Research." *Journal of Research in Crime and Delinquency* 18: (July): 319-350.

Geertz, Clifford. 1973. *The Interpretation of Cultures*. NY: Basic Books.

Glasscock, C.B. 1929. *Bandits and the Southern Pacific*. NY: Frederick Stokes.

Goode, William J. 1978. *The Celebration of Heroes*. Berkeley: University of California Press.

Gordon, Welche. 1891. *Jesse James and His Band of Notorious Outlaws*. Chicago: Laird and Lee.

Gould, R. 1966. "Indian and White Versions of the Burnt Branch Massacre: A Study in Comparative Ethnohistory." *Journal of Folklore Institute*, 3.

Graber, Doris. 1980. *Crime News and the Public*. NY: Praeger.

Halliwell, Leslie. 1979. *Halliwell's Film Guide* (2nd ed.) NY: Granada.

Hearst, Patricia. 1982. *Every Secret Thing*. NY: Pinnacle Books.

Hine, Robert. 1973. *The American West*. Boston: Little, Brown, and Company.

Hobsbawm, Eric. 1959. *Primitive Rebels*. NY: Norton.

———. 1969. *Bandits*. NY: Dell.

———. 1973. "Peasants and Politics." *Journal of Peasant Studies* 1:3-22.

———. 1981. *Bandits* (revised edition) NY: Pantheon.

Hollon, Eugene. 1974. *Frontier Violence*. NY: Oxford.

Horan, James. 1976. *The Gunfighters*. NY: Crown.

Inciardi, James; Alan Block and Lyle Hallowell. 1977. *Historical Approaches to Crime*. Beverly Hills: Sage Publications.

Jackson, Joseph. 1955 "Introduction." in John R. Ridge's *Joaquin Murieta*. Norman: University of Oklahoma Press.

Jones, Daryl. 1973. "Clenched Teeth and Curses: Revenge and the Dime Novel Outlaw Hero." *Journal of Popular Culture*, 7.

—— 1978. *The Dime Novel Western*. Bowling Green: The Popular Press.

Klapp, Orrin. 1962. *Heroes, Villains, and Fools*. Englewood Cliffs, NJ: Prentice Hall.

Klapper, Joseph. 1960. *The Effects of Mass Communication*. NY: Free Press.

Leach, Edmund. 1968. "Myth as a Justification for Faction and Social Change." in R. George (ed) *Studies on Mythology*. Homewood, Ill.: Dorsey Press.

Leeming, David. 1981. *Mythology: The Voyage of the Hero*. NY: Harper and Row.

Levin, Jack and James Fox. 1985 *Mass Murder*. NY: Plenum.

Levine, Lawrence. 1977. *Black Culture and Black Consciousness*. NY: Oxford University Press.

Levi-Strauss, Claude. 1963. *Structural Anthropology*, two volumes. NY: Basic Books.

—— 1966. "Overture to le Cru et le cuit." in *Jacques Ehrmann* (ed.), Structuralism. Garden City, NY: Anchor Books.

—— 1967. "The Story of Asdiwal." in *The Structural of Myth and Totemism*, (ed. Edmund Leach). NY: Tavistock.

McLane, John. 1971. "Archaic Movements and Revolutions in Southern Viet Nam.: in Miller and Aya (eds) *National Liberation*. NY: Free Press.

Mercer, Asa. 1954. *Banditti of the Plains*. Norman: University of Oklahoma, repr.

Miller, Walter. 1958. "Lower Class Culture as a Generating Milieu of Gang Delinquency." *Journal of Social Issues*, 14, (November): 5-19.

Mottram, Eric. 1976. "The Persuasive Lips: Men and Guns in America, the West." *Journal of American Studies*, 10, (April): 53-84.

Munden, Kenneth, Jr. 1958. "A Contribution to the Psychological Understanding of the Cowboy and His Myth." *American Imago*, (Summer): 103-148.

Nachbar, Jack. 1974. *Focus on the Western*. Englewood Cliffs, NJ: Prentice-Hall.

Nash, J. Robert. 1975. *Bloodletters and Badmen*, vol. 3 NY: Warner Books.

Nussbaum, Martin. 1960. "Sociological Symbolism of the Adult Western." *Social Forces* 39 (October): 25-8.

Oberschall, Anthony. 1973. *Social Conflict and Social Movements*. Englewood Cliffs, N.J.: Prentice-Hall.

O'Connor, Richard. 1973. *Iron Wheels and Broken Men*. NY: G.P. Putnam's Sons.

O'Malley, Pat. 1979. "Class Conflict, Land, and Social Banditry: Bushranging in Nineteenth Century Australia." *Social Problems* 26 (February): 271-283.

—— 1981 "Social Bandits, Modern Capitalism and the Tradition of Peasantry." *Journal of Peasant Studies* 6: 489-501.

Orwell, George. 1969. "The Fascination of Crime." in *Sykes and Drabek* (eds) *Law and the Lawless*. NY: Random House.

Quinney, Richard. 1970. *Criminology*. Boston: Little, Brown, and Co.

Rossi, Peter; Waite, E.; Rose, C. and Richard Berk. 1974. "The Seriousness of Crimes: Normative Structure and Individual Differences." *American Sociological Review* 39 (April): 224-37.

Schein, Harry. 1975. "The Olympian Cowboy." in Philip Durham and Everett L. Jones. *The Western Story: Fact, Fiction, and Myth*. NY: Harcourt Brace Jovanovick.

Schudson, Michael. 1978. *Discovering the News*. NY: Basic Books.

Schur, Edwin. 1969. *Our Criminal Society*. Englewood Cliffs, NJ: Prentice-Hall.

Sebba, Leslie. 1984. "Crime Seriousness and Criminal Intent." *Crime and Delinquency* 30/2 (April): 277-44.

Sellin, T. and M.W. Wolfgang. 1964. *The Measurement of Delinquency.* NY: John Wiley and Sons.

Settle, William. 1966. *Jesse James Was His Name.* Columbia: University of Missouri Press.

Sherizen, S. 1978. "Social Creation of Crime News: All the News Fitted to Print." In C. Winick (ed) *Deviance and Mass Media.* Beverly Hills, CA: Sage.

Silberman, Charles. 1978. *Criminal Violence,* Criminal Justice. NY: Random House.

Smith, Henry Nash. 1950. *Virgin Land.* NY: Vintage Books.

Steckmesser, Kent. 1965. *The Western Hero in History and Legend.* Norman: University of Oklahoma Press.

_____ 1966. "Robin Hood and the American Outlaw." *Journal of American Folklore,* 79. (April-June).

_____ 1983. *Western Outlaws: The "Good Badman" in Fact, Film, and Folklore* Claremont, Ca: Regina Books.

Stegner, Wallace. 1942. *Mormon Country.* NY: Hawthorn Books.

Sykes, Gresham and David Matza. 1957. "Techniques of Neutralization: A Theory of Delinquency: *American Sociological Review* 22 (December): 664-70.

Tunstall, Jeremy. 1970. *Media Sociology.* Chicago: University of Illinois Press.

Turk, Austin. 1982. *Political Criminality.* Beverly Hills, CA: Sage.

Turner, Ralph H. 1975. "The Public Perception of Protest." in R.L. Henschel and R.A. Silverman (eds) *Perception in Criminology.* NY: Columbia University Press.

Turner, Victor. 1977. *The Ritual Process.* Ithica: Cornell University.

Warshow, Robert. 1975. "The Westerner." in Philip Durham and Everett L. Jones (eds) *The Western Story.* NY: Harcourt Brace Jovanovich.

Wecter, Dixon. 1941. *The Hero in America.* NY: Charles Scribner's Sons.

Wellman, Paul. 1961. *A Dynasty of Western Outlaws.* Garden City, NY: Doubleday.

White, Richard. 1981. "Outlaw Gangs of the Middle Border: American Social Bandits." *Western Historical Quarterly,* 12 (October): 387-408.

Wiebe, Robert. 1967. *The Search for Order* NY: Hill and Wang.

Wright, Bill. 1975. *Sixguns and Society: A Structural Study of the Western.* Berkeley: University of California Press.

Newspapers
Las Vegas Daily Optic
The New Southwest
Santa Fe New Mexican
Saint Paul Pioneer Press

Bibliography
Chapter 3

Adams, Ramon. 1969. *Six Guns and Saddle Leather.* Norman: University of Oklahoma Press.

Andrews, Sidney. 1971. *The South Since the War.* (David Donald, ed.). Boston: Houghton Mifflin.

Avary, Myrta Lockett. 1906. *Dixie After the War.* NY: Doubleday, Page and Company.

Breihan, Carl W. 1974. *The Escapades of Frank and Jesse James.* NY: Frederick Fell Publishers, Inc.

Brown, Richard Maxwell. 1969. "Historical Patterns of Violence in America," in *The History of Violence in America*. eds. Hugh Davis Graham and Ted Robert Gurr. NY: Frederick A. Praeger, Publishers, pp. 45-83.

Brownlee, Richard S. 1958. *Gray Ghosts of the Confederacy*. Baton Rouge: Louisiana University Press.

Byars, William Vincent. October, 1920. "A Century of Journalism in Missouri." *Missouri Historical Review*. 15:70-2.

Castel, Albert. 1963. "Order No. 11 and the Civil War on the Border." *Missouri Historical Review*. (July) 57:357-68.

Crittenden, H.H., compiler. 1936. *The Crittenden Memoirs*. NY: Putnam's Sons.

Dacus, Joseph. 1882. *Illustrated Lives and Adventures of Frank and Jesse James and the Younger Brothers, The Noted Western Outlaws*. St. Louis: N.D. Thompson and Company.

Davis, Kenneth S. 1976. *Kansas*. NY: W.W. Norton.

Donald, Jay. 1882. *Outlaws of the Border*. Philadelphia: Douglas Brothers.

Edwards, Jennie, compiler. 1889. *John N. Edwards, Biography, Memoirs, Reminiscences and Recollections*. Kansas City: Jennie Edwards, Publisher, .

Edwards, John Newman. 1877. *Noted Guerrillas*. St. Louis: Bryan, Brand and Company.

Ezell, John Samuel. 1978. *The South Since 1865* (2nd ed.) University of Oklahoma Press.

Frantz, Joe B. "The Frontier Tradition: An Invitation to Violence," in *Historical Violence in America*, eds. Hugh Davis Graham and Ted Robert Gurr. NY: Frederick A. Praeger.

Hofstadter, Richard; William Miller and Daniel Aaron. 1970. *The American Republic, Vol. 2*. Englewood Cliffs, NJ: Prentice-Hall.

Horan, James D. 1949. *Desperate Men*. NY: Bonanza Books.

Horan, James D. 1977. *The Outlaws*. NY: Crown.

Love, Robertus. 1940. *The Rise and Fall of Jesse James*. NY: Blue Ribbon Books.

Morison, Samuel Eliot; Henry Steele Commager and William E. Leuchtenberg. 1977. *A Concise History of the American Republic*. NY: Oxford University Press.

Nichols, Roy F. 1961. *The Stakes of Power*. NY: Hill and Wang.

Parrish, William E. 1973. *A History of Missouri, Vol. III*. Columbia: University of Missouri Press.

Rable, George. 1984. *But There Was No Peace: The Role of Violence in the Politics of Reconstruction*. Athens: University of Georgia Press.

Settle, William A. 1966. *Jesse James Was His Name*. Columbia: University of Missouri Press.

Settle, William A. 1942. "The James Boys and Missouri Politics." *Missouri Historical Review*. (July), 36:412-29.

Steckmesser, Kent. 1966. "Robin Hood and the American Outlaw." *Journal of American Folklore*, (April-June), 79:348-55.

Trelease, Allen. 1971. *White Terror: The Ku Klux Klan Conspiracy and Southern Reconstruction*. NY: Harper and Row.

Triplett, Frank. 1882. *The Life, Times and Treacherous Death of Jesse James*. St. Louis: J.H. Chambers and Company.

Wallace, W.H. 1914. *Speeches and Writings of William H. Wallace with Autobiography*. Western Baptist Publishing Company.

Wellman, Paul I. 1961. *A Dynasty of Western Outlaws*. NY: Doubleday.

Wilson, Don W. 1975. *Governor Charles Robinson of Kansas*. Lawrence: University of Kansas Press.

Woodward, C. Vann. 1951. *Origins of the New South: 1877-1913*. Louisiana State University Press.

Newspapers
Chicago *Tribune.*
Cincinnati *Enquirer.*
Gallatin *North Missourian.*

Kansas City *Daily Journal of Commerce.*
Kansas City *Evening Star.*
Kansas City *Journal.*
Kansas City Times.
Lexington *Caucasion.*
Liberty *Tribune.*
Nashville *Banner.*
Sedalia *Democrat.*
St. Joseph *Herald.*
St. Louis *Democrat.*
St. Louis *Globe-Democrat.*
St. Louis *Missouri Republican.*
St. Louis *Republican.*
St. Louis *Times-Dispatch.*
St. Louis *Pioneer Press.*

Notes
Chapter 4

[1]Wallace to Schurz, March 31, 1879 [in Utley, 1987:228]

[2]About fifty men were indicted for offenses related to the Lincoln County War, but virtually all of them would escape trial. For instance, James Dolan was charged with the killings of Tunstall and Chapman, but District Attorney J. Francisco Chavez refused to prosecute him. Utley (1987:154) suggests that both Chavez and Dolan's defense counsel, Thomas Catron, were "among the most politically prominent and powerful men in New Mexico." While the Santa Fe Ring came to the rescue of what was left of the Dolan-Murphy-Riley faction, Billy the Kid had only a newly arrived and uncertain political quantity in Wallace to count on. His other potential source of support, John Chisum, had long since removed himself from the events surrounding the Lincoln County War. Whatever support the Kid might have had among the common citizenry was not particularly useful in saving him from the machinery of the legal system. They might sing to him while he was imprisoned, but they were not going to prevent his execution.

[3]It seems quite likely that Billy Bonney's participation in the Lincoln County struggle really came about because he was a paid gunman, and not because he felt any particular allegiance to Tunstall, as legend suggests (cf. Garrett, 1954:52; Burns, 1926). That this is so may be inferred by letters written by Tunstall. Nowhere does he mention the Kid as a friend or companion, but the Britisher did comment on the cost he was incurring in setting up his "ring" because "men expect to be well-paid for going on the warpath" (in Nolan, 1965:259). Garrett's (1954:49-51) romanticized version of the Kid's life implies, in fact, that originally Billy the Kid worked for Tunstall's rivals but struck a better deal with Tunstall and switched allegiance. There is some circumstantial evidence which suggests, moreover, the Tunstall also tried to enlist Jesse Evans and his men, but perhaps Evans was a better judge of which side was more likely to emerge the victor (cf Utley, 1987:34-6).

[4]This story was also made public in the Las Vegas Daily Optic (June 10, 1881). A rival newspaper, the Las Vegas Gazette (June 16, 1881), however claimed that such an event never took place.

Bibliography

Adams, Ramon. 1960. *A Fitting Death for Billy the Kid*. Norman: University of Oklahoma Press.

Ball, Larry. 1978. *U.S. Marshals*. Albuquerque: University of New Mexico.

Burns, Walter Noble. 1926. *The Saga of Billy the Kid*. NY: Garden City Publishing Company.

Chapman, Arthur. 1905. "Billy the Kid—A Man All 'Bad.' " *Outing* 46: 73-77.

Coe, George. 1951. *Frontier Fighter*, 2nd ed... Albuquerque: University of New Mexico Press.

Delany, Samuel. 1967. *The Einstein Intersection*. NY: Ace Books.

Doughty, Francis. 1890. *Old King Brady and Billy the Kid*. NY Detective Library, No. 411. NY: Frank Tousey.

Drago, Harry Sinclair. 1970. *The Great Range Wars*. NY: Dodd, Mead and Company.

Dykes, J.C. 1952. *Billy the Kid: The Bibliography of a Legend*. Albuquerque: University of New Mexico Press.

Fable, Edmund. 1881. *Billy the Kid, The New Mexican Outlaw*. Denver: Denver Publishing Company.

Fishwick, Marshall. 1954. *American Heroes: Myth and Reality*. Washington, D.C.: Public Affairs Press.

Fulton, Maurice G. 1968. *The Lincoln County War*. Tucson: University of Arizona Press.

Garrett, Pat P. 1954. *The Authentic Life of Billy the Kid*. Norman: University of Oklahoma Press, repr.

Hamlin, William. 1959. *The True Story of Billy the Kid*. Caldwell, Id.: Caxton.

Hinton, Harwood. 1956. "John Simpson Chisum." *New Mexico Historical Review* (July), 31/3:184-205.

Hollon, W. Eugene. 1974. *Frontier Violence*. NY: Oxford Press.

Horan, James. 1975. *The Gunfighters*. NY: Crown Publishers.

Jenardo, Don [John Lewis]. 1881. *The True Life of Billy the Kid*. Wide Awake Library, No. 451. NY: Frank Tousey.

Keleher, William A. 1957. *Violence in Lincoln County*. Albuquerque: University of New Mexico Press.

Klasner, Lily. 1972. *My Girlhood Among Outlaws*. Tucson: University of Arizona Press.

Lamar, Howard L. 1970. *The Far Southwest*. NY: W.W. Norton Company.

Metz, Leon. 1974. *Pat Garrett*. Norman: University of Oklahoma Press.

Nolan, Frederick W. 1965. *John Henry Tunstall*. Albuquerque: University of New Mexico Press.

O'Connor, Richard. 1960. *Pat Garrett*. NY: McGraw-Hill.

Otero, Miguel Antonio. 1935. *My Life on the Frontier*. NY: The Press of Pioneers.

Poe, John. 1936. *The Death of Billy the Kid*. Boston: Houghton Mifflin, reprint.

Rasch, Philip. 1957. "Exit Axtell: Enter Wallace." *New Mexico Historical Review* (July), 32/3: 231-245.

Rasch, Philip. 1966. "The Governor Meets the Kid." *Brand Book* (April), 8:5-12.

Rosa, Joseph. 1968. The Gunfighter: Man or Myth? Norman: University of Oklahoma Press.

Siringo, Charles L. 1931. *Riata and Spurs*. NY: Houghton Mifflin Company.

Sonnichsen, C.L. and William Morrison. 1955. *Alias Billy the Kid*. Albuquerque: University of New Mexico Press.

Steckmesser, Kent L. 1965. *The Western Hero in History and Legend*. Norman: University of Oklahoma Press.

Steckmesser, Kent. 1983. *Western Outlaws: The "Good Badman" in Fact, Film, and Folklore*. Claremont, Ca.: Regina Books.

Stratton, Porter. 1969. The Territorial Press of New Mexico, 1834-1912. Albuquerque: University of New Mexico Press.

Tatum, Stephen. 1982. *Inventing Billy the Kid: Visions of the Outlaw in America, 1881-1981*. Albuquerque: University of New Mexico Press.

Theisen, Lee Scott, ed. 1976. "Frank Warner Angel's Notes on New Mexico Territory, 1878." Arizona and the West (Winter), 18:333-70.

Utley, Robert. 1987. High Noon in Lincoln. Albuquerque: University of New Mexico Press.

Wecter, Dixon. 1941. *The Hero in America: A Chronicle of Hero Worship*. NY: Scribner's.

Newspapers

Cimmaron *News and Press*.

Grant County *Herald*.

Las Cruces *Eco del Rio Grande*.

Las Cruces *Thirty-Four*.

Las Vegas *Daily Optic*.

Las Vegas *Gazette*.

Mesilla Valley *Independent*

San Francisco *Weekly Democrat*.

Santa Fe *New Mexican*.

Whit Oaks *Golden Era*.

Census Data

Vital and Social Statistics in the United States, 10th Census: 1880. Washington, D.C.: Government Printing Office, 1882.

Note

Chapter 5

[1]Pointer meant the Denver *Post*. Recent work by Dan Buck and Anne Meadows (1987, 1988) has questioned much of the information surrounding Cassidy's and Longbough's death.

Bibliography

Betenson, Lula. 1975. *Butch Cassidy, My Brother*. Provo: Brigham Young University.

Buck, D. and A. Meadows. 1987. "The Many Deaths of Butch Cassidy." *Pacific Northwest* 21 (July): 26ff.

Buck, D. and A. Meadows. 1988. "The Aramayo Mule." *South American Explorer* 16 (Feb.): 4-11.

Burt, Struther. 1938. *Powder River*. NY: Farrar and Rinehart.

Chapman, Arthur. 1930. " 'Butch' Cassidy." *Elks Magazine* (April), pp. 30ff.

Chisum, Emmett. 1983. "The Wilcox Train Robbery." *Annals of Wyoming* (Spring) 55/1: 22-31.

Drago, Harry S. 1970. *The Great Range Wars*. NY: Dodd, Mead, and Company.

Gould, Lewis L. 1968. *Wyoming: A Political History*. New Haven: Yale University Press.

Hall, Charles. 1977. "Asa S. Mercer and the 'Banditti of the Plains:' A Reappraisal." *Annals of Wyoming* (Spring) 49/1:43-64.

Hollon, W. Eugene. 1924. *Frontier Violence*. NY: Oxford University Press.

Horan, James D. 1949. *Desperate Men*. NY: Bonanza Books.

———— 1977. *The Outlaws*. NY: Crown Publishing.

Kelly, Charles. 1959. *The Outlaw Trail.* NY: Bonanza Books.

Leech, Margaret. 1959. *In the Days of McKinley.* NY: Harper Brothers.

Mercer, Asa S. 1954. *The Banditti of the Plains.* Norman: University of Oklahoma Press.

Meyer, William. 1979. *The Making of the Great Westerns.* New Rochelle, NY: Arlington House.

Parish, James R. and Michael R. Pitts. 1976. *The Great Western Pictures.* Metuchen, NJ: Scarecrow Press.

Pointer, Larry. 1977. *In Search of Butch Cassidy.* Norman: University of Oklahoma Press.

Smith, Helena H. 1966. *The War on Powder River.* NY: McGraw-Hill.

Newspapers

Anaconda *Standard.*

Basin City *Herald.*

Buffalo *Bulletin.*

Canton *Evening Repository.*

Casper *Weekly Mail.*

Denver *Rocky Mountain News.*

Douglas *News.*

Great Falls *Daily Tribune.*

Green River *Star.*

Helena *Democrat Independent.*

Los Angeles *Times.*

New York *Herald.*

Ogden *Standard.*

Salt Lake City *Herald.*

Bibliography
Chapter 6

Anderson, Paul. 1932. "Tear Gas, Bayonets, and Votes." Nation 135. (Aug. 17): 138-140.

———— 1932. "Republican Handsprings." Nation 135. (Aug. 31): 188-189.

(No author). 1934. "Bad Man at Large." *Time* 23. (May 7): 18-21.

Bellah, Robert. 1979. *Beyond Belief.* NY: Harper and Row.

Bernstein, Irving. 1960. *The Lean Years: A History of the American Worker, 1933-1941.* Boston: Houghton Mifflin Company.

(no author). 1932. "Bombs and Bayonets for the B.E.F." *The Literary Digest 114.* (Aug. 6): 3.

Bryson, Lyman. 1934. "Can the Farmer Be Saved?" *Survey Graphic 23.* 369-371.

California Employment Commission. 1932.

Chandler, Lester. 1970. *America's Greatest Depression, 1929-1939.* NY: Harper & Row.

Cooper, Courtney. 1934. "Bandit Land." *The Saturday Evening Post 207.* (Aug. 4): 879.

(no author). 1932. "Cowardice and Folly in Washington." *Nation 135.* (Aug 10): 116.

Dewey, Ernest. 1933. "The Farmer Turns Gangster." *Commonweal 18* (May 19): 65-67.

DeWitt, W.H. 1935. "Paging Mr. Robin Hood." *North American Review 239* (Jan.): 1-3.

Guthrie, Woodie. 1961. "Pretty Boy Floyd." *Fall River Music, Inc.*

Hobsbawm, Eric. 1969. *Bandits.* NY: Dell.

Kobler, John. 1971. *Capone: The Life and World of Al Capone.* NY: G.P. Putnam & Sons.

Logan, Malcolm. 1931. "Glorifying the Criminal.: *Scribner's Magazine 90.* (July): 43-46.

McMillen, A.W. 1932. "An Army of Boys on the Loose." *Survey Graphic 68*. (Sept. 1): 389-93.

Nash, Jay. 1975. *Bloodletters and Badmen*. NY: Warner Books.

(no author). 1932. "No One Has Starved." *Fortune 6* (Sept.): 18ff.

Pasley, Fred. 1932. *Al Capone: The Biography of a Self-Made Man*. London: Faber and Faber.

Piven, Frances and Richard Cloward. 1932. *Poor People's Movements*. Vintage Books.

Powers, Richard. 1983. *G-Men: Hoover's FBI in American Popular Culture*. Carbondale, Illinois: Southern Illinois University Press.

Purvis, Melvin. 1936. *American Agent*. Garden City, NY: Doubleday, Doran, and Company.

Schlesinger, Arthur M., Jr. 1957. *The Age of Roosevelt, Vol. 1*. Boston: Houghton Mifflin Company.

Spring, G. 1934. "Men Off the Road." *Survey Graphic 23*. (Sept.): 420ff.

Steinbeck, John. 1939. *The Grapes of Wrath*. NY: Viking Press.

Taylor, Paul. 1935. "Again the Covered Wagon." *Survey Graphic 24* (July): 348ff.

Toland, John. 1963. *Dillinger Days*. NY: Random House.

Treherne, John. 1985. *The Strange History of Bonnie and Clyde*. NY: Stein and Day.

Yellin, Samuel. 1974. *American Labor Struggles: 1877-1934*. NY: Monad Press.

Bibliography
Chapter 7

Bradley, R. 1882. *The Outlaws of the Border* or *The Lives of Frank and Jesse James*. St. Louis: J.W. Marsh.

Bugliosi, Vincent. 1975. *Helter Skelter*. NY: Bantam Books.

Burns, Walter. 1926. *The Saga of Billy the Kid*. NY: Garden City Publishing.

Cawelti, John. 1975. *The Six-Gun Mystique*. Bowling Green: Bowling Green University Popular Press.

Cooper, Courtney. 1934. "Bandit Land." The Saturday Evening Post 207:879ff.

Dance, Daryl. 1978. *Shuckin' and Jivin'*. Bloomington: Indiana University Press.

Edwards, John Newman. 1877. *Noted Guerrillas*. St. Louis: Bryan, Brand and Co.

Escarpit, Robert. 1968. "The Sociology of Literature." in D. Sills (ed) *Int. Encyclopedia of the Social Sciences* NY: MacMillan.

Fine, Nathan. 1929. *Labor and Farmer Parties in the United States: 1828-1928*. NY: Rand School of Social Science.

Fishwick, Marshall. 1969. *The Hero: American Style*. NY: David McKay Company.

Fulton, Maurice. 1968. *The Lincoln County War*. Tucson: University of Arizona Press.

Garrett, Pat. 1954 repr. *The Authentic Life of Billy the Kid*. Norman: University of Oklahoma Press.

Guthrie, Woody. 1961. "The Ballad of 'Pretty Boy' Floyd." Fall River Music.

Halliwell, Leslie. 1979. *Halliwell's Film Guide (2nd ed.)*. NY: Granada.

Hobsbawm. Eric. 1959. *Primitive Rebels*. NY: Norton.

———— 1969. *Bandits*. NY: Dell.

Hofstadter, Richard. 1955. *The Age of Reform*. NY: Vintage.

Inciardi, James; Alan Block and Lyle Hallowell. 1977. *Historical Approaches to Crime*. Beverly Hills: Sage Publications.

Keleher, William. 1957. *Violence in Lincoln County*. Albuquerque: University of New Mexico Press.

Kelly, Charles. 1959. *The Outlaw Trail*. NY: Bonanza Books.

Kennerly, Paul. 1980. "The Legend of Jesse James." Rondor Music (London).

Klapp, Orrin. 1962. *Heroes, Villains, and Fools*. Englewood Cliffs, NJ: Prentice Hall.

Klein, Joe. 1980. Woody Guthrie: A Life. NY: Ballantine Books.

Levine, Lawrence. 1977. Black Culture and Black Consciousness. NY: Oxford.

Levi-Strauss, Claude. 1963. Structural Anthropology, two volumes. NY: Basic Books.

——— 1966. "Overture to le Cru et le cuit." in Jacques Ehrmann (ed), Structuralism. Garden City, NY: Anchor Books.

Love, Robertus. 1926. The Rise and Fall of Jesse James. NY: Blue Ribbon Books.

Mercer, Asa. 1954 repr. Banditti of the Plains. Norman: University of Oklahoma.

Merrill, Horace. 1967. Bourbon Democracy of the Middle West. Seattle: University of Washington Press.

Miller, Walter. 1958. "Lower Class Culture as a Generating Milieu of Gang Delinquency." Journal of Social Issues 14:5-19.

Nash, J. Robert. 1975. Bloodletters and Badmen. NY: Warner Books.

Oberschall, Anthony. 1973. Social Conflict and Social Movements. Englewood Cliffs, N.J.: Prentice-Hall.

O'Connor, Richard. 1973. Iron Wheels and Broken Men. NY: G.P. Putnam's Sons.

Otero, Michael. 1935. My Life on the Frontier. NY: Press of the Pioneers.

Powers, Richard. 1983. G-Men: Hoover's FBI in American Popular Culture. Carbondale: Southern Illinois Press.

Powers, Richard. 1987. Secrecy and Power: The Live of J. Edgar Hoover. NY: Free Press.

Schafer, Stephen. 1974. Political Crime. NY: Free Press.

Settle, William. 1942. "The James Boys and Missouri Politics." Missouri Historical Review. 36:412-29.

Settle, William. 1966. Jesse James Was His Name. Columbia: University of Missouri Press.

Sissman, L.E. 1971. "Presenting the Next Great Western Movie." Atlantic Monthly 278:45ff.

Steckmesser, Kent. 1965. The Western Hero in History and Legend. Norman: University of Oklahoma Press.

——— 1966. "Robin Hood and the American Outlaw." Journal of American Folklore, 79:77-82.

——— 1983. Western Outlaws: The "Good Badman" in Fact, Film, and Folklore. Claremont, Ca: Regina Books.

Stegner, Wallace. 1942. Mormon Country. NY: Hawthorn Books.

Sykes, Gresham and David Matza. 1957. "Techniques of Neutralization: A Theory of Delinquency: American Sociological Review 22:664-70.

Tatum, Stephen. 1982. Inventing Billy the Kid: Visions of the Outlaw in America, 1881-1981. Albuquerque: University of New Mexico Press.

Toland, John. 1963. Dillinger Days. NY: Random House.

Triplett, Frank. 1882. The Life, Times, and Treacherous Death of Jesse James. St. Louis: J.H. Chamgers.

Tuchman, Gaye. 1978. Making News. NY: Free Press.

Wecter, Dixon. 1941. The Hero in America. NY: Charles Scribner's Sons.

Wiebe, Robert. 1967. The Search for Order. NY: Hill and Wang.

Note

Chapter 8

[1]Currently there is a debate in the sociology of culture between what might be considered Marxist scholars and theorists influenced by sociologist Max Weber. The Marxist tradition, taken from theorists such as Althusser (1971) and Gramsci (1971), has argued that mass culture plays an important role in maintaining the power of the ruling class by presenting a world-view supporting its position (cf. Gottdiener, 1985; Gitlin, 1979, 1980; Femia, 1975).

Built upon the theory of hegemony, it sees the media as a class weapon used to maintain political and economic control through the production of "ideological false consciousness."

In contrast, a number of theorists have suggested that the mass media might better be understood as a collection of culture industries with their own organizational needs and objectives (cf. Manoff and Schudson, 1987; Peterson, 1976; DiMaggio, 1977). The content of mass media—whether one is talking of news reports or fictional dramas—is shaped more by market structures and organizational demands (i.e., a steady flow of information, formula stories that have proven popular with audiences in the past, a large audience that will attract financial support from advertisers) than by ruling elites (cf. Davis, 1952; Fishman, 1978; Gans, 1980; Garofalo, 1981; Graber, 1980; Humphries, 1981; Sherizen, 1978; Tuchman, 1978; Winick, 1978).

In this work I am suggesting that the organizational interests of media may often coincide with the interests of those in more advantaged positions of power and influence when it comes to presenting images of crime. These media organizations are much more likely to be owned by the affluent than the poor, and revenues critical for their operation are much more readily obtained from the rich and powerful corporations than the poor and relatively powerless individual. However, matters becomed complicated when one considers that many of those managing these media enterprises are political liberals (Lichter, 1986), and the image of corporations and of the wealthy, at least in television dramas, are generally negative (Gitlin, 1983:266-72; Stein, 1979). It seems, as this work shows, that media portrayals of criminality may conflict with political and police versions when market conditions exist that make it appear profitable to do so.

Bibliography

Alexander, Shana. 1979. *Anyone's Daughter*. NY: Bantam Books.

Alix, Ernest. 1978. *Ransom Kidnapping in America/1874-1974*. Carbondale: Southern Illinois Press.

Althusser, L. 1971. "Ideology and Ideological State Apparatuses" in *Levin and Philosophy and other Essays*. NY: Monthly Review.

Brown, Dee. 1976. *Bury My Heart at Wounded Knee*. NY: Vintage Books.

Bugliosi, Vincent. 1975. *Helter Skelter*. NY: Bantam Books.

Cate, Rodney. 1982. "Premarital Abuse: A Social-Psychological Perspective." *Journal of Family Issues* 3:79-90.

Clinard, Marshall B. and Peter Yeager. 1980. *Corporate Crime*. NY: Free Press.

Coleman, James W. 1985. *The Criminal Elite*. NY: St. Martin's.

Davis, F. James. 1952. "Crime News in Colorado Newspapers." *American Journal of Sociology* 57:325-330.

DiMaggio, Paul. 1977. "Market Structure, the Creative Process, and Popular Culture: Toward an Organizational Reinterpretation of Mass-Culture Theory." *Journal of Popular Culture* 11:436-52.

Emmons, Nuel. 1986. *Manson in His Own Words*. NY: Grove Press.

Femia, Joseph. 1975. "Hegemony and Consciousness in the Thought of Antonio Gramsci." *Political Studies* 23:29-48.

Fishman, Mark. 1978. "Crime Waves as Ideology." *Social Problems* 25:531-543.

Fishwick, Marshall. 1969. *The Hero: American Style*. NY: David McKay Company.

Gans, Herbert. 1980. *Deciding What's News*. NY: Vintage.

Garofalo, James. 1981. "Crime and the Mass Media: A Selective Review of Research." *Journal of Research in Crime and Delinquency* 18: 319-350.

Geis, Gilbert and Robert F. Meier (eds.) 1977. *White Collar Crime*. NY: Free Press.

Gitlin, Todd. 1979. "Prime Time Time Ideology: The Hegemony Process in Television Entertainment." *Social Problems* 26:251-266.

Gitlin, Todd. 1980. *The Whole World is Watching: Mass Media in the Making of the New Left.* Berkeley: University of California Press.

Gitlin, Todd. 1983. *Inside Prime Time.* NY: Pantheon Books.

Gitlin, Todd (ed). 1986. *Watching Television.* NY: Pantheon Books.

Gottdiener, Michael. 1985. Hegemony and Mass Culture: a Semiotic Approach. *American Journal of Sociology* 90:979-1001.

Graber, Doris. 1980. *Crime News and the Public.* NY: Praeger.

Gramsci, A. 1971. *Selections from the Prison Notebooks.* NY: International.

Gunther, Max. 1985. . *D.B. Cooper: What Really Happened.* Chicago: Contemporary Books.

Guthrie, Woody. 1961. "The Ballad of 'Pretty Boy' Floyd." Fall River Music.

Hearst, Patricia. 1982. *Every Secret Thing.* NY: Pinnacle Books.

Hobsbawm, Eric. 1959. *Primitive Rebels.* NY: Norton.

———. 1969. *Bandits.* NY: Dell.

———. 1981. *Bandits* (revised edition) NY: Pantheon.

Humphries, Drew. 1981. "Serious Crime, News Coverage, and Ideology." *Crime and Delinquency* 27:191-205.

Inciardi, James; Alan Block and Lyle Hallowell. 1977. *Historical Approaches to Crime.* Beverly Hills: Sage Publications.

Jones, Daryl. 1978. *The Dime Novel Western.* Bowling Green: Popular Press.

Katz, Friedrich. 1981. *The Secret War in Mexico.* Chicago: University of Chicago Press.

Kennerly, Paul. 1980. "The Legend of Jesse James." Rondor Music (London).

Klapp, Orrin. 1962. *Heroes, Villains, and Fools.* Englewood Cliffs. Prentice Hall.

Klein, Joe. 1980. *Woody Guthrie: A Life.* NY: Ballantine Books.

Klockars, Carl. 1980. "The Dirty Harry Problem." *The Annals,* 452:33-47.

Knight, Stephen. 1980. *Form and Ideology in Crime Fiction.* Bloomington: Indiana University Press.

Lichter, Robert. 1986. *The Media Elite.* Bethesda, Adler and Adler.

Makepeace, James. 1981. "Courtship Violence Among College Students." *Family Relations* 30:97-102.

Manoff, Robert and Michael Schudson (eds.) 1987. *Reading the News.* NY: Pantheon.

McKendrick, N., Brewer, J., Plumb, J.H. 1982. *The Birth of a Consumer Society.* Bloomington: Indiana University Press.

Monahan, J., R. Novaco and G. Geis. 1979. "Corporate Violence." in T. Sarbin (ed) *Challenges to the Criminal Justice System* NY: Human Sciences.

Oberschall, Anthony. 1973. *Social Conflict and Social Movements.* Englewood Cliffs, Prentice-Hall.

O'Malley, Pat. 1979. "Class Conflict, Land, and Social Banditry: Bushranging in Nineteenth Century Australia." *Social Problems* 26:271-283.

———. 1981. "Social Bandits, Modern Capitalism and the Tradition of Peasantry." *Journal of Peasant Studies* 6:489-501.

Peterson, Richard. 1976. *The Production of Culture.* Beverly Hills: Sage.

Porter, Dennis. 1981. *The Detective Hero.* New Haven: Yale University Press.

Quinney, Richard. 1970. *Criminology.* Boston: Little, Brown and Co.

Rossi, Peter; Waite, E.; Rose, C. and Richard Berk. 1974. "The Seriousness of Crimes: Normative Structure and Individual Differences." *American Sociological Review* 39:224-37.

Rubin, Lillian. 1986. *Quiet Rage: Bernie Goetz in a Time of Madness.* NY: Farrar, Straus, and Giroux, 1986.

Russell, Diana. 1982. *Rape in Marriage.* NY: Macmillan.

Schudson, Michael. 1978. *Discovering the News.* NY: Basic Books.

Schell, Jonathan. 1976. *The Time of Illusion.* New York: Vintage Books.

Sherizen, S. 1978. "Social Creation of Crime News: All the News Fitted to Print." In C. Winick (ed) *Deviance and Mass Media*. Beverly Hills, CA: Sage.

Smith, Henry Nash. 1950. *Virgin Land*. NY: Vintage Books.

Stein, Ben. 1979. *The View from Sunset Boulevard*. NY: Basic Books.

Sykes, Gresham and David Matza. 1957. "Techniques of Neutralization: A Theory of Delinquency." *American Sociological Review* 22:664-70.

Symons, Julian. 1985. *Bloody Murder* (revised edition). NY: Penguin Books.

Tuchman, Gaye. 1978. *Making News*. NY: Free Press.

Tucker, William. 1985. *Vigilante*. NY: Stein and Day.

Wambaugh, Joseph. 1981. *The Glitterdome*. NY: Bantam Books.

Wecter, Dixon. 1941. *The Hero in America*. NY: Charles Scribner's Sons.

White, Richard. 1981. "Outlaw Gangs of the Middle Border: American Social Bandits." *Western Historical Quarterly*, 12:387-408.

Wilkerson, Michael and Dick Wilkerson. 1981. *Someone Cry for the Children*. NY: Dial Press.

Winick, Charles, 1978. *Deviance and Mass Media*. Beverly Hills: Sage.

Wright, Will. 1975. *Sixguns and Society: A Structural Study of the Western*. Berkeley: University of California Press.

Zevon, Warren. 1973. "Frank and Jesse James." Warner-Tamerlane Music.

Index

Abrahams, Roger 41, 152, 182

Adams, Ramon 9, 43, 98, 181, 185, 188

Alexander, Shana 176, 193

Alix, Ernest 176, 193

Allison, Clay 99

Althusser, L. 192, 193

American Indian Movement 164

Anacostia Flats 123-125

Anderson, Paul 124, 190

Angel, Frank Warner 78, 87-88

Andrews, Sidney 44, 185

Askew, Daniel 55, 71-72

Avary, Myrta 185

Averill, Jim 102, 103

Axtell, Governor Samuel 84, 88

Baker, Frank 84

Ball, Larry 188

Barker, Kate ("Ma") 132

Bass, Sam 9, 99

Bassham, Tucker 64

Becker, Howard S. 14, 40, 181, 182

Bellah, Robert 15, 125, 182, 190

Bell, Daniel 22, 182

Bernstein, Irving 125, 190

Betenson, Lula 9, 108, 181, 189

Blok, Anton 32, 40, 182

Bolton, "Black Bart" 99

Bonney, Billy (The Kid)
  as demon 74, 94-95, 96
  as hero 74, 92, 94, 96
  battle at Lincoln 86-87
  death of 95-96
  early life 74-75
  escape from custody 91, 93-94
  image in the newspapers 92-93, 94
  letter to Wallace 92, 93

  "peace treaty" with Evans 89
  murder of Huston Chapman 89-90
  murder of Sheriff Brady 84-5
  public's view of 91
  relation to Tunstall 81, 88
  rumors of "non-death" 98
  social context 75-78
  surrender to Wallace 90-91
  threatens Chisum 91-92, 95
  with Regulators 83

Bonnie (Parker) and Clyde (Barrow) 9, 117, 132

Bonus Expeditionary Force 123-125

Bothwell, Albert 103

Brady, Sheriff William 80, 83, 84, 85

Bradley, R. 158, 191

Brewer, Dick 83

Bristol, Judge Warren 93

Briehan, Carl 185

Brown, Dee 162, 193

Brown, Richard M. 44, 186

Brownlee, Richard 186

Bryson, Lyman 120, 190

Buck, Dan 189

Buel, James 25, 182

Bugliosi, Vincent 41, 152, 166, 182, 191, 193

Burns, Walter 74, 98, 155, 158, 187, 188, 191

Burt, Struther 103, 106, 107, 189

Byars, William 50, 186

Campbell, Joseph 15, 182

Capone, Al
  as Robin Hood 137-138
  conviction for tax evasion 138-139

196

differs from bandits 139
criminal activities 138
popularity of 138
social context 119-126
Casey, Robert 77
Cassidy, Butch
and Matt Warner 107-109
and Wild Bunch 109
and Spanish-Amer. War 110-111
attempt to reform 115-116
background 107
death of 115
living in New York City 113
living in S. America 114-115
movie of 117
"non-death" of 116-117
robberies 111-113
social context 99-100
Castel, Albert 62, 186
Cate, Rodney 180, 193
Catron, Thomas 85, 88
Cavender, Gray 14, 181, 182
Cawelti, John 18, 26, 182, 191
Champion, Nate 104
Chandler, Lester 31, 119, 120, 182, 190
Chapman, Arthur 98, 114, 115, 188, 189
Chapman, Huston 89-90
Chisum, Emmett 111, 189
Chisum, John 77, 78, 85, 87 91-92, 95
Civil War, in Missouri 44-47
Clarke, James 182
Cleaver, Eldridge 170
Clinard, Marshall 180, 193
Cloward, Richard 124, 125
Coe, George 188
Coleman, James W. 180, 193
Cooper, Courtney 31, 133, 182, 190, 191
Cooper, D.B. 161
Coughlin, Father Charles 125
Cox, Father James 125
Crittenden, H.H. 68, 69, 186
Crittenden, H.H. 63, 65-71
cultural explanations 10, 21-28
Currie, George 109, 110, 111

Dacus, Joseph 186
Dalton, Emmett 181
Dalton, Gang 9, 99
Dance, Daryl 41, 152, 182, 191
Davis, Angela 170
Davis, David 183
Davis, F. James 193
Davis, Kenneth 186
Defleur, Melvin 183
Delany, Samuel 98, 188
Dewey, Ernest 120, 126, 190
Dewitt, W.D. 190
Dillinger, John
background 128
comparison to Jesse James 128-129, 130-131
death of 131
escape from Crown Point 129-130
"non-death" of 132
social context 119-126
visit to family 130
Dimaggio, Paul 178, 193
"Dirty Harry" 171
Dolan, James 77, 79, 84, 85-87, 88, 90, 96-97
Donald, Jay 186
Doolin, Bill 9, 99
Douglas, Mary 183
Doughty, Francis 74, 188
Drago, Harry 77, 188, 189
Dudley, Col. N. 86, 91
due process 144
Dykes, J.C. 188
Edwards, Jennie 186
Edwards, John Newman 8, 49, 50, 62, 65, 67, 71, 154, 186, 191
Edwards, John Newman
"Chivalry of Crime" 49-50
Noted Guerrillas 62, 73
reaction to murder of James 65, 67
role in legend of J. James 50-51, 72-73
surrender of Frank James 67-68
Elkin, Frederick 183
Emmons, Nuel 166, 183, 193
entrepreneurs, role of 39-41,

149-151
Escarpit, Robert 27, 38, 159, 183
Evans, Jesse 79-80, 82, 89-90
extra-legal symbols of justice
    169-176
Ezell, John S. 186
Fable, Edmund 74, 98, 188
farmer turns gangster 126
Faulk, Odie 183
Femia, Joseph 192, 193
Federal Bureau of Investigation
    127-128, 131-132, 135, 139-140
Fine, Nathan 31, 147, 183, 191
Fish, Albert 21
Fisher, King 99
Fishman, Mark 14, 183, 193
Fishwick, Marshall 26, 74, 183,
    188, 191, 193
Flagg, O.H. (Jack) 103, 104
Floyd, Charles (Pretty Boy)
    background 132-133
    charitable acts of 136, 137
    compared to Jesse James 135
    death of 135, 137
    early career 133
    identity 132-133, 136-137
    Kansas City Massacre 134-135
    "non-death" of 137
    public support of 133-134,
    135-136
    Sallisaw robbery 133
    social context 119-126
Folsom, James 183
Ford, Bob 65
Fortune, Jan 181
Fox, James 21
Frantz, Joe B. 186
Fulton, Maurice 31, 77, 79, 81,
    84, 85, 86, 87, 93, 157, 183,
    188, 191
gangsters 119
Gans, Herbert 193
Gard, Wayne 181
Garofalo, James 14, 181, 183,
    192, 193
Garrett, Pat 7, 97, 155,
    158, 181, 187, 188, 191
Garrett, Pat
    first captures Bonney 92
    kills Billy the Kid 95-96

public support of 94
    reaction to killing of Kid 97
    role in legend of Kid 97
Geertz, Clifford 183
Gein, Edward 21
Geis, Gilbert 180, 193
Gitlin, Todd 178, 192, 193, 194
Glasscock, C.B. 31, 183
Goetz, Berhard 12, 171-173
Goode, William 39, 183
Gordon, Welche 25, 183
Gottdiener, Michael 192, 194
Gould, Lewis 189
Gould, R. 182, 183
Graber, Doris 14, 181, 183,
    193, 194
Gramsci, A. 192, 194
Great Depression (1930s)
    impact on farmer 119-120, 126
    homelessness 120, 123
    unemployment in cities 119
Griffith, Bruce 164-166
guerilla war, in Missouri 44-47
Gunther, Max 161, 194
Guthrie, Woody 134, 136, 155,
    156, 157, 158, 181, 190,
    191, 194
Hall, Charles 100, 102, 189
Halliwell, Leslie 151, 183, 191
Hamlin, William 98, 188
Hanes, Bailey 181
Hardin, John W. 181
Hardin, John Wesley 9, 99
Hart, Gene 163-164
Hearst, Patricia 174, 176,
    183, 194
Hearst Patricia 12, 174-176
heroic criminal
    and due process 144
    and identity 39, 142-144
    and mass media 9, 23-24, 117,
    126-127, 152-153, 161-2, 174,
    178-180
    and public 152
    and rock music 174
    and social conditions 32-36,
    160-163, 169
    as cultural product 38-42,
    142-149
    as myth 26-27, 38, 141, 159

as symbol of evil 25
construction of 153-158
cultural explanations 21-28
nature of victims 39, 144, 147
political nature 30-38, 159,
162-3, 179-180
psychological explanations 18-21
resemblance to terrorism 161
role of entrepreneurs 39-41,
149-151
sociological explanations 28-38
Hine, Robert 18, 183
Hinton, Harwood 77, 188
Hobsbawm, Eric 19, 27, 28, 29, 30,
32, 33, 154, 160, 161, 181, 183,
190
Hoffman, Abbie 170
Hole-in-the-Wall 99, 106, 109-110,
111, 117
Hollon, Eugene 31, 75, 183, 188,
189
Hofstadter, Richard 186, 191
homicide, in New Mexico (1880) 75
Hoover, J. Edgar 131
Horan, James 8, 24, 70, 109, 111,
113, 181, 183, 186, 188, 189
Horn, Tom 99
Humphries, Drew 193, 194
identity of criminal 39, 142-144
Inciardi, James 37, 183, 191, 194
Jackson, Joseph 20, 25, 184
James, Jesse
Amnesty Resolution 53-55
and Missouri politics 51, 53-56,
61-67, 71-72
and Zee Mimms 51
assassination of 64-67
attack on mother 52
death of Daniel Askew 55
dramatizing robberies 49, 51
Edwards, John Newman 50-51,
72-73
Gallatin, Mo robbery 47
identity 43, 52, 71
instability in gang 63-64
Kansas City Fair robbery 49-50
letters to the press 48, 49, 50,
54, 55
Northfield (MN) robbery 56-61
Pinkerton detectives 52, 54

social context 43-47, 70
supporters, nature of 72-73
victims, identity of 71-72
James, Frank
public support of 68-69
surrender of 67-68
trials 69-70
Jenardo, Don 74, 188
Johnson County War 100-106
Jones, Daryl 162, 184, 194
Kansas City Massacre 134, 135
Katz, Frederich 162, 194
Keleher, William 81, 157, 188,
191
Kelly, Charles 9, 109, 110, 111,
115, 116, 156, 181, 190, 191
Kelly, George (Machine Gun) 132
Kelly, Ned 161
Kennerly, Paul 8, 181, 191, 194
Kinney, John 96
Kittrell, William 100, 190
Klapp, Orrin 16, 24, 25, 153,
184, 191, 194
Klapper, Joseph 182, 184
Klasner, Lily 77, 188
Klein, Joe 192, 194
Klockars, Carl 171, 194
Kobler, John 181, 190
Knight, Stephen 171, 194
Lemar, Howard 77, 188
Leach, Edmund 182, 184
Leech, Margaret 190
Leeming, David 15, 184
legends as neutralizations 36,
153-158
Leverson, Montague 85
Levin, Jack 21, 184
Levine, Lawrence 41, 152,
184, 192
Levi-Strauss, Claude 26, 38,
141, 159, 184, 192
Lichter, Robert 193, 194
Lincoln County War 79, 86-87
Logan, Harvey (Kid Curry) 110,
111-112, 113
Logan, Lonny 111
Logan, Malcolm 127, 190
Long, Huey 125
Longbaugh, Harry (Sundance Kid)
110, 113, 114, 115

Love, Robertus 54, 55, 62, 64,
    155, 186, 192
Makepeace, James 180, 194
Manoff, Robert 178, 193, 194
Martin, Charles 181
Manson, Charles 41, 152, 166
mass media, role of 9, 23-24,
    152-153, 161-162, 174, 178-180
Matza, David 36, 153, 157
Maxwell, Peter 95
McCarty, Henry 107
McKendrick, N. 178, 194
McKinney, T.L. 95
McLane, John 27, 30, 33, 184
McMillen, A.W. 120, 191
McSween, Alexander
    Angel's view of 88
    background 78
    battle at Lincoln 86-7
    cleared of embezzlement 85
    confrontation with Evans 79-80
    death of 87
    dispute with Murphy 79
    flees Lincoln County 86
    reaction to Tunstall murder 82, 83
Meadows, Anne 189
Mercer, Asa 31, 102, 103, 104,
    105, 106, 184, 190, 192
Mercer, Asa 100, 101
Merrill, Horace 147, 192
methodological problems 12-13,
    142
Metz, Leon 94, 97, 188
Meyer, William 117, 190
Miller, Walter 41, 152, 184, 192
Mimms, Zee 51
Monahan, John 180
Morton, Frank 82, 84
Mottram, Eric 26, 184
Morison, Samuel 44, 186
movie industry 9, 29
Munden, Kenneth 18, 19, 184
Murieta, Joaquin 25-26
Murphy, Lawrence 77, 79, 88
myth, criminal as 26-27, 38, 141,
    159
Nachbar, Jack 184
Nash, Frank 134
Nash, Jay Robert 9, 21, 128, 129,
    132, 134, 136, 137, 138, 155,

    181, 192
Newman, Simeon 93, 94
Nichols, Roy 186
Nolan, Frederick 79, 82, 87,
    187, 188
North, Oliver 180
Nussbaum, Martin 26, 184
Oberschall, Anthony 32, 184, 192,
    194
O'Connor, Richard 31, 97, 149,
    184, 188, 192
O'Day, Tom 110
O'Folliard, Tom 91
Olsen, Marvin 182
O'Malley, Pat 27, 29, 30, 33,
    184, 194
Orwell, George 21, 184
Otero, Michael 7, 98, 158, 181,
    188, 192
Parish, James 117, 190
Parrish, William 46, 47, 186
Pasley, Fred 138, 191
Pecos War (NM) 77
Peppin, George 85, 86-87
Peterson, Richard 178, 193, 194
Phillips, William 116-117
Pinkerton detective 52
Piven, Frances 124, 125, 191
Place, Etta 113, 117
Poe, John 95, 96, 188
Poe, John 95
Pointer, Larry 113, 114, 115,
    116, 190
politics of banditry 12, 29-38,
    141, 162-3, 179-180
Porter, Dennis 171, 194
Powers, Judge Orlando 116
Powers, Richard G. 127, 129, 130,
    137, 138, 151, 191, 192
Preston, Douglas 108, 116, 117
psychological explanations 10,
    18-21
Purvis, Melvin 191
Purvis, Melvin 135, 137
Quantrill, William 45-47
Quinney, Richard 21, 178, 180,
    184, 194
Rable, George 44, 186
Rasch, Philip 77, 88, 90, 188
Richetti, Adam 135

Riley, John 77, 79, 82
Rosa, Joseph 188
Rossi, Peter 7, 182, 184, 194
Rubin, Jerry 166, 170
Rubin, Lillian 171, 172, 194
Rudd, Mark 170
Russell, Diana 180, 194
Ryan, William 64
Rynerson, William 82, 85, 91
Sage, Anna 131
Santa Fe "Ring" 77, 78, 79,
    85, 91
Schafer, Stephen 158, 192
Schein, Harry 18, 184
Schell, Jonathan 169, 194
Schlesinger, A. 125, 191
Schudson, Michael 24, 162, 178,
    184, 194
Schur, Edwin 7, 182, 184
Schurz, Carl 75, 91
Seale, Bobby 170
Sebba, Leslie 182, 185
Sellin, T. 182, 185
Settle, William 24, 32, 50, 51,
    53, 61, 62, 63, 70, 154, 157,
    185, 186
Shelby, Joseph 69
Sherizen, S. 185, 192, 195
Silberman, Charles 22, 185
Siringo, Charles 189
Sissman, L.E. 149, 192
Smith, Helena 102, 104, 106,
    190
Smith, Henry Nash 21, 185, 195
social conditions, role of
    32-36, 160-163, 169
sociological explanations 10,
    28-41
Sonnichsen, C.L. 98, 189
Springer, C.L. 123, 191
Starr, Belle 99
Steckmesser, Kent 25, 33, 36, 74
    77, 93, 98, 143, 147, 155, 156,
    157, 158
Stein, Ben 193, 195
Steinbeck, John 191
Stegner, Wallace 143, 185, 192
Stratton, Porter 78, 189
Symbionese Liberation Army 174-176
Sykes, Gresham 36, 153, 157,

185, 192, 195
Symons, Julian 171, 195
Tatum, Stephen 98, 189, 192
Taylor, Paul 191
Theisen, Lee 189
Thompson, Ben 99
Toland, John 128, 129, 130, 131,
    132, 150, 156, 182, 191, 192
Townsend, Dr. Frances 125
Treherne, John 132, 191
Trelease, Allen 44, 186
Triplett, Frank 55, 154, 186, 192
Tuchman, Gaye 192, 193, 195
Tucker, William 171, 195
Tunstall, Jeremy 182, 185
Tunstall, John
    and Sheriff Brady 80
    background 78
    motives in Lincoln County 79
    murder by sheriff's posse 81-82
    seizure of property 80-81
Turk, Austin 182-185
Turner, Ralph 182, 185
Turner, Victor 27, 185
United States Communist Party 125
Upson, Ash 97
Utley, Robert 93, 187, 189
victims, nature of 39, 144, 147
vigilante justice 170-172
Wallace, Lew 75, 88, 90, 91
Wallace, W.H. 69
Wambaugh, Joseph 170, 195
Warner, Matt 107-109
Warshow, Robert 26, 185
Watson, Ella 102
Wecter, Dixon 24, 74, 185, 189,
    192, 195
Wellman, Paul 182, 185, 186
White, Richard 21, 29, 30, 32,
    185, 195
Widenmann, Robert 81, 84
Wiebe, Robert 147, 185, 192
Wiggins, Ella May 125
Wilkerson, D. 162, 195
Wilson, D. 46, 186
Winick, Charles 14, 182, 193,
    195
Wolfgang, Marvin 182
women as outlaws 19
Woodward, C. Vann 186

Wright, Will 26, 185, 195
Wyoming Cattlemen's Assoc. 102,
    103, 104

Younger, Cole 54, 60-61, 71
Yellin, Samuel 191
Zevon, Warren 8, 182, 195